Minority Rights in Turkey

The issue of minority rights is highly contested in both member and candidate states of the European Union. Compared with other policy areas, the Europeanization process in minority rights is much slower and more problematic. Turkey as a candidate state, though, differs from the majority of the member states by showing positive development, although admittedly, it is still characterized by both accelerations and slowdowns.

This book examines how minority protection, as a highly sensitive and controversial issue, is promoted or constrained in the EU's neighbourhood, by focusing on the case of Turkey. It draws on current external Europeanization theories and suggests a rationalist model comprising both the role of the EU and also domestic factors. It integrates two models of external Europeanization provided by Schimmelfennig and Sedelmier (2005), that is the external incentives and lesson-drawing models, and the framework of the pull-and-push model of member state Europeanization by Börzel (2000), to derive a comprehensive model for external Europeanization. The book argues that the push by EU conditionality and the pull by domestic dissatisfaction are influential in promoting change. Without one or the other, domestic change remains incomplete, as it is either shallow or selective.

Focusing on the Turkish case, the book enhances the theoretical understanding of external Europeanization by shifting focus away from EU conditionality to voluntarily driven change, and by providing a theoretical model that is applicable to other countries. It will therefore be a valuable resource for students and scholars studying minority rights and Turkish and European ethnic politics.

Gözde Yilmaz is an Assistant Professor in Atılım University, Turkey. She completed her Ph.D. in Berlin Graduate School for Transnational Studies (BTS), Free University Berlin. Her further research interests are European integration, Europeanization theories, external Europeanization, EU enlargement policy, European Neighbourhood Policy, Europeanization of Turkey, EU–Turkey Relations and EU–Ukraine Relations.

Routledge Studies in Middle Eastern Politics

For a full list of titles in this series, please visit www.routledge.com

74 **The Europeanization of Turkey**
   Ali Tekin and Aylin Güney

75 **Turkey's Kurdish Question**
   H. Akin Unver

76 **The Israeli Conflict System**
   Harvey Starr and Stanley Dubinsky

77 **Political Violence and Kurds in Turkey**
   Mehmet Orhan

78 **The Europeanization of Turkish Public Policies**
   Ali Tekin and Aylin Güney

79 **Diasporic Activism in the Israeli-Palestinian Conflict**
   Svenja Gertheiss

80 **Israel's Military Operations in Gaza**
   Marouf Hasian, Jr.

81 **The Turkish AK Party and its Leader**
   Edited by Ümit Cizre

82 **Democratic Consolidation in Turkey**
   Edited by Cengiz Erisen and Paul Kubicek

83 **Saudi Arabian Foreign Relations**
   Rene Rieger

84 **Kurdish Politics in Turkey**
   Seevan Saeed

85 **Minority Rights in Turkey**
   Gözde Yilmaz

Minority Rights in Turkey
A Battlefield for Europeanization

Gözde YILMAZ

LONDON AND NEW YORK

First published 2017
by Routledge
2 Park Square, Milton Park, Abingdon, Oxon OX14 4RN

and by Routledge
711 Third Avenue, New York, NY 10017

Routledge is an imprint of the Taylor & Francis Group, an informa business

© 2017 Gözde Yilmaz

The right of Gözde Yilmaz to be identified as author of this work has been asserted by her in accordance with sections 77 and 78 of the Copyright, Designs and Patents Act 1988.

All rights reserved. No part of this book may be reprinted or reproduced or utilised in any form or by any electronic, mechanical, or other means, now known or hereafter invented, including photocopying and recording, or in any information storage or retrieval system, without permission in writing from the publishers.

Trademark notice: Product or corporate names may be trademarks or registered trademarks, and are used only for identification and explanation without intent to infringe.

British Library Cataloguing-in-Publication Data
A catalogue record for this book is available from the British Library

Library of Congress Cataloging-in-Publication Data
Names: Yilmaz, Gözde, author
Title: Minority rights in Turkey : a battlefield for Europeanization / Gözde Yilmaz.
Other titles: Routledge studies in Middle Eastern politics ; 85.
Description: Milton Park, Abingdon, Oxon ; New York, NY : Routledge, 2017. |
Series: Routledge studies in Middle Eastern politics ; 85
Identifiers: LCCN 2016040781| ISBN 9781138639737 (hardback) | ISBN 9781315637020 (ebook)
Subjects: LCSH: Minorities—Legal status, laws, etc.—Turkey. | Turkey—Ethnic relations. | European Union countries—Ethnic relations. | European Union countries—Relations—Turkey. | Turkey—Relations—European Union countries.
Classification: LCC KKX2467.M56 Y55 2017 | DDC 323.1561—dc23
LC record available at https://lccn.loc.gov/2016040781

ISBN: 978-1-138-63973-7 (hbk)
ISBN: 978-1-315-63702-0 (ebk)

Typeset in Times New Roman
by Apex CoVantage, LLC

To Yıldız, Salih and Ozan, to my lovely family

Contents

List of tables viii
List of figures x
Acknowledgements xi
List of abbreviations xii

Introduction: Exploring the puzzle of minority rights 1

1 Theorizing Europeanization through enlargement: Pull-and-push model 9

2 Transformative power of the European union, minority rights and Turkey 23

3 Changing minority rights of Turkey in 1999–2014 37

4 Push without pull in 1999–2004: EU conditionality triggers the reforms 63

5 Transition to pull without push in 2005–2007: From the EU to the 'domestic' 77

6 Pull without push in 2008–2014: Drift from the EU and rule by the 'domestic' 91

7 Alternative explanations 108

Conclusions and prospects 125

Bibliography 131
Index 151

Tables

1.1	Alternative mechanisms of Europeanization	10
1.2	Pull-and-push model: expected outcomes for policy change	13
1.3	Pull-and-push model: possible outcomes for policy change	15
1.4	Outcomes for push factor: the credibility of EU conditionality	19
1.5	Outcomes for pull factor: policy dissatisfaction	21
3.1	The demands of the EU and the response of legal adoption by Turkey: 2002–2004	39
3.2	The demands of the EU and the response of implementation by Turkey: 2002–2004	41
3.3	Minority-related policy change in Turkey: 1999–2004	41
3.4	The demands of the EU and the response of legal adoption by Turkey: 2005–2007	42
3.5	The demands of the EU and the response of implementation by Turkey: 2005–2007	46
3.6	Minority-related policy change in Turkey: 2005–2007	46
3.7	The demands of the EU and the response of legal adoption by Turkey: 2008–2014	50
3.8	The demands of the EU and the response of implementation by Turkey: 2008–2014	56
3.9	Minority-related policy change in Turkey: 2008–2014	60
3.10	Unresolved minority issues: EU demand–Turkish response	60
3.11	Minority-related legal adoption and implementation in Turkey: 2002–2014	62
3.12	Minority-related policy change in Turkey: 2002–2014	62
4.1	Eastern region votes to the AKP and pro-Kurdish DEHAP in the 2002 elections	73
4.2	2002–2004: push without pull	76
5.1	Eastern region votes to the AKP and pro-Kurdish DTP in the 2007 elections	87
5.2	2005–2007: pull without push	90
6.1	Comparing local elections 2004 and 2009	98
6.2	Eastern region votes to the AKP and pro-Kurdish DTP in the 2009 elections	98

6.3	Eastern region votes to the AKP and pro-Kurdish Party in the 2007 and 2011 elections	101
6.4	Eastern region votes to the AKP and pro-Kurdish DTP in the 2014 elections	106
6.5	2008 and 2014: pull without push	107

Figures

1.1	Causal mechanism by the external incentives model	10
1.2	Causal mechanism by the lesson-drawing model	11
1.3	Causal mechanism by the social learning model	12
1.4	Pull-and-push model	15
4.1	Turkish public support for EU membership in 2002–2004	72
5.1	Turkish public support for EU membership in 2005–2007	80
6.1	Turkish public support for EU membership in 2008–2014	92

Acknowledgements

This book is derived from my Ph.D. thesis completed in Berlin Graduate School for Transnational Studies at Free University Berlin, in 2012. Working on the Ph.D. thesis and turning it to a book have been a long and exhausting, but life-changing journey, and I have been very lucky to have amazing people around me in this academic endeavor. First and foremost, I am truly indebted and thankful to my supervisor, Tanja Börzel. Without her guidance, encouragement and invaluable advice, I would not have been able to complete this study. As her current and previous Ph.D. students, we call Tanja — our Doktormutter — 'mama' for her dedicated support like a mother to us. I also owe sincere and earnest thankfulness to my second supervisor, Thomas Diez. His support and intellectual advice have been a great help for my academic venture and this work.

I am very much grateful to the Kolleg-Forschergruppe (KFG) 'The Transformative Power of Europe' for funding my Ph.D. studies and post-doctoral fellowship to work on this book. I would also like to acknowledge the support by the Atılım University, and most importantly, Hasan Ünal, the head of International Relations Department, for his ceaseless support for all academic endeavors I took.

The supportive and stimulating environment at the Berlin Graduate School for Transnational Studies (BTS) and the KFG has been extremely helpful. I am grateful to the directors (particularly to Thomas Risse for his never-ending support), executive committee, and coordination team at the BTS and KFG. I would also like to thank my colleagues and friends at the BTS and KFG for their moral support and comments on different aspects of this work, and special thanks go to Çağlayan, my nearest and dearest friend. I also thank my fellow traveller in life, Ozan, for his true friendship and support.

My work has also benefited greatly from the discussions and insights in my fellowships at ETH Zurich, Koç University and LSE. I am greatly indebted to Bahar Rumelili, Ziya Öniş, Guido Schwellnus, Frank Schimmelfennig and Ulrich Sedelmeier for both hosting me and contributing with thoughtful criticism to my research.

I also owe my deepest gratitude to the academicians and practitioners, who generously found the time to talk to me and help me advance my research.

Last but not least, I would not have been able to complete this book without the encouragement and love of my parents, Yıldız and Salih, and my brother, Ozan. I dedicate this book to them.

Abbreviations

ADD	*Atatürkçü Düşünce Derneği* (Association for Kemalist Thought)
AKP	*Adalet ve Kalkınma Partisi* (Justice and Development Party)
ANAP	*Anavatan Partisi* (Motherlands Party)
ASALA	Secret Army for the Liberation of Armenia
BDP	*Barış ve Demokrasi Partisi* (Peace and Democracy Party)
CEE	Central and Eastern Europe
CEECs	Central and Eastern European Countries
CHP	*Cumhuriyet Halk Partisi* (Republican People's Party)
CoE	Council of Europe
CU	Customs Union
ÇYDD	*Çağdaş Yaşamı Destekleme Derneği* (Association for the Support of Modern Life)
DEHAP	*Demokratik Halk Partisi* (Democratic People's Party)
DSP	*Demokratik Sol Parti* (Democratic Left Party)
DTP	*Demokratik Toplum Partisi* (Democratic Society Party)
EC	European Community
ECHR	European Court of Human Rights
EEC	European Economic Community
EP	European Parliament
EU	European Union
FCNM	Framework Convention for the Protection of National Minorities
GAP	*Güneydoğu Anadolu Projesi* (Southeastern Anatolia Project)
HDP	*Halkların Demokrasi Partisi* (Kurdish People's Democratic Party)
HSYK	*Hakimler ve Savcılar Yüksek Kurulu* (Higher Council of Judges and Prosecutors)
IDP	Internally Displaced Person
IKV	*İktisadi Kalkınma Vakfı* (Economic Development Foundation)
İŞKUR	*Türkiye İş Kurumu* (Turkish Labour Agency)
KCK	*Koma Civakên Kurdistan* (Union of Kurdistan Communities)
Mazlum-Der	*İnsan Hakları ve Mazlumlar İçin Dayanışma Derneği* (Association for Human Rights and Solidarity with the Oppressed)
MHP	*Milliyetçi Hareket Partisi* (Nationalist Action Party)
MP	Member of Parliament

MÜSIAD	*Müstakil Sanayici ve İşadamları Derneği* (Independent Industrialists' and Businessmen's Association)
NGO	non-governmental organization
OSCE	Organization for Security and Co-operation in Europe
PKK	*Partiye Karkeren Kurdistan* (Kurdistan Workers Party)
RoC	Republic of Cyprus
RTÜK	*Radyo ve Televizyon Üst Kurulu* (Radio and Television Supreme Council)
RVRP	Return to Village and Rehabilitation Project
TAF	Turkish Armed Forces
TAYAD	*Tutuklu Hükümlü Aileleri Yardımlaşma Derneği* (Solidarity Association of the Families of the Prisoners and the Sentenced)
TESEV	*Türkiye Ekonomik ve Sosyal Etüdler Vakfı* (Turkish Economic and Social Studies Foundation)
TOKİ	*Toplu Konut İdaresi Başkanlığı* (Housing Administration of Turkey)
TÜSIAD	*Türk Sanayicileri ve Işadamları Derneği* (Turkish Industrialists' and Businessmen's Association)
UN	United Nations
US	United States
YÖK	*Yüksek Öğretim Kurumu* (Higher Education Board)

Introduction
Exploring the puzzle of minority rights

The issue of minority rights is highly contested in both European Union (EU) member and candidate states. Compared with other policy areas, the Europeanization process in minority rights is slower and more problematic. Notably, the practical implementation in candidate states remains incomplete even in the post-accession phase. For instance, the problems of Russian language speakers in Estonia and of Roma in Slovakia remain unsettled (Brosig 2010).

The case of Turkey, though, represents a different pattern, that is positive development in minority rights, and therefore an opportunity for analyzing the conditions that facilitate or limit minority protection in candidate states. Nevertheless, developments in the reform process to date have followed a controversial path, characterized by ups and downs, accelerations and slowdowns: almost no reforms in 1999–2002,[1] an acceleration of legal adoption with a start of implementation in 2002–2004, a period of slowdown in legal adoption with increasing implementation in 2005–2007 and a revival in legal adoption with intensifying implementation in 2008–2014. As seen, the reform process in the area is characterized by different degrees of progress and resistance through these time periods.

Such a process is puzzling due to a number of considerations: the progress in highly sensitive minority issues in a country struggling with the ethnically based conflict with the Kurdistan Workers Party (*Partiye Karkeren Kurdistan* – PKK);[2] increasing implementation of minority rules through time, representing a success story compared with previous EU candidate states; and the continuing reforms in an era of decreased EU leverage.

To clarify further, first of all, minority policy is often regarded as too sensitive or too case-specific, and that is why it is usually neglected in the literature (Liaras 2009: 1). Accordingly, minority protection is the least-likely area for reform in the enlargement process that touches closely a number of sensitive areas such as identity and citizenship or national security, not only for all candidate states, but also specifically for Turkey – due to country-specific factors such as the country's sensitive situation triggered by ethnic conflict with the PKK. Nevertheless, both legal adoption and implementation of minority measures demonstrated considerable progress in Turkey. Most importantly, although the implementation of minority measures still has room for development, the acceleration of the process is puzzling because of the fast transition to the implementation phase in a candidate

2   *Exploring the puzzle*

state of which membership prospect was still being debated. As shown in earlier studies, there is a huge gap between legal adoption and implementation – many EU rules are adopted but not implemented in the pre-membership phase (Falkner *et al.* 2007; Leiber 2007; Schimmelfennig and Sedelmeier 2005). The case of Turkey, therefore, represents a deviant case providing an empirical arena to explore different aspects that influence the implementation process.

Second, the EU reform process including minority-protection reforms in the country slowed down in 2005–2007, immediately after the launch of accession negotiations in 2005. From an incentive-based perspective, the development was quite unlikely due to the sizeable and credible reward of EU membership (Schimmelfennig and Sedelmeier 2005). As can be observed in the accession process of the Central and Eastern European Countries (CEECs), the EU's leverage increased significantly after the launch of accession negotiations (Vachudova 2005). Yet, the case of Turkey demonstrates the opposite outcome, which is puzzling in many aspects.

Third, and even more interesting, the slowdown of reforms in 2005–2007 is usually attributed to a decline in the credibility of EU conditionality (Öniş 2008, 2009; Saatçioğlu 2010; Schimmelfennig 2009). Yet, the incentive-based frameworks would not expect a revival of reforms in any area, let alone minority rights by 2008 due to the significantly weakened credibility of EU conditionality.

Considering all, this book aims to provide an explanation to the aforementioned empirical puzzle of differentiated minority-related change in Turkey over a decade, dividing the process into three time periods – with a background analysis of 1999–2002 – on the basis of the dependent variable (i.e. variation in minority-related change), which is signified by the coupling/decoupling of legal adoption and implementation: shallow policy change in 2002–2004; selective policy change in 2005–2007 (although limited); and 2008–2014.

Notably, the present theoretical frameworks in external Europeanization (see Schimmelfennig and Sedelmeier 2005) do not entirely account for the empirical puzzle. While the incentive-based approach does not explain the continuing reforms by 2005, in an era of decreased credibility of EU conditionality and increasing impact by veto players incurred with adoption costs,[3] the lesson-drawing model has a limited capability to explain the progress in 2002–2004, which signifies low levels of dissatisfaction.[4] The social learning model does also not account for the empirical puzzle due to the low degrees of domestic resonance with and legitimacy of EU minority rules, and the lack of any drastic change in the identification of the Turkish government and society with the EU and its rules in the period under consideration (Duyulmuş 2008: 32–3; Engert 2010: 110–20).[5]

Recognizing the aforementioned limits of the theoretical models, this book starts from an empirically observed phenomenon and addresses how the change in the minority-related policies in Turkey can be explained and under which conditions minority rights measures have been adopted or constrained. Therefore, it aims to uncover the conditions that promote or constrain domestic/policy change and provide a comprehensive theoretical framework for external Europeanization by exploring the case of Turkey. It draws on current external Europeanization

Exploring the puzzle 3

theories and suggests a rationalist model comprising the role of the EU and domestic factors. It integrates two models of external Europeanization provided by Schimmelfennig and Sedelmier (2005), that is the external incentives and lesson-drawing models, under the framework of the pull-and-push model of member state Europeanization by Börzel (2000), to derive a comprehensive model for external Europeanization.

The book argues that domestic change in candidate states, specifically policy change in the Turkish case, depends on a combination of EU-related and domestic factors. Both the push by EU conditionality and the pull by domestic dissatisfaction are influential in promoting change. Without one or the other, domestic change remains incomplete, as it is either shallow or selective.

Focusing on the Turkish case, the book enhances the theoretical understanding of external Europeanization by providing a theoretical model that is applicable to other cases and empirical knowledge with regard to the case of Turkey and its minority policy. Above all, it offers new insights into the literature by shifting the focus away from EU conditionality, which has heavily dominated the research, to voluntarily driven change within the framework of the lesson-drawing model, which is usually neglected and not entirely developed within the literature.

Developing an interactive theoretical framework for external Europeanization: pull-and-push model

This study aims to develop an alternative theoretical framework for external Europeanization to explain policy change in candidate states. Starting from an empirical puzzle, the research aims to uncover the conditions that promote or constrain policy change at the level of policymakers. As is demonstrated in the empirical chapter and alternative explanations, none of the external Europeanization theories fully provides an explanation to the empirical puzzle presented. Therefore, there is a need to develop an alternative causal mechanism to explain the process.

It is seen that external incentives and lesson-drawing models partly explain the puzzle, although each model does so successfully for two different time periods under consideration: the external incentives model for the period 2002–2007 and the lesson-drawing model for the period 2005–2014. The models present explanations in a complementary way, each explaining years the other cannot. While the lesson-drawing model explains minority-related policy change between 2005 and 2014 that the external incentives model cannot account for, the latter sheds light on change between 2002 and 2007. In addition to the aforementioned analysis, interviews conducted in Turkey guide the research to develop an interactive theoretical framework by integrating these two models. These models, therefore, are integrated by employing the pull-and-push framework of Börzel (2000), which combines a domestic-level pull and EU-level push for policy change.

Although the pull-and-push model focuses on compliance of EU member states with EU rules, this study adopts it into external Europeanization. The primary argument of the pull-and-push model is that the government is driven for change by pressure from above (EU push) and pressure from below (domestic

4   *Exploring the puzzle*

pull) (Börzel 2000: 148). Even though domestic pull can be exercised by different actors such as political parties or civil society, this book conceptualizes domestic pull at the decision-making level and is, therefore, concerned with policymakers' motivation for change. While the pull factor for change (dissatisfaction of the government with the status quo) is derived from the lesson-drawing model, the push factor (the credibility of EU conditionality) comes from the external incentives model.

Different combinations of pull and push successfully explain the empirical puzzle of variation in Turkey's minority-related policy change over time. For instance, while push without pull in 2002–2004 accounts for shallow minority-related change, pull without push in the period 2008–2014 explains selective change in minority rights.

The added value of the proposed model is threefold. First, the lesson-drawing model is rather neglected in the external Europeanization literature, and it is the least-researched area in the literature (Börzel and Risse 2009: 8). Scholars focus more on the impact of the EU, and there is a tendency to neglect the possibility of domestic choice theorized by the lesson-drawing model.

The external Europeanization literature primarily focused on the impact of EU conditionality (as top-down approaches) on candidate states through the Eastern enlargement, while treating domestic factors (veto players or domestic opposition) as mediating factors (e.g. Kelley 2004; Schimmelfennig and Sedelmeier 2005; Vachudova 2005). However, prejudging the impact of EU conditionality on domestic change and interventions by domestic factors limits the analysis (Pasquier and Radaelli 2007: 40). Moreover, reliance on top-down research designs in the literature brings the possibility of neglecting further explanatory variables in the domestic arena.

As a result, there has been a gap in the literature, which primarily concentrates on top-down approaches, while treating domestic factors as only mediating and hindering conditions of domestic change. Yet, recently some, among whom the author is also present (e.g. Alpan and Diez 2014; Saatçioğlu 2014), focused on the 'domestic' within the case of Turkey. Despite this, no systematic theoretical and analytical framework is offered in the literature to deal with the aforementioned problematic picture. Therefore, the aim of this book is to fill this gap by bringing the lesson-drawing model as a bottom-up perspective into the analysis to explain the Europeanization of candidate states.

Second, possible interaction between different mechanisms of domestic change is rarely explored in the literature. The tendency to treat different mechanisms as alternative explanations is not fruitful to develop comprehensive frameworks for explaining domestic change. As Börzel and Risse (2009: 8) state, "potential interaction and feedback effects are hardly explored." Therefore, in this study, I provide a theoretical framework comprising the interaction between two different mechanisms of change, ones which are usually considered as alternative mechanisms to each other.

Last, the failure or resistance of/to domestic change in candidate states is not wholly investigated in the literature (Börzel and Risse 2009: 8). I aim to provide an explanation for the conditions under which domestic change is possible and also restrained in the most sensitive area for Turkey: minority rights as an issue often encounter resistance and, therefore, constitute a battlefield for Europeanization.

Pull-and-push driving change in Turkish minority rights: what about the empirics?

The mapping of EU push and domestic pull reveals that there is a trend of declining push of EU conditionality and increasing pull of dissatisfaction for minority rights in Turkey. While the push of conditionality triggered reforms in one of the most sensitive areas, minority rights, through time it was replaced by the pull of dissatisfaction. As a result, a sequential process of these two mechanisms demonstrates itself and that influenced minority-related policy change.

Pull and push, as mentioned, interact at the decision-making process by the government. Most importantly, the primary motivation that drove the Justice and Development Party (*Adalet ve Kalkınma Partisi* – AKP) government in its political calculations between 2002 and 2014 was its survival instinct primarily and later on the consolidation of its rule in the domestic political arena.[6] The issue primarily refers to the AKP's struggle for survival in a hyper-secular and hyper-nationalist state tradition defended by a number of domestic actors fighting for the continuation of the status quo (Dağı 2006: 96). In this, the party employed an electoral strategy relying on keeping and attracting further support to itself at each election. The popular support demonstrated at the elections, in turn, provided legitimacy to its rule.

On the one hand, as a pro-EU, reformist, but historically Islamic-rooted actor, the AKP's fate was strongly depended on the EU accession process that guaranteed the survival of the party referring also to the ban of its predecessors (e.g. the Welfare Party) from political life (Aydın Düzgit and Keyman 2007: 75; Kulahci 2005: 400; Narbone and Tocci 2007: 239). Therefore, the accession process to the EU provided significant legitimacy to the AKP especially in its first years of rule due to the Islamist roots of the party (Sayari 2007: 201). As Aydın Düzgit and Keyman (2007: 75) stresses:

> [T]he AKP viewed EU accession and the necessary reform process as a tool to increase its legitimacy and to guarantee its political survival vis-à-vis the secular establishment in Turkey. In a similar sense, the EU also provided increasing legitimacy for the AKP's heavy emphasis on democracy and the protection of individual rights and freedoms in its political ideology.

On the other hand, receiving a high degree of protest, minority and pro-minority votes the AKP bound its political fate to democratic reforms. As Dağı (2006: 96) emphasizes, the popularity of the AKP displayed via elections has been a valuable asset in the quest of the party to gain recognition from secularists. Therefore, "democracy has turned into be a matter of survival" (Dağı 2006: 96). In this respect, there is a convergence between the AKP's expectations to promote

6 Exploring the puzzle

democracy, human rights and minority rights and EU conditionality (Kulahci 2005: 399).

By 2010, the AKP started to consolidate its rule in the domestic arena with a simultaneous weakening of military and judiciary power over domestic politics. Electoral strategy of the party, though, moved towards creating hegemony more than popularity at the elections by this time. Yet, the AKP still needed the support of minority and pro-minority groups to promote, keep and consolidate its electoral hegemony, and therefore, the party was in need to pursue minority reforms, this time for the consolidation and, again to some extent, legitimacy of its rule.

At the end, AKP's single-party governments have been under constant pressure to maintain its popularity or hegemony due to specific domestic factors. First, the AKP is a party attracting votes from various ideological fronts, various regions and various income levels (Kumbaracıbaşı 2009: 92). The research in the area (e.g. Çarkoğlu and Kalaycıoğlu 2007; Esmer and Sayarı 2002; Kumbaracıbaşı 2009) shows that the Islamic electorate does not surpass a 7 per cent to 9 per cent share of the total vote in Turkey. Therefore, the AKP received a high proportion of protest votes in the elections, supporting the party against the poor performance of previous governments in the 2002 elections (Kumbaracıbaşı 2009: 78). Most importantly, as Liaras (2009: 8) emphasizes, some minority groups, such as Alevis and Kurds, have a population large enough to affect the overall outcome of a Turkish election. The AKP, therefore, had to maintain the support of these different groups to consolidate its 2002 success.

It is important to note that the forthcoming analysis of pull and push between 2002 and 2014 in the next sections exemplifies minority voting with an analysis on the share of Kurdish votes between the AKP and the pro-Kurdish political party. This analysis is critically important because it enables the researcher to demonstrate the significance of minority votes, which constitute a vital component in the AKP's cost–benefit calculations. Because Kurdish votes can be clearly enumerated through analyzing regional distribution of votes, considering that the Eastern and Southeastern Turkey is highly populated by Kurds, the analysis puts special emphasis on the Kurdish share of votes to the AKP and the pro-Kurdish party to explore the impact of minority votes on the AKP's evaluation of the threat of sanctions.

Second, electoral volatility is always extremely high in the Turkish party system, leading to sudden rises and disappearances of political parties (Bahcheli and Noel 2011: 105; Çarkoğlu and Kalaycıoğlu 2007: 34). The dramatic expulsion of coalition partners of the previous government from the Parliament in the 2002 elections and the rise of the AKP demonstrate such high volatility. As Çarkoğlu and Kalaycıoğlu (2007: 35) discuss, "nearly half of the electorate has shifted from one party to another from 1999 to the 2002 elections." Hence, re-election depends mainly on the performance of political parties in office (Patton 2007: 347). In this respect, the AKP adopted a reformist approach in minority rights that gradually relied on selective approximation of minority rules with EU rules – depending on its problem-solving approach in failed areas, such as the Kurdish issue, to attract further votes and preserve its popularity at the elections, and considering the weakening of EU conditionality over time.

Exploring the puzzle 7

These factors thus exerted immense pressure on the AKP to maintain the high level of support it received in the 2002 elections. Losing electoral support from the reformist, pro-minority and minority groups would either change the AKP from being a party of the masses to a small-scale political party, or more radically mean the end of political life. Therefore, high levels of uncertainty in the electoral environment put constant pressure on the AKP through the period between 2002 and 2014.

As a result, both the EU accession process and popular support from the public to the AKP and its policies – demonstrated through election results – provided the AKP government with a strong sense of legitimacy (see Dağı 2006: 97; Narbone and Tocci 2007: 239; Saatçioğlu 2011: 32). At the end, the pull and push for minority reforms operated within this framework in 2002–2014.

Organization of the book

This book explores the conditions that promote or hinder change beyond the EU through explaining the variation in minority-related change in Turkey in 1999–2014. With this, the book provides a comprehensive model for external Europeanization that could be employed for exploring both accession and neighbourhood Europeanization.

Following the Introduction, Chapter 1 builds the theoretical and analytical framework of the book. The chapter first reviews the literature on accession Europeanization providing a theoretical background. Due to the limited capability of the theoretical frameworks in the literature to explain the empirical puzzle, the chapter next provides an alternative theoretical framework (i.e. pull-and-push model) and provides a detailed mapping of scope conditions.

Chapter 2 focuses on the transformative power of the EU, minority rights and Turkey. It starts with an analysis of EU minority policy and, next, explores the case of minority rights in the 2004 big-bang enlargement as a test case for EU's policy. Next, it provides an analysis of minorities and minority rights before the launch of reforms in Turkey by examining the concept of minority and minority rights from the Ottoman period to the Republican period. Last, EU's demands from Turkey regarding minority rights are explored in detail across time in the chapter.

Chapter 3 provides an analysis of the dependent variable: minority-related policy change. This part carefully traces the process to map the variation in minority rights between 1999 and 2014: starting with a preparation phase in 1999–2002; shallow policy change in 2002–2004; selective policy change, though limited in scope and depth, in 2005–2007; and selective policy change in 2008–2014.

Chapters 4, 5 and 6 constitute the main analysis of pull-and-push in the aforementioned time periods with a background analysis of 1999–2002. The chapters map the causal path – in which the push by conditionality and pull by dissatisfaction interacts – to explain variation in minority-related policy change. Chapter 4 focuses on the 1999–2004 period and presents the primacy of push by conditionality over the pull by dissatisfaction, which, in turn, explains shallow policy

8 *Exploring the puzzle*

change in minority rights. Chapter 5 demonstrates that the period of 2005–2007 is rather a transition period from the heavy-hand of EU push to the pull by dissatisfaction that accounts for the selective change to a limited extent in minority protection. Chapter 6 shows the dominance of pull by dissatisfaction without push in 2008–2014 that explains selective change in minority rights.

Chapter 7 reviews alternative explanations to the empirical puzzle. Factors within the social learning model, veto points and domestic adoption costs, and societal mobilization as relevant approaches for policy change in the external Europeanization literature are analyzed in-depth throughout the chapter, concluding that these factors have limited power in explaining Turkey's minority-related policy change.

The conclusion reviews the book and summarizes both theoretical arguments and empirical findings, while locating them in a broader perspective. This part also provides a discussion of the theoretical and empirical implications for existing and future research on external Europeanization and Europeanization of Turkey.

Notes

1 This period is between 1999 and November 2002 elections.
2 The PKK is a militant organization, which was established in 1970s. The original aim of the organization, though changed during time, was to establish a Kurdish state within the borders of Turkey, Iran, Syria and Iraq. The organization used terrorism against both civilians and military targets since that time. Therefore, it is listed as a terrorist organization by a number of states and organizations, including the EU. Later, the PKK has softened its original aim and focused on acquiring cultural and political rights for the Kurds in Turkey (Tocci 2008: 877).
3 Due to the continuing reforms in the area by 2005, especially in an increasing trend by 2008 – despite the growing impact of veto players and high adoption costs – the proposed theoretical model ruled out veto players and domestic adoption costs as one of the primary factors within the external incentives model. For the detailed analysis, please see the empirical section.
4 For the detailed analysis, please see the empirical section.
5 For the details, see the chapter on alternative explanations.
6 The book specifically focuses on the dissatisfaction of the Justice and Development Party (AKP) government in minority rights because the AKP government ruled the country in between 2002 and 2014 as the majority in the Parliament with the power to force change.

1 Theorizing Europeanization through enlargement
Pull-and-push model

The Europeanization of candidate states has become a separate research field in the Europeanization literature, which used to be associated with member state Europeanization (Sedelmeier 2011: 5). In this later-established literature, many scholars (e.g. Kelley 2004; Schimmelfennig and Sedelmeier 2005, 2007; Vachudova 2005) have demonstrated that the EU had a significant impact on candidate states through its conditionality – using both positive and negative means to alter the behavior of a state – in the enlargement process.

Despite the dominance of research relying on EU conditionality, the literature on Europeanization of candidate states provides different perspectives to the process. For a more comprehensive approach to Europeanization and enlargement, Schimmelfennig and Sedelmeier (2005) offer three explanatory mechanisms for rule adoption in non-member states: the external incentives model, the lesson-drawing model and the social learning model. These models differ in two aspects (see Table 1.1). First, the Europeanization process can be either EU- or domestically driven (Schimmelfennig and Sedelmeier 2005: 8). While the EU-driven process relies on EU conditionality to push rule adoption, the latter is a consequence of genuinely domestic initiatives (Schimmelfennig and Sedelmeier 2005: 8). The second distinction concerns the logic of action – either a logic of consequences or a logic of appropriateness – that pushes rule adoption (Schimmelfennig and Sedelmeier 2005: 8). Rule adoption is driven by rational calculations for benefit maximization via a logic of consequences, or it is driven by norms, values and identities through a logic of appropriateness (March and Olsen 1989: 160–2; Schimmelfennig and Sedelmeier 2005: 9).

The external incentives model

The external incentives model as a rationalist bargaining approach follows a logic of consequences, one that treats actors as strategic utility maximizers. According to the model, the EU employs a strategy of 'reinforcement by reward', in which EU rules are set as a precondition for candidate states to receive rewards from the Union (assistance and institutional ties) (Schimmelfennig and Sedelmeier 2005: 10).

10 Theorizing Europeanization

Table 1.1 Alternative mechanisms of Europeanization

Principal actor	Logic of consequences	Logic of appropriateness
EU – Conditionality	External incentives model	Social learning model
Domestic – Voluntary	Lesson-drawing model	Lesson-drawing model

Source: Schimmelfennig and Sedelmeier (2005: 8)

The starting point of the model is the domestic status quo determined by the 'goodness of fit', reflecting the misfit between European and domestic processes, policies and institutions (Börzel and Risse 2000; Risse *et al.* 2001). As a top-down perspective, the model assumes that the launch of EU conditionality upsets the domestic status quo by providing incentives for rule adoption and changes the domestic-opportunity structure (Magen and Morlino 2008: 33; Schimmelfennig and Sedelmeier 2005: 11).

The general proposition of the approach is, "A government adopts EU rules if the benefits of EU rewards exceed the domestic adoption costs" (Schimmelfennig and Sedelmeier 2005: 12). Research (e.g. Kelley 2004; Schimmelfennig and Sedelmeier 2005; Vachudova 2005) indicates that the credibility of EU conditionality and size of adoption costs are the key factors regarding domestic change in candidate states. However, the external incentives model conceptualizes domestic factors under undifferentiated one, veto players and adoption-costs factor, and such underspecification leads to ad hoc operationalization and different conceptualizations of adoption costs (Sedelmeier 2011: 30). Moreover, the number of veto players cannot be expected to vary over a short period of time, as the current study covers approximately 15 years. Therefore, rather than conceptualizing veto players based on their number, present research argues that the weight and impact of the veto players incurring adoption costs – the relevant costs to minority rights – matter.[1]

Figure 1.1 Causal mechanism by the external incentives model
Source: Author's own elaboration

The lesson-drawing model

The lesson-drawing model,[2] which is usually neglected in the literature, is based on the idea of non-member states adopting EU rules without the motivation of EU incentives (Schimmelfennig and Sedelmeier 2005: 20). The EU, therefore, is not the primary factor behind policy change; rather, change is domestically driven and voluntary. Lesson-drawing is a response to policymakers' dissatisfaction with the status quo, leading them to learn lessons about more effective policies and rules from abroad in order to remedy problems or failures (Rose 1991: 11; Schimmelfennig and Sedelmeier 2005: 21). The model's general proposition is, "A government adopts EU rules if it expects these rules to solve domestic policy problems effectively" (Schimmelfennig and Sedelmeier 2005: 22). In this regard, rule adoption increases as the perception that domestic rules are working satisfactorily decreases and dissatisfaction with domestic rules increases (Rose 1993; Schimmelfennig and Sedelmeier 2005). Therefore, the lesson-drawing model starts from a specific policy failure leading to domestic dissatisfaction with the status quo; this becomes the stimulus for policymakers to search elsewhere for new policies (Rose 1991: 11).

The model assumes that dissatisfaction works via sanctions (Rose 1991: 12). If policymakers ignore or heed domestic dissatisfaction, they may face loss of support or even loss of public office (Rose 1991: 12). Being aware that current policy is not working (policy failure), policymakers search for alternative policy models to adopt voluntarily. Therefore, failure in a specific policy area is a sufficient condition for the rise of policy dissatisfaction (Rose 1993: 50).

Figure 1.2 Causal mechanism by the lesson-drawing model

Source: Author's own elaboration

The social learning model

The social learning model[3] is rooted on the sociological institutionalism. The model defines the EU as a community that relies on a collective identity and a set of common norms and values. Following the logic of appropriateness, rule adoption by non-member states depends on the perception of EU demands and rules as appropriate regarding the collective identity, norms and values (Kelley 2004; Schimmelfennig and Sedelmeier 2005: 18). Therefore, the model places substantial emphasis on the impact of the EU's persuasive power in the Europeanization process (Kelley 2004: 32–3; Schimmelfennig and Sedelmeier 2005: 18). The EU can persuade either the government or societal actors of the appropriateness of its rules, norms and values – therefore, pushing domestic change (Schimmelfennig and Sedelmeier 2005: 18). The general proposition of the social learning model is, "A government adopts EU rules if it is persuaded of the appropriateness of EU rules" (Schimmelfennig and Sedelmeier 2005: 18).

The causal mechanism via social learning starts with the presentation of new norms, ideas and collective understandings by the EU to non-member states. If these are accepted as legitimate and resonate with the domestic arena, and if the government and society identify themselves with the EU in which the rules embedded, rule adoption is likely (Börzel and Risse 2003; Schimmelfennig and Sedelmeier 2005).

Figure 1.3 Causal mechanism by the social learning model
Source: Author's own elaboration

In summation, Schimmelfennig and Sedelmeier (2005) provide a clear research guide through different causal mechanisms to explore Europeanization in candidate states. Despite the heavy emphasis on the external incentives model as the most empirically successful causal mechanism to explain the Europeanization process in candidate states, all the causal paths provided by the authors have been the most influential in the literature. Yet, an analysis of these causal mechanisms to explain the variation in minority-related policy change in Turkey demonstrates limited explanatory power. Neither of these mechanisms can fully account for the change in Turkish minority rights between 1999 and 2014 – considering the period between 1999 and 2001 as a preparation phase. While the external incentives model explains minority-related change between 2002 and 2007, the lesson-drawing model is able to provide an explanation between 2005 and 2014. These two models have limited but complementary explanations for the variation in minority-related change in Turkey in different time periods between 1999 and

2014. As a result, the present research integrates the two models into a broader pull-and-push model, which is explained in the next sections.

The explanandum: policy change in minority rights

The Europeanization literature basically concerns with domestic change as the outcome of the Europeanization processes (Radaelli 2003: 37; Schimmelfennig and Sedelmeier 2005: 7). Although the literature is well-established in terms of what the possible outcomes of the process are (e.g. inertia, absorption), such an approach is highly static for the case of Turkey, in which the process is significantly dynamic. Therefore, this study focuses on the legal adoption and implementation as primary indicators of policy change and identifies outcomes of policy change through whether there is a coupling or decoupling between legal adoption and implementation (see Table 1.2). Important to note is that, in a wider context, implementation includes a wide perspective from deep societal internalization of the rules to the translation of the rules into action. However, here implementation simply refers to the process of "translating policy into action" (Barrett 2004: 251).

Table 1.2 Pull-and-push model: expected outcomes for policy change

Legal adoption / Implementation	High	Low
High	Effective policy change	Rule-confirming policy change or selective policy change
Low	Shallow policy change	Inertia

Source: Author's own elaboration

As Table 1.2 shows, different combinations of legal adoption and implementation lead to different outcomes characterized by the coupling/decoupling of legal adoption and implementation. If there is a decoupling of legal adoption and implementation, policy change is either shallow due to the low levels of implementation or it is selective depending on the scope for further legal adoption. If there is a coupling of these two, policy change is effective. In contrast, in the case of decoupling of the two, the outcome is, as expected, inertia.[4]

The analysis of minority-related change demonstrates variation across time and the research divides the process into three periods, with an additional preparation phase (1999–2001) as a background to the analysis, on the basis of the variation: acceleration of legal adoption with very limited implementation (2002–2004), slowdown of legal adoption with limited implementation (2005–2007) and revival of legal adoption with intensified implementation (2008–2014).

An interaction-oriented mechanism for external Europeanization: pull-and-push model

In the external Europeanization literature, conditionality – using positive and negative means to alter the behavior of a state – is the most explored area, and research

14 Theorizing Europeanization

has shown that the EU had a significant impact on candidate states through the enlargement process (e.g. Schimmelfenning and Sedelmeier 2005). Adopting a top-down perspective, scholars of external Europeanization (e.g. Schimmelfenning and Sedelmeier 2005) focus on domestic factors as obstacles rather than as possible drivers of change. In return, top-down research designs as such have restricted the research area and brought the danger of neglecting possible explanatory factors in the domestic arena, such as the internal pressure for change (Pasquier and Radaelli 2007: 40).

The focus on top-down approaches also represents a common tendency in the research regarding domestic change in Turkey (e.g. Grigoriadis 2008; Keyman and Öniş 2007). Some scholars (e.g. Narbone and Tocci 2007; Yilmaz 2014a) argue, though, that Europeanization is not a linear process based on EU conditionality. Instead, it is an interactive process between domestic and EU-related factors. Such an understanding, adopted by this research, prevents over-determination of EU factors and the neglect of possible domestic drivers of change.

In an attempt to avoid this kind of limitation, this study starts with the pull-and-push model that approaches external- and internal-level factors in the same vein and contributes to the literature with its equal focus on the EU level and the domestic level, highlighting Turkey as one of the most challenging and interesting cases among EU candidate states. The next section explores the proposed theoretical model.

It is the combination of external and domestic factors! Pull-and-push model

The main proposition of the pull-and-push model is that pressure from below (i.e. pull) and pressure from above (i.e. push) increase the adoption and implementation of EU rules (Börzel 2000: 147–8). When a government is sandwiched between pressure from above and from below, the likelihood of adoption and implementation of EU rules increases, even if domestic actors incur high adaptation costs (Börzel 2000: 148).

While the external push originates from EU pressure, the domestic pull comes from societal actors, such as political parties and civil society organizations (Börzel 2000: 148). This research, however, considers the direct pull within the government level instead of the indirect pull by societal actors, although the source for this comes from voter dissatisfaction.[5] Moreover, the pull-and-push model focuses on the compliance of EU member states with EU rules. The present study builds its framework on the model by adjusting it to external Europeanization. As the purpose of the research to integrate external- and domestic-level mechanisms to explain change in candidate states, while putting equal emphasis on both levels, the model provides an appropriate framework that prioritizes neither level, but treats both equally.

Under the umbrella of the pull-and-push model, scope conditions (i.e. credibility of EU conditionality and policy dissatisfaction) are primarily derived from the external Europeanization literature addressing the impact of EU conditionality (i.e. external incentives model) and domestic choice of candidate states on domestic change (i.e. lesson-drawing model) (see Figure 1.4) (Schimmelfenning and Sedelmeier 2005).

Theorizing Europeanization 15

Push for policy change

                    Credibility of EU conditionality
                                ↓
                      (Interaction point)
                  Policymakers/Government → Policy change
                                ↑
                Policy dissatisfaction with the status quo

Pull for policy change

Figure 1.4 Pull-and-push model
Source: Yilmaz (2014b: 241)

    The pull-and-push model suggests that EU push and domestic pull empower each other at the decision-making level. Policy change becomes more likely when there is a convergence between credible commitments for rewards and sanctions by the EU, and policy dissatisfaction working through the threat of sanctions by means of elections.[6]

    Different combinations of pull by dissatisfaction and push by conditionality lead to different outcomes for policy change characterized by the coupling/decoupling of legal adoption and implementation (see Table 1.3). If there is a decoupling of legal adoption and implementation, policy change is either shallow due to the low levels of implementation, or it is selective, depending on the scope for further legal adoption. If there is a coupling of these two, policy change is effective.

Table 1.3 Pull-and-push model: possible outcomes for policy change

		Push	
		Low	High
Pull	Low	Q2 *Inertia*	Q1 *Shallow policy change*
	High	Q3 *Selective policy change*	Q4 *Effective policy change*

Source: Yilmaz (2014b: 242)

    The pull-and-push model thereby provides an explanation for the variation in policy change through different combinations of empowerment between pull and push as the following:

> *Pull and push*: The combination of the push by the credibility of EU conditionality and the pull by policy dissatisfaction increases the likelihood of effective policy change.

Neither pull nor push: The absence of both pull and push decreases the likelihood of policy change.

Pull without push: The likelihood of policy change is high, though remaining selective, via the pull by policy dissatisfaction despite the lower levels of the push by the credibility of EU conditionality.

Push without pull: The likelihood of policy change is high, though remaining shallow, via the push of the credibility of EU conditionality despite the lower levels of the pull by policy dissatisfaction.

While the combination of EU push and domestic pull increases the likelihood of effective policy change,[7] policy change remains shallow in case of EU push without domestic pull. This trend was evident in the accession process of CEECs. As previous studies (e.g. Schimmelfennig and Sedelmeier 2005) demonstrate, legal adoption in the pre-accession phase was successful due to EU push, primarily relying on EU conditionality. Moreover, the newly adopted EU rules in these countries, in many cases, were not fully implemented and most often remained lagging (see Brosig 2010; Schimmelfennig and Sedelmeier 2005). Such trend of decoupling – dutiful legal adoption and lower levels of implementation – in the accession process of CEECs strongly implies that legal adoption in candidate states is driven by EU push, in which the compliance goal overrides domestic concerns (Falkner and Treib 2008).

In contrast, implementation depends primarily on domestic factors: domestic concerns prevail, either positively or negatively, in a clash of interests for implementation. Accordingly, in the pull-and-push model, the existence of pull increases the likelihood of implementation. Furthermore, in a situation with pull without push, policy change remains selective because government dissatisfaction directed by failure determines the focus of the government on providing solutions to domestic problems, and the government strategically uses reforms to attract electorate. Therefore, instead of focusing entirely on EU demands, the government is directed towards providing solutions to problematic issues.

Important to note is that the model assumes the direction of change designated by the EU in candidate states since they are under the constant pressure of EU conditionality for accession. Therefore, in the search for alternative solutions in response to a specific failure, the EU determines the direction of the policy if the country is subject to accession pressure. In the case of Turkey, the AKP government's policy dissatisfaction with previous minority policies and the process of EU membership candidacy overlapped at some point. Due to this circumstance, the government did not need to search for alternative policies abroad as expected by the lesson-drawing model, but took the EU model and adopted it into national circumstances.

Adopting the EU model, however, does not imply that it is the best possible policy alternative. The pressure of EU conditionality, pushing for the EU model to be adopted by candidate states, is a powerful source that influences the direction of policy change. However, policymakers can still pick and adopt specific features of the model, while ruling out others due to various issues like national circumstances, strategic calculations for elections. This can include considering the sensitivity of an issue that may cause significant public reaction and weighing EU-related factors, such as the credibility of EU conditionality.

Most importantly, this study considers a possible interaction of external push and domestic pull at government-level decisions for policy change. The research adopts a two-step approach in line with the impact of the two levels on decisions taken in the policy-making process. On one hand, policy dissatisfaction from the domestic sphere convinces the government of the need for policy change. On the other, EU conditionality instrumentally pushes the government towards policy change. Both levels involve different degrees of rewards and threat of sanctions in different settings. While the government faces EU sanctions in the case of non-compliance and is promised rewards in response to compliance, it is also confronted with sanctions in the domestic sphere by voters. Weighing costs and benefits at both levels, the government decides whether to adopt policy change in a given area. Therefore, the interaction of external- and domestic-level factors emerges in the decision-making process, incurring the motivational impact of dissatisfaction in the domestic sphere and EU conditionality.

Moreover, a sequential process might dominate the pull-and-push process. EU conditionality could act as a trigger for reforms by providing new opportunities and constraints to the government, and this might, in the long run, empower and intensify policy dissatisfaction. Therefore, a sequential process from push of EU conditionality to pull of policy dissatisfaction is also possible. The next sections provide a detailed explanation of pull and push factors.

External-level push factor: credibility of EU conditionality

A credible and conditional EU membership perspective is widely recognized in the literature as vital for the EU to promote domestic change in candidate states (Kelley 2004; Saatçioğlu 2010; Schimmelfennig 2008; Schimmelfennig and Sedelmeier 2005, 2007). Even though credible conditionality necessitates a fertile domestic ground for domestic change according to these scholars, it remains as the most important factor for the EU to push domestic change (Kelley 2004: 41; Saatçioğlu 2010: 7; Schimmelfennig 2008: 919; Schimmelfennig and Sedelmeier 2005: 13–14).[8]

The credibility of EU conditionality stems from two factors: capabilities of and costs for the agency that employs conditionality and the consistency of the institution's allocation of rewards (Schimmelfennig and Sedelmeier 2005: 14–15). First, compliance of candidate states necessitates both the superior bargaining power of the rule-setting agency in terms of credible threats and certainty for target states concerning conditional payments for credible promises (Schimmelfennig and Sedelmeier 2005: 13–14). In this situation, in order to promote credible conditionality, the EU needs to be able to both withhold rewards and pay them with a low cost to itself (Schimmelfennig and Sedelmeier 2005: 14). However, the process involves "sunk costs" of rewarding, which involves costly preparations and arrangements for enlargement (Schimmelfennig and Sedelmeier 2005: 14). Therefore, the credibility of EU conditionality increases with the opening of accession negotiations due to the increasing costs of withholding membership

18 Theorizing Europeanization

through the advancement of the pre-accession process (Schimmelfennig and Sedelmeier 2005: 14).

Second, the EU needs to link the behavior of candidate states to institutional membership for the application of credible conditionality (Kelley 2004: 41). The EU, here, binds the possibility of the ultimate reward of membership to the compliance record of candidate states. This record is determined by the Copenhagen political criteria, the conditions for the application of accession conditionality, formulated in the Copenhagen European Council (1993) as "stability of institutions guaranteeing democracy, the rule of law, human rights, and respect for and protection of minorities".

The application of EU conditionality on the basis of 'community context',[9] which requires accession conditions as common constitutive norms of the EU, is the main principle to support the credibility of conditionality (Engert *et al.* 2003: 8; Saatçioğlu 2010: 8). Therefore, credible conditionality of the EU requires consistent and fair application of the threat to withhold rewards in the case of non-compliance and the EU's promise to deliver the rewards in response to compliance for all candidate states (Schimmelfennig and Sedelmier 2005: 13). If other political, economic or strategic considerations of the EU prevail in the accession process, this leads to a decrease in the credibility of conditionality due to the fact that the target state may either hope to receive the rewards without fulfilling necessary requirements or perceive that it will not receive the rewards in any case (Schimmelfennig 2008: 919; Schimmelfennig and Sedelmeier 2005: 15).

At the end, the credibility of EU conditionality depends on the normative consistency of the EU guided by linking the membership perspective to the democratic and human rights performance of the target country – conditioned for accession to the Union and built on the constitutive norms of the Union (Schimmelfennig 2008: 920–1).

EU conditionality, usually presented as purely objective and technical by the EU, enables the Union to frame the accession process as a "game of trust and dependable expectations" (Tocci 2007: 9–10). Moreover, objective or technical conditionality – based on an established and uniform basis through the Copenhagen criteria and applied equally to all candidate states at all times – represents the key in the accession process of candidate states and strengthens the credibility of the EU (Tocci 2007: 10–11). However, EU conditionality is usually political rather than technical and objective in practice. As Tocci (2007: 14) states, "The choice of which conditions to emphasize, how to interpret them and what benchmarks to set is inevitably subjective and 'political'" depending on considerations other than the Copenhagen criteria, such as national interests of member states or regional and international contexts. As a result, EU conditionality is a politicized tool in many instances and politicization of conditionality leads to a decrease in normative consistency and an increase in discrimination among candidate states, therefore weakening the credibility of EU conditionality.

For the credibility of EU conditionality, one needs to question the extent to which the EU consistently links accession progress – as well as the ultimate reward of membership – to the Copenhagen criteria (consisting of democratic

Table 1.4 Outcomes for push factor: the credibility of EU conditionality

Democratic Conditionality	
Politicized Conditionality (PC) Technical Conditionality (TC)	
More linkage to Copenhagen criteria than non-Copenhagen criteria TC > PC	More linkage to non-Copenhagen criteria than Copenhagen criteria TC < PC
Credible	**Not credible**
Strong push	**No push**

Source: Author's own elaboration

norms, values and rules of the EU) and to the non-Copenhagen criteria (such as absorption capacity). While the linkage of fulfillment of the Copenhagen criteria to progress towards accession leads to credible conditionality, the linkage of fulfillment of the criteria other than Copenhagen to progress in the accession path (denoting politicized conditionality) causes a decline in credible conditionality. Therefore, the more the normative consistency of the EU guided by linking the prospect of membership to the performance of the target country based on the fulfillment of the Copenhagen criteria is, the more EU conditionality becomes credible, and the more the push for policy change is strengthened.

As a result, the main question regarding EU conditionality – with the potential to weaken its credibility – is whether conditions other than the Copenhagen criteria dominate the accession process of candidate states (see Table 1.4). If the EU extends its membership conditions to other circumstances such as a candidate's size, population or budgetary impact on the EU, the credibility of EU conditionality is politicized and weakened (Saatçioğlu 2010: 8; Schimmelfennig 2008: 920).

Domestic-level pull: policy dissatisfaction with the status quo

Rose (1993: 50) emphasizes the tendency of policymakers when everything is satisfactory in a given policy: "If it ain't broke, don't fix it." However, policymakers can become dissatisfied if a particular policy is not working properly, noted by Rose (1993: 61) as "You can't afford not to do." Failure, as the most important and sufficient factor for dissatisfaction in a given policy (such as a sharp increase in unemployment) creates policy dissatisfaction that leads to a search for alternative solutions to the problem by policymakers (Rose 1993: 60).[10]

Due to the stimuli by failure, policymakers search for a solution "that will reduce the gap between what is expected from a program and what government is doing" (Rose 1993: 50). Therefore, dissatisfaction is directly related to the action policymakers take in a policy area wherein something went wrong. Dissatisfaction of policymakers leads to, first, a search for alternative solutions and, second, taking necessary measures to fix the problematic policy. As a result, policy dissatisfaction arises in two steps. First, policy dissatisfaction needs to be stimulated by failure. Second, policymakers evaluate the status quo as unsatisfactory and diagnose the problem in a specific policy area (Rose 1993: 59). After these steps, policymakers search for policy programs abroad, and the policy is modified or completely changed.

It is important to note that the case of Turkey did not necessitate a broad search for alternative solutions to minority-related problems due to the launch of EU candidate country status in 1999. As Schimmelfennig and Sedelmeier (2005: 21) emphasize, if the rules in question are subject to EU conditionality, policymakers might only look to the EU model rather than search for a superior model abroad. Therefore, EU conditionality limits the search. Policymakers dissatisfied with a given policy might voluntarily import the EU model due to perceived domestic utility rather than the impact of EU conditionality (Schimmelfennig and Sedelmeier 2005: 21). The case of Turkey represents such an overlap of EU conditionality and voluntary action for policy change.

To detect policy dissatisfaction, it is necessary to take the aspirations of policymakers and policy problems into account. If a gap between aspirations (what is possible to attain) and achievements (signified by existence of policy problems in this analysis) exists, this creates dissatisfaction (Rose 1991: 10–11, 1993: 58). Due to the fact that minority-related policy problems are evident in Turkey, as is further explained in the next pages, the degree of AKP aspirations[11] determines the dissatisfaction with minority-related policy. Nevertheless, the analysis of policy dissatisfaction needs an analysis of diagnosis in minority-related failure as shown through AKP government representatives' speeches. This is because problems in a policy area may exist in principle, but are not diagnosed or recognized by policymakers. Alternatively, policymakers, who may be among status quo defenders, can diagnose policy failure without taking any action in the problematic area. For instance, in the 1990s, a number of politicians who acted as Prime Minister in Turkey – such as Süleyman Demirel, Tansu Çiller and Mesut Yılmaz – recognized the Kurdish reality and Kurdish problem; however, no concrete initiative followed from their statements (Bahcheli and Noel 2011: 101–2).

Importantly, as in line with Rose (1991: 10), "the relation between aspiration and achievement is the critical determinant of action or inaction." As long as a policy works smoothly matching with aspirations, there is satisfaction (Rose 1991: 11). Thereby, it can work by routine. However, in the case of a gap between the policy at work and aspirations, dissatisfaction arises and policymakers are pressured to find a solution (Rose 1991: 11).

For dissatisfaction, therefore, policy aspirations need to be questioned with the question of the extent to which AKP government representatives refer to the necessity of change in minority-related policy and for a solution to a specific policy problem (e.g. alternative models or solutions such as a tolerant and peaceful minority policy, integration with minorities, or citizenship-based model etc.). At the end, the more the gap exists between aspirations of policymakers and achievements signified by the existence of policy failure, the more policymakers become dissatisfied and the more the pull for policy change is strengthened. Therefore, the gap or mismatch between aspirations of policymakers and achievements,

Table 1.5 Outcomes for pull factor: policy dissatisfaction

Achievements: The Existence of Policy Failure \ Aspirations	Existed	Absent
Existed	Match (gap) Dissatisfaction of reformers = Effective pull	Mismatch (no gap) Satisfaction of status quo defenders = No pull
Absent	Mismatch (no gap) Dissatisfaction of reformers with ambitious policy ideals = Competitive pull	Match (no gap) Satisfaction of the status quo powers = No pull

Source: Author's own elaboration

signified by the existence of policy problems, is the key for outcomes ranging from satisfaction to dissatisfaction.

Because dissatisfaction is directly linked to the action or inaction of policymakers, outcomes for policy dissatisfaction caused by the gap also comprise the behavior of policymakers, action or inaction, and the characteristics of policymakers, reformers or status quo defenders (See Table 1.5). In the case of a gap between aspirations of reformers for further policy change and policy failure, dissatisfaction arises and thus demonstrates an effective pull. There is no pull consequential to the satisfaction of status quo defenders with any aspirations for policy change even in the existence or non-existence of policy failure. Where there are aspirations for policy change without any case of failure, dissatisfaction of reformers – who aim to reform the existing policy to compete with other political actors – emerges as a competitive pull.

Conclusions: it is pull and push that matters for external Europeanization!

The Europeanization process beyond the Eastern enlargement necessitates new approaches to explore external Europeanization. New enlargement rounds, new candidates, new parameters, new issues need new approaches, and the pull-and-push model provides a comprehensive approach for all the 'new'.

The model aims to bring two levels together without judging the 'domestic' as only a hindering factor for Europeanization, but a possible driver of Europeanization. Bringing the external EU factor and domestic dissatisfaction together, the model offers a comprehensive perspective not only to accession Europeanization, but also neighbourhood Europeanization. The empirical part details the model at work and discusses the implications for future research.

Notes

1 It is important to note that the adoption-costs factor is not able to provide an explanation of variation in Turkey's minority-related change – as explored in the section of alternative explanations.
2 Schimmelfennig and Sedelmeier (2005) draw on the work of Rose (1991, 1993) on lesson-drawing to provide a systematic explanatory model for accession Europeanization. Even though the elaborated model includes a rationalist and sociological variant, the present research departs from the rationalist conceptualization of lesson-drawing by Rose and further elaborates on the model using these scholars' work in the next section of the pull-and-push model.
3 The social learning mechanism is ruled out from the analysis due to its limited explanation of the variation in minority-related change in Turkey, which will be demonstrated at the part of alternative explanations.
4 Different outcomes regarding the pull-and-push model will be analyzed in the next sections, and it will be detailed why certain combination of pull and push leads to a certain outcome.
5 The focus on the direct mechanism of pull and push is related to the weak societal impact on policy-making in Turkey. For instance, the limited impact of Turkish civil society (which is still in the making) on policy-making is a vital illustration of this (see Bertelsmann Stiftung 2010: 10, 2012: 12, 2014: 13; CIVICUS 2010: 11–14).
6 As in the original model for member state Europeanization by Börzel (2000), the existence of pull-and-push factors leads to change in external Europeanization even if veto players and other domestic actors incur high adaptation costs. The empirical case also supports this argument. Therefore, veto players as an obstructing factor is ruled out from the analysis.
7 Although the empirical case does not demonstrate the outcome of effective policy change, in cases of the push with pull the original pull-and-push model by Börzel (2000: 148) expects an increase in the likelihood of adoption and implementation of EU rules, therefore, coupling in legal adoption and implementation, which can be conceptualized as effective policy change.
8 It can be argued that the size and speed of conditional rewards are equally important to promote domestic change. In this context, the ultimate reward of membership is the main trigger for domestic change as well as the distance to the reward. Although the importance of the factor is evident, the size and speed of conditional rewards also depend on the credibility of EU conditionality. If the EU provides membership perspective for a candidate state and draws membership up through proceeding to accession negotiations, it still depends on the EU's ability and credibility to keep its promise of membership to the candidate state in response to the fulfillment of the Copenhagen criteria. If the EU is not credible in this aspect, both size and speed of rewards are influenced negatively and become weakened.
9 Community context relies on three features: legitimate conditions, impartial treatment and consistency of enlargement practice (Saatçioğlu 2010: 8).
10 Dissatisfaction can be a direct and indirect consequence – direct impact of policy failure on policymakers in the government and indirect impact of failure via societal pressure on the policymakers, respectively (Rose 1991: 11–12, 1993: 60–1). Because the impact of societal actors on policy-making in Turkey is still weak and in the making, this study rules out the indirect mechanism and adopts the direct mechanism of policy dissatisfaction.
11 Because the AKP government constituted the majority in the parliament with the power of pulling policy change between 2002 and 2014, the aspirations of the AKP is relevant to the study.

2 Transformative power of the European union, minority rights and Turkey

From the EU member states to the candidate states and later to the neighbourhood states, the Europeanization phenomenon has travelled across Europe and beyond in the last decades. Beginning within its borders, the EU has successfully exported its rules, values and norms to a wider area. The accession process of CEECs provided a laboratory for scholars to explore Europeanization in candidate states in detail and the magnetic impact of the EU pulling these countries to itself has been identified as the primary driving force of transformation in Central and Eastern Europe (CEE). Such magnetic pull of the EU in its neighbourhood demonstrated the transformative power of the EU motivating states in its near abroad to transform themselves to a European model. However, the transformative power of the EU needs to be unpacked for different issues. As the least likely area for reform, minority rights constitute a challenging issue for the EU's transformative power.

The EU and minority rights

After the dissolution of the Soviet Union and end of the Cold War, the dominance of hard security issues was replaced with the increasing place of soft security issues like illegal migration, corruption or low-intensity conflicts and civil wars at the world agenda. Especially ethnic conflicts of this era in the Balkans had a significant impact on the European approach on minorities and minority rights. Having had various ethnic, religious and linguistic minorities, the European states felt threatened by the spill over potential of the conflicts to all Europe, and this led to the increasing European attention on minority issues.

At the first half of the 1990s, the European agenda was dominated with the discussions on the preparation of standards for minority protection. In this process, the role of European organizations (i.e. the Council of Europe (CoE), the Organization for Security and Co-operation in Europe (OSCE) and the EU) in addition to the European states was critically important. At the end, a consensus emerged among the European states and organizations to deal with the imminent 'minority threat' through creating norms and standards at the minimum level and building the necessary mechanisms to monitor the implementation (Kymlicka 2007: 197).

In spite of the consensus and concrete effort in Europe for building minority standards up, this does not lead to the establishment of a minority regime like the well-established human rights regime of Europe. Yet, a European minority regime has still been in the making and it is gradually emerging with the efforts of three European organizations (i.e. CoE, OSCE, EU) (Nancheva 2016). Collaboration among these organizations led to some common standards on minority protection through referring to the documents of each other and, therefore, the standards regarding minority protection, and paved the way for a European minority rights regime (Galbreath and McEvoy 2013: 11).

While efforts for establishing minority standards in Europe have started to progress by the 1990s, interestingly, there is still no consensus on the definition of minorities. Despite their reputation as the most active organizations advocating the protection of minorities, neither the United Nations (UN), the CoE, the OSCE, nor the EU have clarified the definition of 'minority' and their rights within their documents. Though, Capotorti's (1979) definition of minorities has been widely recognized, but not officially accepted by the international community, including the EU. Capotorti (1979) defines minorities on the basis of four characteristics:

(1) a group of citizens who are different from the majority on the basis of race, religion, or language;
(2) a relatively small group;
(3) non-dominant; and
(4) determined to protect their identity, which differs from that of the majority.

Considering the development of minority rights in Europe, the role of three European organizations (i.e. the CoE, OSCE and the EU) is critical as mentioned. To start with, the CoE, as an active actor in human rights before the 1990s, has increasingly focused on minority rights and standards in 1990s. The Council established the Committee for the Protection of National Minorities in 1993 to prepare a European treaty on minority protection (Galbreath and McEvoy 2013: 12). Accordingly, Framework Convention for the Protection of National Minorities (FCNM), a binding, multilateral and comprehensive text for minority protection, was adopted in 1994 and entered into force in 1998. The Framework constitutes the cornerstone of minority protection in Europe, as it determines the fundamental standards on minority rights in the continent. While the implementation of the Framework is left to the member states, a monitoring mechanism preparing regular reports on the implementation was established and strictly oversaw the process (Gilbert 1996: 174). Despite some countries like France or Turkey refuse to sign the Framework, it is still the most important instrument on minority protection in Europe.

Together with the Framework Convention, European Charter for Regional or Minority Languages has been the most referred documents in European minority protection. Though, the Charter provides neither individual nor collective rights for the ones who speak regional or minority languages; rather it aims to promote and protect those languages (Thornberry 2001: 58).

The OSCE, as another active actor regarding minority rights, also plays a key role in the embedding of minority standards in Europe. Like the CoE, OSCE focused on human rights issues rather before the 1990s and later on minority rights. The organization aims to prevent any kind of oppression on minorities wherever they live, to minimize the conflicts between the majority and minority and formulate state policies on minority protection (Preece 1998). Starting with the 1989 Concluding Document of the Vienna Meeting, OSCE released many documents dealing with minority protection (e.g. 1998 Oslo Recommendations regarding the Linguistic Rights of National Minorities) (Galbreath and McEvoy 2013: 11). However, the impact of all these documents that constitute the minority standards of OSCE remains limited due to the non-binding nature of them (Wright 1996: 197). Most importantly, High Commissioner on National Minorities established within the OSCE in 1992 to detect potential conflicts and develop early-warning strategies has taken an important role in European minority protection (Johns 2003: 689). Yet, the Commissioner was envisaged as an instrument for European security, and accordingly, it was designed as an institution about minorities, but not for minorities (Wright 1996: 200).

Despite gradually developing a significant role in promoting minority rights in Europe, the EU has still pursued a rather low profile in European minority rights. The Union has still not established its own minority standards, and therefore, it has been compelled to refer minority standards of different European organizations (i.e. CoE and OSCE) (Toggenburg 2000; Schwellnus *et al.* 2009). Not having any established minority standards, the EU does not have any jurisdiction over the protection of minorities within its borders and leaves the issue to the jurisdiction of individual member states. At the end, minority protection has remained a vague issue within the Union (Schwellnus 2005: 56).

The words of an EU official in an interview by Galbreath and McEvoy (2013: 175) clarifies the EU's approach on minority rights and frankly puts why there is no need of explicit minority standards of the EU: "there is 'no need to reinvent the wheel' as 'the wheel was invented perfectly by the Council of Europe'".

With the aforementioned approach in mind, the EU has nevertheless begun to encourage and actively promoted minority protection through its enlargement processes, in which minority protection was determined as a precondition for membership by the Copenhagen criteria. Such increasing attention and concrete efforts to promote minority rights was due to the increasing ethnic and religious tensions in Europe after the end of the Cold War (Kurban 2008: 272). As a result, security concerns outweighed for the inclusion of minority rights in the Copenhagen criteria, referring to the transition process of post-communist countries (e.g. the violent disintegration of the former Yugoslavia or any potential conflict in CEE) (Sasse 2008: 847). At the end, the EU has expanded the boundaries of its enlargement policy to include minority rights (Kurban 2008: 272).

In this process, the differential treatment of the EU regarding member and candidate states has generated concerns on double standards in minority rights (Schwellnus 2001: 3). While candidate states have to adopt and implement various measures on minority protection to be a member of the EU, the EU left the issue to the member states' own jurisdiction. For instance, in 2010, France dismantled Roma camps and deported Roma, who were mostly Romanian citizens (BBC News Europe 2010). Although the European Commission and Parliament reacted to the French actions on the ground that they violated freedom of movement and the principle of non-discrimination, these incidents demonstrate the aforementioned double standards for member and candidate states.

Despite the concerns on double standards and even no standard at all on minority protection within the EU, the 2009 Lisbon Treaty constituted milestone for the EU regarding minority rights as it refers to 'minorities' explicitly for the first time in EU primary law. Article 2 of the Treaty on European Union mentions the rights of persons belonging to minorities as one of the values on which the Union is founded (Consolidated Versions of the Treaty on European Union 2010: 17). Article 2.3 also states that the EU "shall respect its rich cultural and linguistic diversity" (Consolidated Versions of the Treaty on European Union 2010: 17). However, the Treaty has still not provided a definition of the term 'minority' and left the issue open. Besides, there is no reference to 'national' minorities and their rights as collective rights; rather the phrase 'persons belonging to minorities' within a larger human rights context is referred in the Treaty. Nevertheless, through the Lisbon Treaty, the rights of persons belonging to minorities are accepted as a value on which the Union is founded; therefore, such rights can no longer be an exclusive condition for accession to the EU.

Since the EU considers protection of minorities as only a part of the Copenhagen criteria, the EU's impact on minority rights as collective rights still remains basically in the domain of enlargement policy. First of all, the Union expects candidate states to join the CoE and comply with its standards of both human and minority rights (Ram 2003: 34). Second, candidate states are required to sign two primary documents for minority protection: the Council Directive 2000/43, comprising of the principle of non-discrimination, and the Council of Europe Framework Convention for the Protection of National Minorities. The latter document was the first legally binding agreement on minority rights that required the promotion of equality and conditions for the preservation of minority cultures and identities (Ram 2003: 35). Third, the Union monitors the protection of minorities in candidate states by clarifying measures, specified for each country in the individual country reports and Accession Partnerships, to adopt and improve minority rights (Rechel 2008: 174; Toktaş 2006: 2).

In conclusion, minority protection has not been developed as a EU rule applicable to both member and candidate states. The issue is still a highly contested issue due to its nature, touching to the sovereignty of states, which wish to keep their jurisdiction on the issue. Within the EU, older member states do keep their jurisdiction over minority protection, while candidate states are responsible to take the necessary measures for minority protection that are put as priorities for action by the EU – varying across candidate states according to the level of their problems in the area and the protection already provided.

Transformative power of the EU, minority rights and the big-bang enlargement

The EU had a significant transforming impact on the post-communist states in its neigbourhood through the enlargement process. Yet, minority protection has always been a problematic and contested issue since it remains within the sovereignty of a state. In comparing Europeanization of other policy areas, the process in minority rights is slower and more problematic in CEECs, and change in the area varies within and across countries (Rechel 2009c: 227).

Many factors are identified by scholars (Hughes and Sasse 2003; Johnson 2006; Sasse 2005; Schwellnus 2005) for the problematic passage to minority protection in CEE: the controversial approach of the EU on minority rights (i.e. double standards for member and candidate states); the contested definition of what constitutes a 'national minority' and the lack of common minority standards within the EU; the lack of emphasis on minority protection within the pre-accession funding of the EU; and EU's tendency to accept candidates as members that do not fully implement minority rules.

Despite the aforementioned problems, research on minority rights in the CEECs (Brosig 2010; Kelley 2004; Ram 2003; Rechel 2008, 2009a; Sasse 2008) demonstrate that legal adoption in minority protection was considerably better than in any of the old member states. All CEECs adopted the primary EU legislation for minority rights: they transposed EU directives on non-discrimination with varying degrees of speed though; ratified the FCNM; adopted integration programs for Roma; and established governmental bodies dealing with minority issues (Rechel 2009b: 7). However, the Europeanization of minority rights represents a trend of accommodation rather than a real transformation in CEECs considering the implementation problems.

The legal adoption of minority rules as one of the most sensitive areas for reform in the CEECs confirms the positive impact of the EU through credible and technical application of its conditionality, empowered domestic actors to overcome domestic opposition in such a contested issue area (Brosig 2010; Kelley 2004; Rechel 2008, 2009a; Schimmelfennig and Sedelmeier 2005). At the end, the accession process of the CEECs demonstrates the successful strategy of the EU conditioning accession in return for compliance with EU priorities on minority protection, even though the issue constitutes the most contested area for reform.

In contrast to the aforementioned picture, scholarly work on minority rights in CEE finds only limited impact of the EU on the implementation of minority rules in CEECs (Brosig 2010; Kelley 2004; Rechel 2008, 2009a; Sasse 2008). Such trend of dutiful legal adoption with the lack of or low levels of implementation in the accession process of the CEECs strongly confirms that legal adoption in candidate states, including minority rights, has been driven by EU conditionality and, in contrast, the practical implementation of EU's minority rules have been shaped by different factors, mostly found in the domestic arena (Yilmaz 2012). At the end, there is still room for the improvement of the minority rights in CEECs as well as the EU member states.

Minorities and minority rights in Turkey prior to the reforms

Although there is no official recognition, when applying Capotorti's (1979) definition of minorities on the basis of four characteristics, a significant number of minority groups exist in Turkey – irrespective of their self-identification.

28 Transformative power of the EU

Therefore, Turkey is a multicultural and multiethnic state with approximately 50 different Muslim and non-Muslim minority groups living in it (Kaya 2013: 47). However, accurate numbers of individuals belonging to minority groups remain unknown, and the quantitative data need to be read cautiously.

Minorities in Turkey can be grouped on the basis of their religious, ethnic and linguistic differences from the majority. First, Turkey has historically been a home of various religious groups. They include Alevis, Caferis, Armenians, Jews, Rum Orthodox Christians and Assyrians. Although the precise population of these groups is unknown, the total estimated population is somewhere between 10 per cent and 33 per cent of the entire country (Kaya 2009: 10; Minority Rights Group International 2007: 11–14; Yıldız 2007: 791). Second, Turkey has also been the home of different ethnic and linguistic minorities. These minorities include Kurds, Arabs, Caucasians, Roma and Laz with the estimated population cited between 10 per cent to 23 per cent of the entire Turkish population (Kaya 2009: 10; Minority Rights Group International 2007: 11–14). However, the differentiation of minorities on the basis of religion, ethnicity and language is hardly reliable, since many minority groups are interlinked on the basis of overlapping religion, ethnicity or language, such as Christian Roma or Alevi Kurds.

Even though the information on minority populations in Turkey should be read with caution due to the estimation range, their existence alone warrants protection. However, with the exception of three non-Muslim minority groups, official approach to minorities in Turkey excludes various minority groups due to the restricted definition of the term 'minority'.

Who is a 'minority'? From the Ottoman Empire to the Turkish Republic

The concept of minority in Turkey simply means 'non-Muslim' citizens for the official authorities. The concept is derived from the 1923 Lausanne Peace Treaty, which is still in force today and cited by many as the source of the official policy regarding minorities and their rights. While the Treaty defines minorities in Turkey as non-Muslims without mentioning any communities granted with minority status, 'non-Muslim' phrase was interpreted in the Republic of Turkey as the 'prominent non-Muslim communities' (i.e., Armenians, Greeks and Jews) and, consequently, the rights of these minorities are under the protection of the international arena (i.e. the League of Nations at the time the Treaty was signed) for Turkish authorities (Dressler 2015: 16). Therefore, Turkey still rejects the international definition of minority on the basis of racial, linguistic or religious differences, and denied the existence of Muslim minorities such as Kurds or Alevis and their rights (Grigoriadis 2008: 31; Oran 2004: 64).

It is widely confirmed in the literature (e.g. Bayır 2013; Cagaptay 2006; Kaya 2013; Oran 2004, 2014) that the denial of Muslim minorities has historical roots in the Ottoman Empire's system of *millet* – referring to 'confessional community'. The *millet system* divided subjects of the Sultan on the basis of religion: Muslims, regardless of ethnic origin, as one Muslim community, as the 'Dominant

Community', and non-Muslims as the 'Dominated Community' (Cagaptay 2006: 5; Oran 2014: 18–19). As noted by Oran (2006: 50), the system was both multicultural and discriminatory. While Muslims were considered to be the first-class members of the Empire, non-Muslims were treated as second-class members (Oran 2007: 37). Despite granting international protection for minorities in the 17th century, Ottoman rulers and society perceived minorities as a 'threat' and a potential tool for international powers to interfere in the internal matters of the Empire, which also persevere in the Turkish Republic (Grigoriadis 2008: 34).

By the *Tanzimat* reforms in the 19th century, *millet* as a term referred to religious minority groups that were legally protected (i.e. Greek, Orthodox, Jewish, Armenian and Syrian Orthodox groups) and *millets* were subjected to strict regulations in their relationship with the ruling Muslims (e.g. building new churches only under license, limits imposed to inter-marriage) (Kaya 2013: 33–4). Therefore, the *millet* system held *millets* with their collective non-Muslim identity rather than members of a group as individuals (Kaya 2013: 34).

As Oran (2009) stresses, the *millet* system has been transferred to the Republic with modifications. The Treaty of Lausanne codified the system by preserving non-Muslims as the Dominated Community and changed the Dominant Community to mean not only Muslims, but also Turks (i.e. Muslim Turks) (Oran 2014: 18–19). The discriminatory character of the *millet system* has been preserved in the Republic of Turkey with the denial of Muslim minorities and restricting the definition of non-Muslim minorities to only Armenians, Greeks and Jews.

Another explanation for the restricted approach to minorities and minority rights in the Republican era is provided by Bayır (2013), challenging the aforementioned dominant perspective in the literature (i.e. *millet* system). Bayır (2013: 15) argues that Turkish approach to minorities and minority rights needs to be analyzed considering the transition from an imperial-state to a modern nation-state and the Republican elites' perspective of diversity and nation-state structure as incompatible.

Whether it is the *millet* system or the transitionary era that led to the limited approach of the Republic, various groups with different backgrounds have existed in Turkey. However, in line with the restrictive definition of minority, rights for minorities also remained restricted until the reforms launched in 2000s.

Minority rights in the Turkish Republic

Until the reforms, Turkey did not have any legal document regarding minority rights except the Lausanne Treaty. In addition, in the 1982 Constitution, no article concerned with minority rights was present. As stated in the Minority Rights Group International report on Turkey (2007: 10), "the Turkish constitutional scheme 'solves' the question of minorities without ever addressing it. There is no reference in the Constitution to the word 'minority', not even the Lausanne minorities." In addition, some articles of the 1982 Constitution were even used to restrict minority rights so often within the Republic.

As the only official document for minority protection, the Lausanne Treaty has also not been fully implemented due to its security-oriented roots and restrictive interpretations of authorities (Soner 2010: 26). As Oran (2009) emphasizes, there were three types of standard violations in minority rights of non-Muslims granted by the Lausanne Treaty: "Restrictions in education (violation of arts 40 and 42/3); Language restrictions ('30s and '60s; violation of art. 40); Restrictions imposed on minority religious foundations (violation of art. 42/3)".

Rights for some groups other than specified by the Turkish authorities (e.g. citizens speaking languages other than Turkish in their daily lives) were also not implemented and even bans were imposed in conflict with the Lausanne Treaty (Oran 2007: 40–1). For example, Article 42 of the Turkish Constitution stated that "No language other than Turkish can be taught as a mother language", and it banned the use of languages other than Turkish spoken in the daily life of Turkish citizens in education and in the political life with the following clause in the Law on Political Parties: "No language other than Turkish can be used by political parties in congresses, meetings" (in violation of Lausanne 39/4) (Minority Rights Group International Report on Turkey 2007: 15; Oran 2009). A number of judicial cases were also launched against individuals and political parties (e.g. the closure of pro-Kurdish political parties) by citing different articles of the Constitution (Minority Rights Group International Report on Turkey 2007: 15).

After all, the reasons for such a restricted minority policy were grounded in Turkish nationalism and Turkish identity, which were constructed during the early years of the Republic. Even though different discourses of Turkish nationalism (i.e. official nationalism or Atatürk nationalism, Kemalist nationalism or *Ulusculuk*, liberal neo-nationalism, Pan-Turkist radical nationalism and nationalism in Islamism) exist in Turkey, official nationalism as the 'root-language' of Turkish nationalism is the one that needs to be unpacked regarding minorities and minority rights (Bora 2011). Official nationalism of Turkey is the sum of French-style territorial citizenship and German-style ethnicist assumptions (Bora 2011: 63). Two elements or, as Kadıoğlu (2011: 35) states, twin motives of Turkish nationalism are critically important to understand the official minority policy of Turkey: the unity of the state and Westernism with secularism as its cornerstone.

First of all, as Article 3 of the 1982 Constitution clearly reflects, Turkish nationalism relies on the principle of 'indivisibility of the state': "The Turkish state, with its territory and nation, is an indivisible entity." This approach refers to, first, national unity and, second, territorial integrity of the state. In the early years of the Republic, the concept of nation was framed as a monolithic entity that cannot be divided (Oran 2007: 45). Due to homogeneous nation being a myth, as Özkırımlı (2011: 83) puts it, a territorial citizenship, defining citizenship on the basis of residence within the borders of the Republic, was used to achieve national unity in the Republic (Kaya 2013: 47). Therefore, an inclusive citizenship-based approach was constructed regarding the 'nation' and 'national unity' (Dressler 2015: 17). Yet, within time starting by 1931, the inclusive citizenship defined on the basis of *jus soli* has become an exclusive and ethno-cultural one based on *jus sanguinis* (Cagaptay 2006: 57; Kaya 2013: 47; Oran 2004: 65). This approach developed later was exclusive and restrictive, denying the existence of minorities and their rights other than translated from the Lausanne Treaty by the Turkish authorities (Oran 2007: 45).

As a result, citizenship as an ethnically defined concept of 'Turkishness' implying citizens as ethnically Turkish and religiously Sunni Muslim was evident in practice, although the citizenship was framed within civic republican borders with an emphasis on universal values in rhetoric (Karaosmanoğlu 2010: 1 94; Kaya 2013: 47; Özkırımlı 2011: 94). Besides, equality within the citizenship framework was mostly identified with national uniformity, and therefore national homogenization, within the Republican tradition (Soner 2010: 24). Therefore, diversity was seen as a 'threat' by the authorities, and accordingly, the idea of national uniformity left no room of tolerance to ethnic, linguistic and religious differences within the Turkish society (Soner 2010: 24). As Kadıoğlu (2011: 43) emphasizes:

> Citizenship certificates mask the absence of minority rights. Thus state officials and ordinary people take a false pride in saying that they are all Turkish citizens, without realizing that such homogenization masks difference and therefore is discriminatory.

Other component of the 'indivisibility of state' refers to the territorial integrity, which is a prominent feature of Turkish national identity and Turkish nationalism. This basically denotes the preservation of the state regarding the irreversibility of its borders (Kadıoğlu 2011: 42–3). Stressing the exclusive focus on the territorial indivisibility and on the potential enemies targeting it within the Turkish nationalism, Özkırımlı (2011: 94) explains the place of mind that the threat perception leads to in the end:

> A perpetual concern for survival continues to be the defining feature of official nationalism, as manifested by the credo 'Turks have no friends but Turks', which in turn gives birth to a thriving industry of conspiracy theories and a laborious process of inventing enemies, both within and outside.

The aforementioned imminent threats and enemies against the Republic are best reflected in the Sevrés syndrome, which is also the most referred issue behind the security-oriented perspective of minorities and minority rights. The syndrome, named after the Sevrés Treaty that led to the partition of the Ottoman Empire, refers to the fear of separatism and disintegration of the Turkish Republic (Aydın-Düzgit and Keyman 2007: 80; Kaya 2013: 65; Oran 2014: 47–8). The primary idea behind the Sevrés syndrome is that Turkey is encircled by both external and internal threats (i.e. the aim of the Christians and West to divide Turkey; of Kurds to split up the country; of Islamists to bring an Islamist rule to the country; and of Armenians to claim lands and properties from Turkey) (Oran 2009).

The particular relevance of the syndrome with the minority issue is the idea of possible collaboration among foreign powers and minorities to break up Turkey like once done in the past with the Sevrés Treaty for the Ottoman Empire (Oran 2007: 52). Through the 1970s to 1990s, the fear further fuelled by the intensifying clashes with and activities of the Secret Army for the Liberation of Armenia (ASALA)[1] and the *Partiye Karkeren Kurdistan* (PKK) (Oran 2007: 52).

Interestingly, Oran (2014: 47–8) considers the Sevrés syndrome as a chosen trauma, in which collective grief as much as collective victory unites people. Whether it is a trauma, syndrome or paranoia, it does not matter: the Sevrés issue securitized the minority issue in Turkey and led to a problematic picture for years in the area.

As seen, minorities are historically considered as 'threats' to the "indivisible unity of the state and of the nation" (Oran 2009). The narrow definition of national identity on the grounds of homogeneity and indivisibility of the state and nation, excluding minorities and denying minority rights, has been the primary reason behind Turkey's restrictive minority approach (Engert 2010: 110; Toktaş 2006: 489–90). Most importantly, minority rights have long meant for the Turkish authorities a solid threat that would harm national unity and lead to social fragmentation on the basis of demands for autonomy and secession by minorities, especially referring to the Kurdish issue (Engert 2010: 111).

Second, the approach of Westernization via secularism dominated the scene by 1924 and led to the construction of a secular-Westernist Turkish identity in the early years of the Republic (Kadıoğlu 2011: 40). While secularizing reforms such as the change of Muslim Sabbath from Friday to Sunday, closing the religious seminaries (i.e. *madrasa*) and Sufi Dervish lodges, imposing to wear Western-style hats dominated the early era of the Republic, legal measures such as the 1926 secular civil code followed the symbolic acts of secularism (Cagaptay 2006: 13–14).

Most importantly, secular reforms were accompanied by assimilationist and homogenizing state policies towards both non-Muslim and non-Turkish-speaking Muslim groups, who were also exposed to a Turkification process (Kadıoğlu 2011: 40). To achieve this, the authorities implemented many restrictive measures such as the "Citizen! Speak Turkish" campaign, making Turkish classes compulsory in minority schools and changing non-Turkish names of places (Çapar 2006: 83; Karaosmanoğlu 2010: 198; Kaya 2013: 47; Yeğen 2006: 107). Such policies reflect the exclusion of non-Muslims and the official denial of cultural, religious and ethnic differences of Muslim minorities. Furthermore, active pressure and bans on exercising minority languages and cultural traditions led to the eradication of differences among minorities (Çapar 2006: 85; Kaya 2013: 47).

In addition to the denial and exclusion of minorities through restrictive policies, the history of young Republic includes many tragic events that minorities experienced. For instance, in the beginning of 1940s, the Turkish government issued a tax called 'Wealth Tax' (*Varlık Vergisi*) to be paid by the people with high income. Because the state commission determined the amount of the tax for each individual to pay, especially non-Muslims faced very high amounts and many had to close their businesses, sell their property or even work in a labour camp, called *Aşkale*, in the case of non-payment (Karaosmanoğlu 2010: 196). The source of such policies came from the common belief that minorities constitute a group of rich and privileged people, who work against the unity and integrity of Turkey (Karaosmanoğlu 2010: 196).

Consequently, such perceptions and policies alienated both non-Muslim and Muslim minorities (Oran 2009). The report of Minority Rights Group International on Turkey (2007: 3) clearly reflects the aforementioned problematic picture and, accordingly, the historical setting of minority rights in the country – broadcasting in minority languages and using minority languages in political life and in public services were forbidden for years; more than a million people, mainly Kurds and Assyrians, were displaced from their homes in the Southeast; violence was a part of daily life for minorities (e.g. lootings of minority shops, murders of minority rights supporters); and an electoral threshold of 10 per cent prevented minority political parties from entering the Parliament.

To conclude, minority rights in Turkey, prior to the launch of the reforms, constituted both rhetorically and practically a restricted policy area. The denial of non-Muslims, other than three mentioned groups, along with various other Muslim minorities, was part of the official policy. Besides, the Lausanne Treaty, which granted certain rights to the officially chosen minorities, was not fully implemented. Both the official and societal stances concerning minorities were shaped by the perception of minorities as 'threats' to the integrity of the state, as a tool of foreign interference and as second-class citizens. Yet, reforms of the previous policies concerning minority rights changed the picture at the turn of the 21st century.

The EU, Turkey and minority rights

EU–Turkey relations endured ups and downs for decades due to a number of issues such as the divisions among EU member states on the prospective membership of Turkey and military interventions experienced in Turkey several times. Starting with the 1959 Turkey's application for association with the European Economic Community (EEC), the relations entered to a phase of closer engagement. In 1963, Ankara Agreement was signed to realize a gradual establishment of Customs Union (CU) between parties, and in 1987, Turkey applied for full membership to the EC. Yet, between those years, the relations were quite unstable (e.g. increasing doubts from the Turkish side on the benefits of association with the EU, unilateral freezing of the Ankara Agreement by Turkey in 1978) (Müftüler-Baç 2005: 19–20). At that time, the Commission recommended to the Members sticking to the Association Agreement with Turkey rather than adopting an accession perspective for the country, and accordingly, the Customs Union Agreement was signed between parties in 1995 (Müftüler-Baç 2005: 120).

Completing the first step to closer integration with the EU through CU, Turkey was disappointed with the EU's decision not to include the country on the list of EU candidate states in the 1997 Luxembourg Summit. After two years of anger and disappointment and tense relations with the EU, Turkey entered a new phase of its relations with the EU through the 1999 Helsinki Summit, which declared Turkey as a candidate state to the Union. Accordingly, by 1999, the EU provided a route map to Turkey for wide range of reforms in several areas, including minority rights, primarily through its reports.

As mentioned before, minority protection has been problematic in the Union because of the absence of a EU standard on the issue. Nevertheless, some guiding principles for minority protection are set up in the enlargement process, which

34 Transformative power of the EU

are tailor-made for each candidate country and detailed in the EU regular and progress reports on the country (Toktaş 2006: 13).

To understand what is demanded by the EU from Turkey in its accession process regarding minority rights, a thorough analysis of EU regular and progress reports on the country is needed. Considering the period of 1999–2014, EU priorities in minority protection, consistently demanded from Turkey, include the ratification of the CoE FCNM; eliminating bans on broadcasting and education in languages other than Turkish used by Turkish citizens in their daily lives and ensuring the implementation; eliminating the limited interpretation of the 1923 Lausanne Treaty – restricted definition of 'minority' limited to three non-Muslim groups (i.e. Armenians, Greeks and Jews); resolving the problems in the Southeast of the country, both culturally and socio-economically (including the issue of Internally Displaced Persons (IDPs)),[2] and the Kurdish issue; resolving the problems of non-Muslims and their foundations, such as granting property rights or removing the ban on training clergy and opening the *Halki* Seminary for the training;[3] and, eliminating the problems of non-Sunni minorities (Alevis) (e.g. see European Commission 1999, 2005a, 2006a, 2007, 2008, 2009, 2012, 2013, 2014).

To go into detail, in 1999–2002, and compared to other periods, the EU placed significant emphasis on the Kurdish question. The Union emphasized the necessity to find a civilian solution to the problem and provide democratic rights to the Kurds, such as eliminating the ban on broadcasting in Kurdish (European Commission 1999: 14, 2000: 18). Besides, the underdevelopment in the Eastern and Southeastern part of the country primarily populated by the Kurds was a consistent reference in the EU regular reports on Turkey (European Commission 1999: 14, 2000: 18). Interestingly, in this period the EU tended to stress minority rights to provide a civilian solution to the 30-year Kurdish–Turkish conflict. Overall, EU demands regarding minority rights focused highly on the ratification of European and international agreements, broadcasting and education in other languages than Turkish used in daily life of citizens, the Kurdish problem and the problems in the Southeast region of Turkey, and the recognition of minorities in broader terms than the Lausanne Treaty.

During 2002–2004, the EU continued its stress on the issues regarding the East and Southeast Turkey (e.g. lifting emergency rule in the region, finding a solution to the problem of IDPs and the removal of village guard system).[4] The problems of non-Muslim religious communities including the legal personality and property rights of their foundations, the training of clergy, minority schools and their internal management and the restrictions on the exercise of cultural rights and on broadcasting in languages and dialects traditionally used by Turkish citizens in their daily lives – all were stressed by the EU for further improvement (European Commission 2002, 2003, 2004).

Notably, the Union enlarged its demands to include the implementation of the rules adopted in this period, such as the broadcasting and teaching in different languages and dialects traditionally used by Turkish citizens in their daily lives, measures regarding for property rights and the construction of places of worship (European Commission 2002, 2003, 2004).

The most important difference of the years between 2002 and 2004 from the previous period was the EU's approach to Kurdish problem and minority rights. Since 2002, the EU has changed its strategy from insisting on a specific solution to the Kurdish problem through providing rights to Kurds to a wider call for improvement in minority rights for all minorities (e.g. European Commission 2004). Such a broader approach enabled the EU to put pressure on Turkey regarding specifically the Kurdish issue and generally minority protection and give, at the same time, the Turkish government more scope for action in such a domestically contested area.

In 2005–2007, the EU stressed the implementation issue more, focusing primarily on ongoing restrictions concerning previously granted minority rights. The Union consistently stressed that Turkey should further remove restrictions on minority rights (e.g. use of other languages other than Turkish used by Turkish citizens in their daily lives), referring to the duty of the Turkish government to ensure the exercise of the rights provided to minorities by recent legal reforms (European Commission 2005a, 2007). Additionally, the priorities stressed in the EU reports became more specific like abolishing the religion information on ID cards, addressing the difficulties experienced by non-Muslim minorities in acceding to the administrative and military positions, or eliminating discriminatory language in school books (European Commission 2005a, 2007; European Commission against Racism and Intolerance 2005).

Seeking active participation of other European organizations and cooperation with them to improve minority protection was another highly stressed issue in the EU reports for Turkey in 2005–2007. For instance, the EU has emphasized the necessity of building dialogue between Turkey and the OSCE High Commissioner on National Minorities on issues like the participation of minorities in public life (European Commission 2005a, 2007).

In the last period of 2008–2014, the EU provided an even more detailed roadmap for Turkey to improve minority protection. First, the focus thoroughly shifted to the implementation problems. Second, the issues emphasized intensely were the ones left untouched by the Turkish government, such as the elimination of restrictions on using languages other than Turkish in political life (European Commission 2009, 2012). Third, Roma and their rights were put to the forefront in this period comparing it to the previous years. Many issues were raised by the EU regarding Roma, such as the need to build a strategy to solve problems of Roma, or to amend the Law on the Movement and Residence of Aliens, which discriminated against Roma (European Commission 2008, 2009, 2010, 2012, 2013, 2014, 2015). Fourth, the elimination of hate speech and hate crimes has increasingly been underlined starting by 2011 (European Commission 2011, 2013, 2014, 2015). Last but not least, notably, the EU increasingly focused on the Kurdish problem in this period, most likely due to the launch of Kurdish peace process by the Turkish government (European Commission 2008, 2009, 2010, 2013, 2015).

All in all, since 1999, the EU has stressed detailed priorities for the improvement of minority protection in Turkey each year and further specified them through time. Three points arise from the analysis of EU demands from Turkey regarding minority rights. First, the EU consistently put pressure on Turkey to solve its fundamental problems, such as eliminating the restrictive definition of minorities based on the Lausanne Treaty and ensuring broadcasting and education in other languages used in the daily life of Turkish citizens.

Second, the EU detailed its roadmap for improving minority protection over time. Especially since 2008, such detailed recommendations have become explicit. However, this is not a surprise since as much as the Turkish side tackles the fundamental issues, the issues left untouched came to the upfront and deepened critiques and recommendations, which remained hidden behind the fundamental ones.

Third, the EU has put increasing attention on the problems of the implementation since 2005. While still stressing further legal adoption in areas that are not handled by the government, the EU has ever-increasingly put pressure on the Turkish authorities to ensure implementation of the rules previously adopted. Issues like education and broadcasting in other languages other than Turkish used by Turkish citizens in their daily life, Foundations Law regarding property rights for religious foundations, or the Law concerning IDPs constitute the main issues for implementation (e.g. see European Commission 2009, 2010, 2013, 2015).

Conclusions

The transformative power of the EU has been successful in promoting minority protection beyond its borders through the enlargement policy. Although many problematic issues exist within the EU regarding minority rights, such as the vague or no common standards of minority protection at the EU level, as the transformation process of the CEECs demonstrated, the EU successfully promoted legal change in minority rights and to some extent implementation of the rules in the region through its enlargement policy.

Turkey as a candidate state to the EU has also been under the direct attention of the EU starting in 1999. At the time of the launch of candidate country status for Turkey, a significant gap or misfit existed between the minority regime of the country and the demands of the EU detailed for Turkey to take action in the area. While a threat perception grounded in a security-oriented approach was dominant regarding minorities in the country, reforms concerning minority protection at the turn of the 21st century changed the picture, which will be explored in detail in the next chapter.

Notes

1 Having assassinated many Turkish diplomats, ASALA was a militant group formed in 1975 to force Turkey accept responsibility for the1915–1916 events.
2 During the 1990s, around 380,000 Kurdish villagers were forcefully displaced by Turkish security forces due to the conflict with the PKK in the Southeastern part of the country (Human Rights Watch 2004; UN Human Rights Council 2010: 15). This led to a number of problems concerning the IDPs.
3 The *Halki* Seminary is the training college for priests, which was closed in 1971 by a decision of the Turkish Ministry of National Education on the grounds that the Seminary did not have enough students. Since then, it has been closed.
4 The village guard system, armed civilians against the PKK, was launched after 1985 by the Turkish state (Ayata and Yükseker 2005: 16; Freedom House 2005: 6).

3 Changing minority rights of Turkey in 1999–2014

Minority rights constitute a highly sensitive area for reform connected to various areas, such as identity issues, citizenship matters and national security, and therefore, promoting minority protection in any country is highly challenging, which makes the issue the least likely area for reform (Liaras 2009: 1). However, reforms for minority rights in Turkey were successfully launched in the 2000s.

After the launch of candidate country status for Turkey in 1999, the reforms did not begin automatically, but rather until the AKP's rule, no significant change was observed regarding minority rights. The 1999–2002 period under the coalition government of the Democratic Left Party (*Demokratik Sol Parti* – DSP), the Nationalist Action Party (*Milliyetçi Hareket Partisi* – MHP) and the Motherland Party (*Anavatan Partisi* – ANAP) is, therefore, more of a preparation phase for reforms to establish necessary institutions like the Secretariat General for EU Affairs and conclude necessary documents (e.g. the National Program for the Adoption of the *Acquis*) and agreements like the Accession Partnership with the EU signed in 2000.

Additionally, in 1999, the arrest of Abdullah Öcalan, the leader of the PKK, and the ceasefire between the PKK and the Turkish government, were vital developments regarding minority rights. These developments can be considered preparatory steps that enabled the government to launch reforms in the following years without having enormous reaction from the public; minority-protection measures in the past were often seen by the public as giving concessions to the PKK (Öniş 2003: 14).

Beginning in February 2002, the coalition government kicked off reforms for legal harmonization of Turkish laws with the EU's. However, the only change related to minority rights brought about in 1999–2002 was indirect through the 2001 Constitutional amendments by removing of the sentence "No language prohibited by law can be used to express and diffuse thoughts" (European Commission 2001: 25). The amendment granted negative rights to the minorities by removing or amending the sentence in the Constitution that was formally used to prosecute minorities (Oran 2004: 119).

Except for the removal of the aforementioned language ban from the Constitution, the preparation phase did not witness any legal adoption or implementation. Therefore, two years until the November 2002 elections passed without the adoption of any significant minority measures, and this period represents inertia in minority-related policy change.

2002–2004: slowdown in legal adoption with increasing implementation leading to shallow policy change

After the 2002 elections, the reform process accelerated in a number of policy areas, including minority rights, under the AKP government. Started by the previous government, eight reform packages passed through the Parliament until 2004 including both amendments of rules restricting minority rights and the adoption of new measures to improve minority protection. Comparing the policies adopted over time with the initial policy, the period from 2002 to 2004 represents a considerable break from the previous policies, which were characterized by the denial of minorities and their rights as well as the restriction of the rights of minorities recognized by Lausanne together with assimilation and Turkification of different groups other than the majority (Oran 2009).

To start with legal adoption, the 2002–2004 period represents vital changes from previous policies. One of the most challenging issues, the bans on broadcasting and education in languages other than Turkish used in daily life of Turkish citizens, were eliminated during this period (Official Gazette 2002).

To improve the socio-economic and cultural development in Eastern and Southeastern Turkey, populated mainly by Kurds, emergency rule was lifted entirely in 2002. Additionally, by signing the Ottawa Convention in 2004, the government launched its program to remove landmines in the region (Hammarberg 2009: 14).

Regarding the problems of non-Muslim minorities, difficulties in property rights of non-Muslim foundations were eased via an amendment to Article 1 of the Law on Foundations, including the extension of the application period for community foundations to register real-estate holdings to 18 months (Official Gazette 2003a). Another amendment to Article 2 of the Law on Construction was also adopted to allow the building of places of worship for various religions and faiths (Official Gazette 2003b).

Minority protection was further enhanced through the ratification of international agreements: the 1965 UN Convention on the Elimination of All Forms of Racial Discrimination in 2002, and both the International Covenant on Civil and Political Rights and the International Covenant on Economic, Social and Cultural Rights in 2003 (Secretariat General of the Turkish Republic for EU Affairs 2007: 19).

With the 2004 Constitutional Reform Package, an indirectly minority-related amendment was adopted in the Article 90 concerning the ratification of international agreements to the Constitution (Secretariat General of the Turkish Republic for EU Affairs 2007: 19). The amendment confirmed that, in the case that a conflict between a domestic and ratified international convention on human rights occurs, the latter takes precedence (Grigoriadis 2008: 36). Such a clause protects minorities through bypassing any discriminatory domestic law (Grigoriadis 2008: 36).

To summarize, legal adoption of minority rules progressed significantly in 2002–2004 – turning away from the historical legacy. A number of rules were

Changing minority rights in 1999–2014 39

adopted and amended by the coalition and AKP governments starting by 2002 (see Table 3.1).

While legal changes accelerated starting by 2002, interestingly, in such an early phase implementation also progressed. To start with, the government launched the "Return to Village and Rehabilitation Project" (RVRP) to facilitate the return of the Kurdish villagers that were forcefully displaced by Turkish security forces during the 1990s, due to conflict with the PKK in the Southeastern part of the country (Human Rights Watch 2004; UN Human Rights Council 2010: 15). Although it is difficult to monitor actual implementation of such programs, official statements from Turkey suggested that the RVRP was further implemented in 2002. According to Turkish authorities, 37,000 persons returned to their villages by 2002, such as Diyarbakır, Bingöl, Van and other areas of Eastern and Southeastern Turkey (European Commission 2002: 43). However, the numbers provided by the Turkish government are under suspicion because there are sources asserting that these figures were falsified: for instance, the report by Human Rights Watch (2004) states that the RVRP was not implemented in this period.

Table 3.1 The demands of the EU and the response of legal adoption by Turkey: 2002–2004

EU Demand*	Turkish Response
Ratification of the UN International Covenant on Civil and Political Rights with its Optional Protocol and of the UN International Covenant on Economic, Social and Cultural Rights (3)	In 2003 with reservations
Ratification of the UN Convention on the Elimination of All Forms of Racial Discrimination (3)	In 2002
Recognition of the use of languages other than Turkish for broadcasting and elimination of restrictions (3)	In 2002, 2003 and 2004
Recognition of the use of languages other than Turkish for education and elimination of restrictions (3)	In 2002, 2003 and 2004
Improvement to the situation in the Southeast in terms of socio-economic development and cultural rights (1)	Improvement starting by 2003
Lift of emergency status in the Southeast (1)	In 2002
Provision and implementation of property rights to religious foundations (2)	Improvement through an amendment in foundations law
Clearance of landmines (3)	Ottawa Convention signed
Elimination of bans and restrictions on minorities to exercise their rights (1)	Series of amendments in many laws to provide negative rights

Source: Author's own elaboration

*1 stressed in almost all EU documents under consideration
 2 stressed in around ¾ of the EU documents under consideration
 3 stressed in around ½ of the EU documents under consideration
 4 stressed in less than ¼ of the EU documents under consideration[1]

Keeping the aforementioned issue in mind, again according to information provided by the Turkish government, implementation of the RVRP continued to proceed in 2003. The Commission's regular report (2003: 40) states that 82,000 people were authorized to return to their villages between January 2000 and January 2003. Moreover, Turkey started a dialogue with international organizations to address the weaknesses of the RVRP highlighted by the UN Secretary General's Special Representative for Displaced Persons in 2002 (European Commission 2002: 43; Human Rights Watch 2004: 26). Nevertheless, the existence of village guards, who occupy the deserted lands in the region, constitutes a problem for the successful implementation of the RVRP (Human Rights Watch 2004).

Regarding property rights, 2,234 applications for the registration of property in line with the January 2003 Regulation were submitted, but only 287 were accepted (European Commission 2004: 43). Furthermore, only the 160 minority foundations listed in the Regulation could apply (European Commission 2004: 43), because many non-Muslim religious communities are not entitled to establish foundations, and they are deprived of the right to register, acquire and dispose of property. Another development in 2003 was the finalization of redrafting the descriptions of Christian denominations in religious educational textbooks, which were criticized by minorities for being subjective and inaccurate (European Commission 2003: 35).

Concerning non-Sunni Muslim communities, there were few developments. The banned Union of Alevi and Bektashi Associations were granted legal status in April 2003, allowing them to pursue activities (European Commission 2003: 36). However, the problem of Alevis regarding the compulsory "religious culture and ethics class" in schools continued (Hammarberg 2009: 9).

The implementation of freedom of associations regarding minorities was mixed and incoherent. For instance, the Kurdish Writers' Association, which was established in Diyarbakır in 2004, despite the restriction in Law banning the establishment of any association on the basis of race, ethnicity, religion, sect, region or any other characteristics of minority groups, were charged due to the meeting with representatives of the European Commission without seeking prior permission (European Commission 2004: 42).

In 2004, both broadcasting and teaching in languages used in the daily life of Turkish citizens other than Turkish began. Although there were some restrictions, greater tolerance was achieved. For instance, six private schools started teaching Kurdish (Kirmanchi dialect) in several cities (European Commission 2004: 49; Hammarberg 2009: 4).

Additionally, in October 2004, Istanbul's main synagogue was reopened after the 2003 bombing with an official ceremony attended by Prime Minister Erdoğan (European Commission 2005a: 430). In December 2004, a complex comprising a mosque, church and synagogue – 'the Garden of Religions' – was opened in Belek (European Commission 2005a: 30).

To conclude, in the early phase of enacting the reforms, legal adoption in minority rights was complemented, to some extent, by implementation (see Table 3.2).

Table 3.2 The demands of the EU and the response of implementation by Turkey: 2002–2004

EU Demand*	Turkish Response
Solution to the problems of IDPs (1)	Further implementation of the RVRP
Provision of rights to non-Sunni Muslims (i.e. Alevis) (1)	Some improvement on the legal status of non-Sunni associations
Provision and implementation of property rights to/of religious foundations (2)	Applications began for the registration of foundations
Elimination of restrictions on broadcasting in languages used in the daily life of Turkish citizens other than Turkish and implement them (1)	Limited implementation in state television
Elimination of restrictions on education in languages used in the daily life of Turkish citizens other than Turkish and implement them (1)	Teaching in private schools – but limited implementation
Revision of the curricula in schools and removal of discriminatory language from textbooks (3)	Finalization of redrafting descriptions of Christian denominations in religious education textbooks
Provision and implementation of freedom of religious associations (1)	Establishment of the Kurdish Writers' Association
	-Reopening Istanbul's main synagogue
Elimination of the problems with construction permits for places of worship (3)	-Opening a complex comprising a mosque, church and synagogue – 'the Garden of Religions'

Source: Author's own elaboration

*1 stressed in almost all EU documents under consideration
2 stressed in around ¾ of the EU documents under consideration
3 stressed in around ½ of the EU documents under consideration
4 stressed in less than ¼ of the EU documents under consideration

Although the implementation process was restricted, implementation that went hand-in-hand with legal adoption in such early phase of reforms represents a critical development in such a sensitive area.

At the end, the period of 2002–2004 signifies shallow change in minority rights, due to high degree of legal adoption and low degrees of implementation, therefore, due to the decoupling of the two (see Table 3.3). There is still much room for improvement in both legal adoption and implementation regarding minority protection, which progressed further in the following years.

Table 3.3 Minority-related policy change in Turkey: 1999–2004

Legal Adoption	Implementation	Policy Change
High degree	Low degree	=
Progress	**Very Limited**	Shallow Policy change

Source: Author's own elaboration

42 *Changing minority rights in 1999–2014*

2005–2007: progressing legal adoption with implementation leading to selective policy change

In 2005–2007, legal adoption for minority protection slowed down significantly (see Table 3.4). Although there were legal changes to some extent, such as the new Law on Foundations, legal adoption was inconclusive when compared to the previous period, and developments in the area are as follows.

In July 2005, the Ministry of the Interior issued a circular for facilitating the voluntary return of IDPs, raising public awareness of the process and initiating further collaboration with non-governmental organizations (NGOs) (European Commission 2005a: 39). The circular aimed to clarify the Governorships' duty to take necessary measures to facilitate voluntary return to the places in which security was successfully achieved, and to make the process more transparent and participatory (Secretariat General of the Turkish Republic for EU Affairs 2007: 22). Moreover, the Council of Ministers issued a strategy document (i.e. the Internally Displaced Persons Problem and Measures on Village Return and Rehabilitation Project) on August 17, 2005, to clarify official aims and principles of IDP strategy (Secretariat General of the Turkish Republic for EU Affairs 2007: 22).

On April 12, 2006, the ninth harmonization package was announced. The package included the legislation of the Law on Private Education Institutions, which entered into force on February 14, 2007. The new law changed the previous law by removing the citation of "Turkish origin" and through that eased limitations in schools established by foreigners, including minority schools where the language of education is not Turkish (European Commission 2007: 21; Secretariat General of the Turkish Republic for EU Affairs 2007: 24).

On November 9, 2006, the Law on Foundations improving the status of minority foundations and allowing minority groups to reclaim their previously seized

Table 3.4 The demands of the EU and the response of legal adoption by Turkey: 2005–2007

EU Demand*	Turkish Response
Solution to the problem of IDPs (1)	-Circular for facilitating voluntary return of IDPs -Strategy document titled the Internally Displaced Persons Problem and Measures on Village Return and Rehabilitation Project
Improvement in the situation of Roma (2)	New Law on Settlement
Solution to the problems of minority schools (2)	New Law on Private Education Institutions

Source: Author's own elaboration

*1 stressed in almost all EU documents under consideration
 2 stressed in around ¾ of the EU documents under consideration
 3 stressed in around ½ of the EU documents under consideration
 4 stressed in less than ¼ of the EU documents under consideration

property was adopted by Parliament and sent to the President for approval. However, the President returned the law to Parliament for clarification and discussion of some articles (European Commission 2007: 21; Secretariat General of the Turkish Republic for EU Affairs 2007: 23). In addition, on September 26, 2006, a new Law on Settlement eliminating discriminatory provisions against Roma was adopted (Secretariat General of the Turkish Republic for EU Affairs 2007: 23).

Starting by 2005, the slowdown – especially in legal adoption – was dramatic as seen. However, implementation of minority-protection measures continued to progress. As the report by Freedom House (2007: 2) stresses, despite the slowdown in almost all areas, "progress has not stopped altogether. For example, in 2005–06 a new penal code went into effect, an ombudsman office was established, and implementation of earlier reforms was systematically improved".

To begin with, broadcasting in languages other than Turkish, including Kurdish, proceeded in 2007, despite some restrictions (Freedom House 2009: 3; UN Committee of the Elimination of Racial Discrimination 2007: 27). In March 2007, a new radio channel in Diyarbakır, Çağrı FM, received authorization to broadcast in Kırmanchi and Zaza Kurdish (European Commission 2007: 22). Although four local radio and TV stations broadcasting in Kurdish were established, there were still restrictions (European Commission 2007: 22; Freedom House 2009: 3). For instance, all broadcasts, except songs, had to be either translated or subtitled into Turkish, making broadcasts, especially live broadcasts, highly cumbersome (European Commission 2007: 22). Besides, educational programs teaching Kurdish are not allowed neither on TV nor in radio broadcasts (European Commission 2007: 22).

The teaching of Kurdish also faced a backlash in August 2005, due to the closure of all existing Kurdish courses by the owners of five remaining schools (European Commission 2005a: 37; Freedom House 2007). Furthermore, two schools in Adana and Batman closed down earlier in the same year, due to financial difficulties (European Commission 2005a: 37). Most importantly, education in Kurdish in public schools was still banned by Turkish authorities at that time (Kurdish Human Rights Project 2004: 26).

Considering the role of the judiciary in guaranteeing the right to use Kurdish, the picture was mixed. Although the Court of Cassation revoked a decision banning the use of Kurdish music during the election campaign in May 2005, a Criminal Court in Diyarbakir ordered the confiscation of a number of music albums, on the basis of Article 312 of the former Penal Code, with the statement that the Kurdish language lyrics constituted propaganda in support of an illegal organization (European Commission 2005a: 38). The use of languages other than Turkish by public officials in their services was also problematic. For instance, in 2007, the Council of State dismissed the Mayor of Sur (Diyarbakır) municipality on the basis of initiating multilingual (Turkish, Kurdish, Armenian, Syriac, Arabic and English) municipal services (Hammarberg 2009: 5).

The registration of names other than Turkish also started to be implemented in this period by the civil registry offices (European Commission 2005a: 38). However, implementation varied throughout the country and faced problems concerning the registration of certain Kurdish names (European Commission 2005a: 38). In addition, a circular was still in force, at the time under investigation, prohibiting names including the letters Q, W and X, which exist in Kurdish, but not in Turkish (European Commission against Racism and Intolerance 2005: 22).

Although Prime Minister Erdoğan, while visiting Diyarbakır in August 2005, met with Kurdish intellectuals and stressed the necessity of resolving the Kurdish problem through democratic means, members of the pro-Kurdish Democratic Society Party (*Demokratik Toplum Partisi* – DTP) were repeatedly prosecuted for speech-related crimes (European Commission 2005a: 38; Human Rights Watch 2007: 13).

Further efforts, in this period, ensured the opening and functioning of places of worship other than mosques (European Commission 2005a: 30). For instance, in March 2005, a Protestant church was established as an association; in May 2005, the request of the Bahai community to renovate its garden was approved and, in June 2005, another Protestant church in Diyarbakır was registered as a place of worship (European Commission 2005a: 30).

Regarding property rights, in 2005 religious communities made 2,285 applications for the registration of property, in line with the 2003 Regulation, with 341 being approved (European Commission 2005a: 30). However, a number of non-Muslim religious communities were not recognized by Turkish authorities to establish foundations and, therefore, they were not granted the right to register and exercise property rights (European Commission 2005a: 30; Minority Rights Group International 2007: 27).

Regarding the demands for legal status to non-Muslim foundations, the government took no action in this period. By the same token, the Ecumenical Patriarch was not allowed to use the ecclesiastical title (Freedom House 2008: 15). Considering the situation of *Halki* Seminary, the training college of priests in Turkey closed in 1971 by a decision of the Turkish Ministry of National Education on the grounds there were not enough students to continue to operate, it remained closed. However, no restriction was imposed on the employment of foreign clergy in the country as there were 122 foreign clergy registered with working permits to serve in places of worship in 2006 (UN Committee on the Elimination of Racial Discrimination 2007: 21).

Interestingly, hate crimes and acts of intolerance against non-Muslim minorities increased in 2005–2007 (Freedom House 2008: 15). For example, in 2006, a Catholic priest in Trabzon was murdered (Freedom House 2008: 15); in 2007, three Protestants in Malatya were murdered (Freedom House 2008: 15); and also in 2007, the editor of the bilingual Turkish-Armenian newspaper *Agos* and human rights defender Hrant Dink was murdered (Human Rights Watch 2007: 12). It is important to note that Dink was prosecuted three times for speech-related charges (e.g. insulting Turkish national identity), which could be an example of the deadly consequence of such prosecutions and their publicization (Human Rights Watch 2007: 12). Notably, judicial cases of these murders were merged together with the case against *Ergenekon* case, defined as a criminal organization accused of plotting to overthrow the government (Today's Zaman 2008).

In 2007, there were rather some positive developments regarding the registration of religious associations. To illustrate, the Association for Supporting Jehovah's Witnesses, which had explicit religious objectives, was granted the right of official registration after the decision of the Court of Cassation, which confirmed the acquittal in a case against the association (European Commission 2007: 15).

Another important development of 2007 was the launch of the 'Alevi Opening'. This initiative was followed by many workshops organized by the AKP to reach out Alevis and discuss their demands (Pinar 2013: 512). Yet, the Opening remained rather symbolic, and no concrete change regarding Alevis and their rights was realized in this period.

The Law on Compensation of Losses Resulting from Terrorist Acts, adopted in 2004, also begun to be implemented in 2005–2007 with some delay and uncertainty (European Commission 2005a: 38). By August 2005, Turkish authorities reported that 173,208 applications had been made to the authorities and decided to provide compensation for the losses for 2,200 applications (European Commission 2005a: 38). By March 2005, 212,000 Turkish Lira had been paid to 22 people whose applications were considered eligible by the evaluation commissions (European Commission 2005a: 38). By May 2007, 269,759 persons had further applied to the Damage Assessment Commissions for compensation under the Compensation Law, and 37,309 applications got a positive response (European Commission 2007: 23; Minority Rights Group International 2007: 27). Moreover, the number of Damage Assessment Commissions increased to 106 (European Commission 2007: 23).

As seen the implementation of new laws and amendments in Turkish minority rights increased in 2005–2007 compared to the previous years (see Table 3.5). However, still a large room for development existed in those years for further implementation, and this denotes rather a limited degree of implementation in 2005–2007.

All in all, the period of 2005–2007 demonstrates a significant slowdown, with a very much low degree of legal adoption, in minority reforms and increasing implementation attempts of the rules previously adopted by the Turkish authorities concerned, although still limited. Such an outcome denotes selective policy change in 2005–2007 – still limited in scope compared to the other periods – due to the room for further legal adoption and implementation (see Table 3.6).

2008–2010: revival in legal adoption with intensifying implementation leading to selective policy change

The year 2008 represents a revival of legal adoption in minority rights, demonstrating a medium degree in comparison with other time periods (see Table 3.7). To begin with, after a slowdown in reforms since 2005, a new Foundations Law was adopted in 2008 (Hammarberg 2009: 11). The law provided non-Muslim foundations to be represented in the Foundations Council and provided for further property rights (Hammarberg 2009: 11). In addition, in October 2011, the provisional Article 11 of the Foundations Law that regulates the conditions for

Table 3.5 The demands of the EU and the response of implementation by Turkey: 2005–2007

EU Demand*	Turkish Response
Elimination of restrictions on broadcasting in languages used in the daily life of Turkish citizens other than Turkish (1)	-Broadcasting in languages other than Turkish/limited -Radio station broadcasting programs on Christianity -Further implementation of broadcasting in languages other than Turkish.
Elimination of restrictions on education in languages used in the daily life of Turkish citizens other than Turkish (1)	Teaching in languages other than Turkish/limited
Elimination of restrictions on the use of languages used in the daily life of Turkish citizens other than Turkish in public life (1)	Registration of names in languages used in the daily life of Turkish citizens other than Turkish /limited and varied
Elimination of the problems of religious foundations (1)	-Establishment of equal treatment for mosques and Christian churches regarding free access to water -Establishment of a Protestant church as an association in Ankara -Further registration of religious associations -The approval of the Bahai community's request to renovate its garden
Provision of rights to non-Sunni Muslims (i.e. Alevis) (1)	The launch of 'Alevi Opening'
Provision and implementation of property rights to/for religious foundations (2)	2,285 applications for registration of property
Elimination of the problem of IDPs (1)	-The Law on Compensation of Losses Resulting from Terrorist Acts with 173,208 applications -Continuing process of compensation with respect to IDPs

Source: Author's own elaboration

*1 stressed in almost all EU documents under consideration
2 stressed in around ¾ of the EU documents under consideration
3 stressed in around ½ of the EU documents under consideration
4 stressed in around less than ¼ of the EU documents under consideration

Table 3.6 Minority-related policy change in Turkey: 2005–2007

Legal Adoption	Implementation	Policy Change
Low degree **Slow down**	Medium degree **Increasing**	= **Selective Policy Change (Limited)**

Source: Author's own elaboration

applications for properties and compensation payments was amended through a decree law detailing the implementation of the Article (UN Committee on the Elimination of Racial Discrimination 2014: 27).

In regard to the problems in Eastern and Southeastern Turkey, the government announced guidelines of a plan aiming to further develop the region (European Commission 2008: 27; Freedom House 2009). The government ensured the allocation of funding – equivalent to 14 billion Euros –to complete the Southeastern Anatolia Project (*Güneydoğu Anadolu Projesi* – GAP), launched for supporting the socio-economic development of the Southeast Turkey, in 2008–2012 (European Commission 2008: 27). The GAP was later extended for further five years (European Commission 2012: 33). In April 2012, an incentive package was also adopted to increase investment in the underdeveloped regions and reduce regional disparities (European Commission 2012: 33).

In 2009, the government started both a parliamentary and public discussion to solve the Kurdish problem, which is called officially 'Unity and Fraternity Project', but also 'Kurdish initiative' or 'Kurdish Opening' (Freedom House 2010; Hürriyet 2010). The discussion initiated public and political awareness for making peace with the PKK through the democratization of Turkey and the granting of further rights to Kurdish people, while also encompassing other minorities (Freedom House 2010; Hürriyet 2010). This was the second attempt by Turkish officials after President Turgut Özal, in the 1990s, aimed to bring an end to the war in the East and Southeast of Turkey through further democratization (Sabah 2009).[2]

In 2009, Erdoğan as the Prime Minister of the Republic recognized the existence of the Kurdish people and the existence of a Kurdish problem (Hürriyet 2009). After the recognition and diagnosis of the problem, a debate emerged about making peace with the PKK and solving the Kurdish problem. As a result of the debate, 34 PKK members – as a peace activation group who were not related to any violent acts – returned to Turkey from a PKK base in Kandil, Northern Iraq, and were not charged with any crimes (Konuralp 2009). However, due to problems in the following months, 14 of them returned to the PKK Camp in Northern Iraq (Burulday 2010).

No matter how difficult, the Kurdish initiative of 2009 represents a vital development. The initiative, as it sought to extend cultural and linguistic rights to the Kurdish minority, was an important step for further progress in the protection of minorities (Freedom House 2010: 4). However, the fate of the initiative remained uncertain due to the ban of the pro-Kurdish party (i.e. DTP) and the protests, against the initiative, following it and later the process halted (Freedom House 2010: 4).

As a part of the Kurdish settlement process, in March 2013, some legislation as a part of the 'democratization package' including the private education in the languages used in the daily life other than Turkish and allowing the use of non-Turkish letters like X or Q largely used in Kurdish was adopted (European Commission 2014: 62; Freedom House 2015a). In June 2014, a law for the elimination of terrorism and strengthening social integration was adopted as a part of the legal basis for the settlement process, which provides legal protection to the people involved in talks with the PKK and facilitation of rehabilitating PKK militants that give up arms (European Commission 2014: 17).

In regard to the removal of landmines, in June 2009, Parliament adopted a Law on De-mining the Turkish–Syrian Border, allowing private companies to de-mine and to receive a right to farm the land for up to 44 years after the de-mining is concluded (European Commission 2009: 30).

In 2010, a minority circular was published by Prime Minister Erdoğan, declaring the right of non-Muslim minorities to exercise their cultural rights as part of their identities (Official Gazette 2010). The circular states the problems faced by non-Muslim minorities in public institutions with the necessity of removing any problems caused by representatives of public institutions and specifically stresses the necessity of implementation of the rights granted in the previous years (Official Gazette 2010).

In May 2010, another round of constitutional amendments was accepted by Parliament. The amendments comprised a number of issues that did not directly deal with minority rights. However, one of the amendments indirectly improves minority protection by setting higher obstacles to the closure of political parties and, as a result, minority parties (e.g. 2009 closure of pro-Kurdish DTP). After the amendment, proposals for closure of political parties can only be done by Parliament, though previously proposed by the Constitutional Court (CNN Türk 2010).

In March 2012, the Ministry of Education issued a new regulation on private education institutions that allows children of Armenian, Greek and Jewish minorities without holding Turkish citizenship to get education in minority schools (European Commission 2012: 31; Official Gazette 2012). Through the regulation, the old regulation allowing only children of minorities holding Turkish citizenship to be educated in minority schools was removed (Kaya 2012).

In February 2012, newspapers run by non-Muslim minorities were enabled to publish official notices in case they make a written application (European Commission 2012: 31). In June 2012, a new curriculum was issued for primary schools obligating them to add courses on living languages like Kurdish if there is a demand by 10 pupils minimum (European Commission 2012: 31). Moreover, a law that allows private education in the languages used in the daily life of Turkish citizens other than Turkish was adopted in 2013 as a part of the 'democratization package' (European Commission 2014: 62; Freedom House 2015a).

In 2013, an amendment was adopted to allow campaigning in languages used in the daily life of Turkish citizens other than Turkish by political parties and candidates, thus the ban on using those languages in political life was eliminated (European Commission 2014: 62). In January 2013, the Criminal Procedure Code was amended to enable defendants to use a language they prefer at some stages of judicial proceedings (European Commission 2013: 15, 62). Through this, the use of languages spoken in the daily life of Turkish citizens other than Turkish in public life was partly eliminated.

The Ministry of Interior issued a circular in 2014 to facilitate the registration of Roma as Turkish citizens (European Commission 2014: 61). Most importantly, in March 2014, an amendment in the Criminal Code was adopted focusing on hatred and discrimination that increased penalties for hate crimes, which, in turn, demonstrates an increasing attention on these issues (European Commission 2014: 60).

While legal adoption demonstrates progress compared to the previous years, the implementation of the rules adopted previously significantly accelerated as follows. In the area of broadcasting in languages used in the daily life of Turkish citizens other than Turkish, following the June 2008 amendments to the relevant Law, in January 2009, TRT (the public service broadcaster) started operating channel TRT-6, broadcasting in Kurdish 24-hours a day (Hammarberg 2009: 5; Freedom House 2009). At the inauguration ceremony of TRT-6, the Prime Minister spoke a few words in Kurdish. While, in 2009, the public radio network of the country began to broadcast in Armenian, more than 10 private companies applied for regional and local broadcasting licenses in Kirmanchi, Zaza and Arabic in January 2010 (UN Human Rights Council 2010: 8).

In 2010, the movie *Min Dît* ("The Children of Diyarbakır") was released in theaters in Turkey (Gökçe and Özbudak 2010). For the first time, a movie completely in the Kurdish language was allowed to be released in the country. Onatlı (2010) emphasizes that the movie is the first instance of professional Kurdish cinema, which was applauded by the public and even given awards in Turkey.

In March 2012, a Syriac monthly newspaper started publication for the first time in the Republic's history; in September 2013 Anatolia News Agency started broadcasting in Kurdish; in March 2015 a private children's channel started broadcasting in different dialects of Kurdish (European Commission 2012: 32, 2013: 63, 2015: 69). In addition, *Agos*, the Armenian-Turkish bilingual newspaper, has become available at the airport stands of Turkish Airlines by February 2013 (Akşam 2013).

Despite the positive developments in the area of broadcasting, restrictions in the Law on the RTÜK (*Radyo ve Televizyon Üst Kurulu* – Radio and Television Supreme Council) continue to be applied for private, local, and regional TV and radio programs (European Commission 2009: 30). For instance, educational programs in Kurdish are still not allowed; several court cases and investigations have been launched against GÜN TV – the only private TV channel broadcasting in Kurdish (European Commission 2009: 30).

In the area of education in languages used in the daily life of Turkish citizens other than Turkish, a number of positive developments have occurred. In September, the Higher Education Board's (*Yüksek Öğretim Kurumu* – YÖK) approved the application from Artuklu University in Mardin to establish an Institute called "Living Languages Institute" providing post-graduate education in Kurdish and other languages spoken in the country (European Commission 2009: 29). After a judgment by the European Court of Human Rights (ECHR) in 2009, the president of the YÖK decided to include Kurdish in language courses offered in

Table 3.7 The demands of the EU and the response of legal adoption by Turkey: 2008–2014

EU demand*	Turkish Response
Provision and implementation of property rights to/for religious foundations (2)	-New Foundations Law -2011 Decree Law to revise the Article 11 of the Foundations Law
Elimination of restrictions on the languages used in the daily life of Turkish citizens other than Turkish in public life (1)	Amendment in the Criminal Procedure Code 2013
Elimination of ban on the languages used in the daily life of Turkish citizens other than Turkish in political life (2)	Amendment to allow campaigning in languages other than Turkish by political parties and candidates
Improvement of the situation in the Southeast in terms of socio-economic development and cultural rights (1)	-Adopted plan and incentive package for development of the Eastern and Southeastern regions -Extension of the GAP project
Recognition of the languages used in the daily life of Turkish citizens other than Turkish for broadcasting and elimination of restrictions (1)	Legislation for non-Muslim minorities with running newspapers to publish official notices -Legislation to allow private education in Kurdish
Recognition of the languages used in the daily life of Turkish citizens other than Turkish for education and elimination of restrictions (1)	-New curriculum obligating primary schools to add courses on living languages such as Kurdish or Circassian in case minimum 10 pupils demand it.
Clearing the area of landmines (3)	Legislation to remove landmines
Removal of the village guard system (1)	Preparations to remove village guard system
Solution to the Kurdish Question (2)	-Kurdish initiative -Legislation to eliminate terrorism and support social integration as a legal basis of the settlement process -Legislation for the implementation of the democratization package of 2013 -The abolition of Article 10 of Anti-Terror Law and the reduction of maximum detention period to five years
Solution to the problems of minority schools (2)	New regulation allowing children of Armenian, Greek and Jewish minorities without Turkish citizenship to get education in minority schools
Ensuring the exercise of minority rights and establishing dialogue with minorities and their representatives (1)	Minority Circular
Improvement in the situation of Roma (2)	Circular to facilitate the registration of Roma as citizens
Closure of parties (2)	2010 Constitutional amendments
Elimination of hate speech and hate crimes (4)	Amendment in the Criminal Code

Source: Author's own elaboration

*1 stressed in almost all EU documents under consideration
2 stressed in around ¾ of the EU documents under consideration
3 stressed in around ½ of the EU documents under consideration
4 stressed less than ¼ of the EU documents under consideration

universities' curriculum. A Kurdish language course was also made available in the winter semester of 2009 at Bilgi University, Istanbul (Hammarberg 2009: 5).

Additionally, implementation has extensively continued in the recent years: in public schools elective courses in Kurdish are available; in various universities (e.g. Mardin Artuklu University, Bingöl University) departments on minority languages and culture are established, such as the Arabic and Syriac language and culture departments in Mardin Artuklu University or Kurdish language and literature department in Muş Alparslan University; post-graduate education in Kurdish and elective Kurdish courses at the undergraduate level are available in some universities (e.g. Mardin Artuklu University) (European Commission 2015: 69; UN Committee on the Elimination of Racial Discrimination 2014: 36).

With the amendment of Criminal Procedure Code in 2013, restrictions on using languages used in the daily life of Turkish citizens other than Turkish in public life was eliminated and implemented in the following years, such as at some stages of judicial proceedings and in letter exchanges or visits at the prisons (European Commission 2013: 14–15, 62).

Although the use of minority languages in political life was forbidden by the Law on Elections and Political Parties, in the 2009 local-election campaign, Kurdish was used by politicians and political parties without provoking any legal consequences (European Commission 2009: 28). Moreover, most of the court cases against Kurdish politicians for using the Kurdish language resulted in no penalty (European Commission 2009: 28). Furthermore, a number of governorships in the Southeast have begun to provide public services in Kurdish (European Commission 2009: 28).

Despite these positive developments, the use of minority languages in political life continued to be problematic for that time, and results were mixed in practice. For instance, in July 2009, the Court of Cassation charged DTP members for using Kurdish in political life (European Commission 2009: 28). The charges resulted with the closure of the DTP in 2009 and the ban of 37 members of the DTP from political life (BBC Türkçe 2009). The 2013 legislation allowing political campaigns in languages used in the daily life of Turkish citizens other than Turkish during local and general elections changed this picture and was smoothly implemented in the 2014 local elections and 2015 June and November general elections (European Commission 2014: 62, 2015: 69; UN Committee on the Elimination of Racial Discrimination 2014: 36).

The use of Kurdish in public has also been normalized, especially in the recent years through its use by official figures in public, such as in the 2013 celebration of the International Women's Day by the Diyarbakır police chief, or the speech by the President of the Diyanet and prayers said in Kurdish to celebrate the birth of the Prophet (European Commission 2013: 63, 2014: 16; Mynet 2013). Moreover, in the same year, preparation started for a Kurdish Quran as well as Kurdish Quran courses by the Diyanet, and prayers in Kurdish were allowed in mosques (European Commission 2013: 63).

The rights of non-Muslims have also been subjected to some developments regarding the implementation. The authorities responded positively to requests by non-Muslim students for exemption from compulsory religious and ethics classes, and the 2013 introduction of questions on Islam in the university entrance and secondary school examinations is followed by a declaration informing the public about the alternative questions prepared for non-Muslim students (European Commission 2013: 54, 61). Moreover, authorities accepted the request for reopening the Greek minority school on the island of Gökçeada, and the school was opened in 2013, while the secondary part began to function in 2015 (Gezen and Bozok 2015; UN Committee on the Elimination of Racial Discrimination 2014: 27). Besides, in minority schools, children without Turkish citizenship continue to have an option to attend courses as guest students, although without any graduation certificates (European Commission 2013: 62).

On the problems of religious foundations regarding the foundation status or legal personality, the foundation status was granted or restored to the Greek Orphanage in Büyükada, the patriarchal church of the Armenian Catholics in Istanbul, the Jewish Community in İzmir, the Greek primary school for girls in Istanbul and Armenian Tibrevank Lycee in Istanbul (European Commission 2012: 30; 2013: 60, 2015: 66). Moreover, regarding the problems with construction permits for places of worship, the Malatya Municipality reconstructed the Armenian cemetery in the city and opened it in 2013, and the Istanbul Metropolitan Municipality accepted the land request by the Istanbul Syriac Orthodox Church to construct a new church (UN Committee on the Elimination of Racial Discrimination 2014: 27).

Regarding property rights, the implementation of the Law on Foundations proceeded smoothly (European Commission 2009: 21; UN Human Rights Council 2010: 17). The revised Law was also implemented despite few problems: 116 minority foundations applied for restitution of properties (numbered as 1,560), and by April 2014, the Foundations Council decided to return 318 properties and pay compensations for 21 properties (European Commission 2014: 16, 59–60).

Some progress has also been achieved on providing work permits for foreign clergy (European Commission 2009: 21, 2012: 25; UN Human Rights Council 2010: 11). In 2008, the application of the Ecumenical Patriarchate for work permits was answered positively, including one-year visas for foreign clergy, though (European Commission 2009: 21; UN Human Rights Council 2010: 11). Furthermore, although the Syriac community informally started training outside official schools, the elimination of problems on training clergy remains intact (European Commission 2013: 55, 2015: 63). The *Halki* Seminary, the training college for priests, has remained closed since it was first closed in 1971 (Hammarberg 2009: 10; USCIRF 2015: 186).

The revision of curricula and removal of discriminatory language from textbooks continued with different initiations: the new religious education textbooks and new religious culture and ethics course textbooks including the Alevi faith; the revision of 10th grade history textbook of for its discriminatory rhetoric on Syriacs; and the preparation of textbooks and curricula by the authorities collaborating with stakeholders for Christianity courses at school (European Commission 2012: 24, 2013: 54, 61–2; USCIRF: 2015: 187).

Considering the rights for non-Sunni Muslims, Alevis specifically, there were some positive movements as well. The Turkish authorities participated in a number of Alevi gatherings, such as the opening of the first Alevi Institute in 2008, the Alevi fast-breaking ceremony in 2009, the President's hosting Alevi representatives for a first ever official fast-breaking dinner in 2012 (European Commission 2009: 22; Sabah 2012). Moreover, the government organized workshops to discuss the problems and expectations of the Alevis (European Commission 2009: 22). The public service broadcaster also began to broadcast some programs on the Alevi Muharram celebrations (European Commission 2009: 22).

Although Alevi places of worship (i.e. Cem houses) are not recognized as such and do not receive financial aid from the state, they were recognized by three municipal councils as places of worship and granted the same financial advantages as mosques (European Commission 2009: 22; Hammarberg 2009: 9). Moreover, several courts ruled that Alevi students do not have to attend the mandatory religion and ethics course (European Commission 2009: 22). However, some developments caused discontent among Alevis, such as naming the third bridge of Bosporus as I. Sultan Selim, who is perceived by Alevis responsible of mass Alevi killings (Milliyet 2013).

For the Kurdish settlement, the legislation adopted within the framework of democratization package was implemented in this period. Bans and restrictions using Kurdish in broadcasting and education and in public and political life were eliminated and further implemented: the use of Kurdish in public was normalized with the state officials speaking Kurdish in many public occasions; in addition to the open debates on the Kurdish issue and the settlement, a civic commission called 'wise persons' was established to trigger public support to the peace process; with abolishing the Article 10 of Anti-Terror Law and reducing the maximum detention period to five years, many defendants with cases related to the Kurdish issue (e.g. Union of Kurdistan Communities (Koma Civakên Kurdistan – KCK)) were released (European Commission 2013: 63, 2014: 17, 53; Kozan 2013). However, the peace process has halted in the recent years, and violence has escalated after the end of ceasefire by the PKK in 2013 (European Commission 2015: 24).

The GAP has also been implemented further with vital improvement in infrastructure (European Commission 2009: 30, 2012: 33, 2013: 15, 2014: 17, 2015: 25). However, disparities among the regions remain, and the refugee flux from Syria to the Eastern and Southeastern regions necessitates further attention on the region (European Commission 2015: 25). Besides, in regard to the exercise of cultural rights, Newroz (New Day Feast celebrated by Kurds) and some other Kurdish celebrations in general passed peacefully in the years under investigation (European Commission 2009: 30, 2012: 34, 2014: 53).

The implementation of the RVRP proceeded as well; by the end of 2009, 151,469 citizens returned to their former places of residence (UN Human Rights Council 2010: 16). Moreover, the government implemented the "Support for the Development of an IDP Program in Turkey Project" in cooperation with the United Nations Development Program (UN Human Rights Council 2010: 16). Despite these developments, village guards have still not been removed.

Regarding the IDPs, the law on compensation of losses resulting from terrorism and the fight against terrorism was extended and compensation process continued, without a national strategy adopted for the IDPs: 340,000 applications were assessed by 2015 by the Damage Assessment Commissions, and almost half of them got compensation (European Commission 2009: 32, 2012: 35, 2013: 16, 2015: 25; Freedom House 2009). Yet, progress on payment of compensation continued slowly, and some of the IDPs returned to their villages compelled to stay there for a limited time period due to the lack of infrastructure (European Commission 2009: 32, 2014: 18). Furthermore, IDPs has fallen from the government's agenda due to the increasing number of Syrian refugees arrived to Turkey starting by 2011 (Internal Displacement Monitoring Centre 2013).

The problem of removing landmines remains an important security concern as there have been casualties among civilians and security forces caused by explosions (European Commission 2009: 32). After ratifying the Ottawa Convention in 2004 to gradually remove landmines, the government began to destroy anti-personnel mines in mined areas to conclude the de-mining process by 2014 (European Commission 2009: 32). Because the de-mining process could not be finished, the government asked for an extension period to destroy the landmines until 2022, and therefore, the clearance of the landmines in the region was in progress (European Commission 2012: 33, 2013: 15, 2014: 17).

Interestingly, this period, unlike other periods, reflects an increasing focus on the situation of Roma and, accordingly, developments about the issue: dialogue between the Roma NGOs and the authorities accelerated; in 2013, the Roma People Forum of Turkey was established by several Roma associations and federations; Roma Language and Culture Research Institute was established in 2015 in Trakya University; efforts were taken by the Ministry of Labour and Social Security and Turkish Labour Agency (*Türkiye İş Kurumu* – İŞKUR) to promote the employment of Roma in temporary public benefit jobs and vocational training; health services have become accessible for Roma after the introduction of General Health Insurance in the country in 2012; one television series with discriminatory language was taken off the air; the Housing Administration of Turkey (*Toplu Konut İdaresi Başkanlığı* – TOKİ) constructed housing in many places for Roma living in poor conditions (ERRC 2013; European Commission 2012: 33, 2013: 62, 2014: 61, 2015: 69; UN Committee on the Elimination of Racial Discrimination 2014). Although a National Strategic Action Plan for Roma is under preparation, which would provide an official Roma strategy, Turkey still lacks an official Roma policy and, therefore, a solid base for the improvement in the situation of Roma (UN Committee on the Elimination of Racial Discrimination 2014: 14). In addition, there are still no quantitative data on the situation of Roma.

Notably, the years between 2008 and 2014 signify attempts for eliminating hatred and discrimination, which was neglected in the previous years. For instance, in December 2012, fines were issued to six people for their anti-Armenian banners at a rally, and in January 2015, a judicial case was launched against two columnists for inciting hatred in regard to the *Charlie Hebdo* caricatures (European Commission 2013: 60, 2015: 64).

Changing minority rights in 1999–2014 55

In addition to the aforementioned developments, the dialogue between the authorities and minorities, as well as minority representatives, intensified in 2008–2014 (UN Committee on the Elimination of Racial Discrimination 2014: 28). For instance, the President hosted a delegation of Syriacs from Sweden and visited the community in Sweden in 2013; Prime Minister and non-Muslim religious leaders met in 2013; the Parliament issued an invitation to the minority representatives – beyond the official definition of minorities – to receive their views on the new Constitution under preparation in 2011; and the Prime Minister gave a first ever message on the 1915 Armenian events (European Commission 2012: 31, 2013: 14, 60, 2014: 61).

To conclude, this period demonstrates an intensifying implementation of the measures adopted for the protection of minorities (see Table 3.8). In spite of the high degree of implementation, the process still remains selective like the one in the previous time period, because there is still room for further implementation of minority measures, such as the opening of *Halki* Seminary.

All in all, in 2008–2014, both legal adoption and implementation of minority rights showed progress. While legal adoption demonstrates a revival with a medium degree of change, implementation of minority rules signifies an intensifying and high degree of progress (see Table 3.9). This, in return, leads to selective policy change in 2008–2014.

What is left out? Cherry-picked reforms and selective change

Although Turkey has progressed in adopting measures for minority protection, there is still room for both legal adoption and implementation. For instance, Turkey has not signed the CoE FCNM; has not eliminated the restrictive interpretation of the Lausanne Treaty; has not adopted a national strategy and action plan for both Roma and IDPs; has not provided education in mother tongues other than Turkish; and has not published a regulation on election procedures in non-Muslim foundations, which were consistently demanded by the EU (European Commission 2012: 31, 2014: 16, 18, 2015: 68–9).

Besides, the process of implementation still remains problematic in many areas of minority protection stressed by the EU for improvement. Some of the issues are problems experienced by Syriacs, Yazidis and Greeks for registering property, especially in the Southeast of the country; existence of religion information in the identity cards and, to some extent, of discriminative language in school textbooks; restrictions on training clergy; continuing removal of landmines despite the commitment under the Ottawa Convention to finish clearance by 2014 (European Commission 2014: 17, 60, 2015: 63, 66, 68).

At the end, comparing the current situation in minority rights with the previous decades, significant improvement is observed. However, the process remains incomplete with significant room for further legal adoption despite increasing implementation (see Table 3.10). This suggests increasingly selective adoption of minority measures by the government over time. While selectively adopting legal measures as well, the implementation of the rules proceeded smoothly in most cases. For instance, providing legal rights to non-Sunni groups, mainly Alevis,

Table 3.8 The demands of the EU and the response of implementation by Turkey: 2008–2014

EU Demand*	Turkish Response
Elimination of restrictions on broadcasting in languages used in the daily life of Turkish citizens other than Turkish (1)	-National broadcasts, all day long, in languages used in the daily life of Turkish citizens other than Turkish on state television (i.e. TRT) -Start of the TRT-6, broadcasting in Kurdish 24-hours a day -Four local TV and radio channels broadcasting in languages and dialects traditionally used by Turkish citizens -Broadcast in Armenian began on state television TRT for half an hour, twice a day -Approval of the applications to broadcast in three dialects in Kurdish and Arabic by radio stations -The beginning of the public radio network to broadcast in Armenian -The first Syriac monthly newspaper -The beginning of Kurdish broadcasting in Anatolia news agency -Making *Agos* available at the Turkish Airlines stand at airports -The first private children's channel broadcasting in several dialects of Kurdish
Elimination of restrictions on education in languages used in the daily life of Turkish citizens other than Turkish (1)	-Continuing elective courses in Kurdish in public schools; post-graduate education in Zaza and Kırmanchi in Mardin Artuklu University; undergraduate elective Kurdish language course in Muş Alparslan University -The offer of Kurdish as a language course at Bilgi University -Establishment of Arabic and Syriac Language and Culture Departments in Mardin Artuklu University; establishment of the "Living Languages Institute" providing post-graduate education in Kurdish and other languages in Artuklu University; establishment of Kurdish Language and Literature Departments in Muş Alparslan University and Bingöl University; establishment of Kurdish Language Department in Diyarbakır University and Dicle University; establishment of a Department of Eastern Languages and Literatures in Tunceli University; organization of a Kurdish Language course in Tunceli University. -Public services offered in Kurdish
Elimination of restrictions on languages used in the daily life of Turkish citizens other than Turkish in public life (1)	-Continuing use of Kurdish in prisons during visits and exchange of letters -Progress of implementation in the right of the accused to use a language of their preference other than Turkish at certain stages of judicial proceedings, even if they can express themselves adequately in Turkish

Elimination of restrictions on languages used in the daily life of Turkish citizens other than Turkish in political life (2)	Implementation of legislation allowing campaigning in languages other than Turkish by political parties and candidates during local and parliamentary elections without impediment in the March 2014 local elections and in 2015 June and November general elections
Provision of rights to non-Sunni Muslims (i.e. Alevis) (1)	-Opening of the first Alevi Institute -Recognition of the Cem Houses as a place of worship by some municipal councils that granted the Houses the same financial advantages as mosques -The exemption given to Alevi students from attending the mandatory religion and ethics course by administrative courts in Antalya, Ankara, Izmir and Istanbul -The host by the President of the Republic a first ever official fast-breaking dinner for Alevi representatives
Ensuring the exercise of minority rights and establishing dialogue with minorities and their representatives (1)	-Peaceful Newroz and Kurdish celebrations that was given permission by governorates -Making classes on religious culture and ethics non-compulsory for non-Muslim students -Alternative questions for non-Muslim students in the university entrance and secondary school final examinations, following the introduction of questions on Islam -The approval of the request for the reopening of a Greek minority school on Gökçeada Island and the opening of the school -Option to attend courses as guest students without any graduation certificates in minority schools -First message in the Republic's history on 1915 Armenian events and offer of condolences to the descendants of the victims by the Prime Minister -Minister of EU Affairs attending a commemorative mass, in which a message by the President read -Many commemoration events for the 1915 tragedy peacefully held -Conferences on the 1915 Armenian deportation -Activities organized by civil society groups and initiatives to mark Armenian Genocide Commemoration Day, to commemorate the events in 1915 held peacefully -Visit by the Turkish Deputy Prime Minister to the Syriac community in Germany -Visit to the President by a delegation of Syriacs from Sweden and another by the President to the Syriac community in Sweden -Meeting between the Prime Minister and religious leaders of non-Muslim communities held -Call issued by a Deputy Prime Minister and the Minister of Culture for minorities to return Turkey -Minority representative (beyond the official recognition) invited to the Parliament for the first time in the Republic's history to express their views on a new Constitution -Open and lively debates on sensitive issues like Kurdish and the Armenian issues

(Continued)

Table 3.8 (Continued)

EU Demand*	Turkish Response
Elimination of the problems of religious foundations (1)	-Re-gained its foundation status of the Greek Orphanage in Büyükada -Foundation status granted to the Jewish Community in İzmir, the Greek primary school for girls in Istanbul and Armenian Tibrevank Lycee in Istanbul -Restoration of the legal personality of the patriarchal church of the Armenian Catholics in Istanbul
Provision and implementation of property rights to/for religious foundations (2)	Implementation of the new Law on Foundations and after the 2011 amendment of the law
Elimination of the problems with construction permits for places of worship (3)	-The land request by the Istanbul Syriac Orthodox Church to construct a new church granted -Reconstruction and opening of the Armenian cemetery in Malatya
Elimination of ban on training clergy (1)	-Positive answer to the Ecumenical Patriarchate's applications for work permits -Informal training for the Syriac Orthodox community, although only outside official schools, becoming possible
Revision of the curricula in schools and removal of discriminatory language from textbooks (3)	-New religious education textbooks including information on Alevi faith -New textbooks for religious culture and ethics courses, including information on the Alevi faith -Revision of 10th grade history school textbook on the basis of the discriminatory rhetoric for Syriacs -Preparation of textbooks and curricula collaborating with stakeholders for Christianity courses at school
Improvement to the situation in the Southeast in terms of socio-economic development and cultural rights (1)	Continuing GAP
Solution to the problem of IDPs (1)	-Progress in compensation of losses due to terrorism -Extension of the period of implementation of the law on compensation of losses resulting from terrorism and the fight against terrorism -Damage Assessment Commission assessment of over 340,000 applications and compensation granted to half of them

Removal of landmines (3)	-Under the Ottawa Convention, mostly anti-personnel mines destroyed by March 2014, but an extension needed. Continuing clearance of anti-personnel landmines
Solution to the Kurdish problem (2)	-Wide-ranging public debate to address the Kurdish issue -Continuing Kurdish settlement process -A civic commission of wise persons to boost public backing for the peace process -Releasing most defendants accused in cases related to Kurdish issue like KCK -Officials using Kurdish for their public speeches
Improvement in the situation of Roma (3)	-A Roma Language and Culture Research Institute at the University of Thrace in Edirne -Ad hoc contacts between Roma NGOs and relevant ministries -Efforts of Labour Ministry and İŞKUR for promoting employment of Roma in temporary jobs of public benefit and to providing vocational training -Regular contacts between Roma NGOs and the administration. -Preparation of a National Strategic Action Plan for Roma -Establishment of the Roma People Forum of Turkey -Continuing provision of temporary public benefit jobs for Roma -A Roma Language and Culture Research Institute in Trakya University -Taking a TV series off the air due to discriminatory language -Accessible health services for Roma
Elimination of hate speech and hate crimes (4)	Fines issued for incitement to hatred and enmity

Source: Author's own elaboration

*1 stressed in almost all EU documents under consideration
2 stressed in around ¾ of the EU documents under consideration
3 stressed in around ½ of the EU documents under consideration
4 stressed in less than ¼ of the EU documents under consideration

Table 3.9 Minority-related policy change in Turkey: 2008–2014

Legal Adoption	Implementation	Policy Change
Medium degree	High degree	=
Revival	**Intensifying**	**Selective Policy Change**

Source: Author's own elaboration

Table 3.10 Unresolved minority issues: EU demand–Turkish response

EU Demand*	Turkish Response
Signing the CoE FCNM (1)	*Not* signed
Lifting the reservation regarding minority rights in the UN Covenant on Economic, Social and Cultural Rights/Civil and Political Rights (3)	*Not* lifted
Starting a dialogue with OSCE High Commissioner on National Minorities (3)	*Not* started
Official recognition of all minorities (Muslim and non-Muslim) through eliminating the restricted interpretation of Lausanne Treaty (2)	*Not* recognized
Provision of education in mother tongues (1)	*Not* provided
Abolishment of the requirement to indicate religion on ID cards (3)	*Not* abolished
Elimination of the 10 per cent threshold in the election system (3)	*Not* eliminated
Revision of the curricula in schools and removal of discriminatory language from textbooks (3)	*Not* wholly revised, still there are problems
Removal of compulsory religious classes in public schools (2)	Partially removed; only for non-Muslim students
Provision of rights to non-Sunni Muslims (i.e. Alevis) (1)	-No concrete steps in regard to the problems of non-Sunni Muslims -No recognition of Cem houses as places of worship -Continuing compulsory religious classes in public schools -No regulation on election procedures for non-Muslim foundations
Elimination of the problems of religious foundations (1)	-No legal personality and foundation status provided for Catholic churches -Difficulties in property and land registration -Continuing hate crimes and speeches that necessitate a comprehensive response
Provision to the Ecumenical Patriarch to publicly use the ecclesiastical title of Ecumenical (2)	-No indication from the authorities for the use of the title freely

Table 3.10 (Continued)

EU Demand*	Turkish Response
Elimination of ban on training clergy (*Halki* seminary problem) (1)	-Some limited initiatives permitted, but bans not eliminated wholly -*Halki* Seminary still closed
Improvement to the situation in the Southeast in terms of socio-economic development and cultural rights (1)	-Some improvement -Continuing regional disparities
Removal of landmines (3)	Significant improvement, but still removal not wholly concluded
Solution to the problem of IDPs (1)	Some improvement, but no national strategy on the IDPs
Solution to the Kurdish problem (2)	-Settlement process halted, still no settlement in the Kurdish question
Improvement in the situation of Roma (3)	-No national strategy and action plan for Roma -No quantitative data on the situation of Roma -Continuing discrimination -Continuing problems and difficulties of Roma, such as accessing health and social security services

Source: Author's own elaboration

*1 stressed in almost all EU documents under consideration
2 stressed in around ¾ of the EU documents under consideration
3 stressed in around ½ of the EU documents under consideration
4 stressed in less than ¼ of the EU documents under consideration

progressed slightly, while property rights to non-Muslim foundations or broadcasting and education in languages used in daily life other than Turkish significantly improved. At the end, the government ignored some priorities related to minority rights highlighted by the EU and rather took into consideration of some and adopted these measures, which demonstrates at the later stages of reforms-selective minority-related change.

Conclusions: mapping policy change in minority rights

Since 2002, Turkey has attained significant change in minority protection through considerable legal adoption with intense implementation in recent years. Analyzing legal adoption and implementation in minority rights in 2002–2014 with background information on 1999–2002 preparation phase, the research revealed that variation in both legal adoption and implementation is significant. While legal adoption varies from a high to medium degree, implementation starts with a very limited degree and increases through time to medium and high degrees (see Table 3.11).

62 *Changing minority rights in 1999–2014*

Table 3.11 Minority-related legal adoption and implementation in Turkey: 2002–2014

Time Period / Action	2002–2004	2005–2007	2008–2014
Legal Adoption	High	Low	Medium
	Progress	**Slowdown**	**Revival**
Implementation	Low	Medium	High
	Very limited	**Limited**	**Intensified**

Source: Author's own elaboration

Table 3.12 Minority-related policy change in Turkey: 2002–2014

2002–2004	2005–2007	2008–2014
Legal adoption: High with Implementation: Low **Shallow policy change**	Legal adoption: Low with Implementation: Medium **Selective policy change (Limited)**	Legal adoption: Low Medium with Implementation: High **Selective policy change**

Source: Author's own elaboration

Such a process, characterized by differentiated policy change, is puzzling for a number of reasons. First, minority rights constitute a least likely area for reform because of its highly sensitive nature touching upon even more sensitive issues. Second, recent developments demonstrate an intensification of rule-consistent behavior in Turkey. This development is surprising because implementation is often the most problematic area in the accession process, and implementation of minority-protection rules was even more problematic in previous candidate states.

According to the different degrees of the legal adoption and implementation, minority-related policy change is indicated as shallow policy change in 2002–2004; selective policy change in 2005–2007, though limited; and selective policy change in 2008–2014 (see Table 3.12).

Notes

1 Progress reports and regular reports of the EU Commission and Council decisions between 1999 and 2014.
2 At the beginning of the 1990s, Özal recognized the existence of Kurds by declaring that his grandmother was a Kurd, and declared his aim to solve the Kurdish issue (Sabah 2009). However, the President died before solving the Kurdish problem, and his Kurdish initiative was dropped until the 2009 initiative of Prime Minister Erdoğan.

4 Push without pull in 1999–2004
EU conditionality triggers the reforms

Starting by the decisive point in EU–Turkey relations and the Turkish Europeanization process (i.e. the 1999 Helsinki decision granting Turkey the candidate country status), the study focuses on, in this part, first the transition or preparation phase for Europeanization from 1999 to November 2002 elections, which led to establishment of the AKP government, and second the period with the AKP's single-party government in 2002–2004 and the pull-push mechanism.

1999–2002: kicking off the reforms? The coalition government and minority rights

The period of 1999–2002 represents a preparation or a transitional phase for reforms and almost no change in minority rights. With the EU's declaration of Turkey as a candidate country in 1999, the following years were mostly focused on the EU accession process, and the coalition government of DSP-MHP-ANAP attempted to improve the institutional structure for launching reforms. For instance, the Accession Partnership with the EU was signed in 2000, and the National Program for EU reforms was launched in 2001.

Outside the external-level developments, two important domestic-level developments interlinked to each other emerged in1999 as the arrest of Abdullah Öcalan, the leader of the PKK, and the ceasefire between the PKK and the Turkish government. Such developments paved the way for the future Turkish governments to launch minority reforms without having enormous reactions from the public, because minority-protection measures in the past were often seen by the public as giving concessions to the PKK (Öniş 2003: 14).

In the years under investigation, the only change brought about was the 2001 Constitutional reform. Regarding minority rights the sentence "No language prohibited by law can be used to express and diffuse thoughts" was removed from the 1982 Constitution through an amendment (European Commission 2001: 25). Rather than positive rights, the amendment granted negative rights to the minorities by amending the Constitution that was formally used to prosecute minorities (Oran 2004: 119).

Except for the removal of the aforementioned language ban from the Constitution, the preparation phase did not witness any further legal adoption or implementation in minority rights. Therefore, this period is a transitional period from inertia to the acceleration of reforms in minority protection later on.

Towards the golden age of Europeanization: Helsinki Summit and beyond

The vague picture in EU–Turkey relations, which started with the country's application to the European Economic Community for closer integration in 1959, changed significantly with the 1999 Helsinki Summit (Tanıyıcı 2010: 184). The EU decision to recognize Turkey as a candidate country in the Summit was a turning point. As Uğur (2003: 172) stresses, "For the first time in the history of EU–Turkey relations, the decision set clear markers about Turkey's obligations . . . signaled a clear EU commitment to start accession negotiations when these obligations are fulfilled". Following the decision, the credibility of EU conditionality and incentives to push reforms in Turkey considerably increased (Öniş 2003: 9).

The decision taken at the Helsinki Summit was a surprising one, since Turkey was not included as a candidate state to the list of candidates at the 1997 Luxembourg Summit. The Luxembourg Summit was perceived with disappointment and responded by hostile reactions in the domestic arena with doubts about the EU's commitment to Turkish accession process (Müftüler-Baç and McLaren 2003: 21). Just two years before the Helsinki Summit, EU's conditionality was seen as not credible, and so the EU as not reliable, by Turkey. Therefore, the decision of the EU at the Helsinki Summit led to a burst in Turkish perception of EU conditionality overly credible.

As mentioned at the beginning, the years in between 1999 and 2002 represent a preparation phase with the establishment of an institutional framework with the EU, as well as adjustment of the necessary domestic structures to the new circumstances. In the first years, Turkey needed to build up the necessary administrative structures to prepare the country for EU membership (Sozen and Shaw 2003: 116). The country established the Secretariat General for EU Affairs in 2000 to ensure effective coordination of relations with the EU. Moreover, almost all ministries and public institutions established their own department for relations with the EU in addition to the increasing number of independent regulatory bodies in the country (Sozen and Shaw 2003: 117).

While Ankara dealt with necessary preparations for the adjustment of domestic structures to the new phase of EU relations, the Union strengthened the credibility of its conditionality as a starting point. It was initially made clear that the rewards of the EU are conditional, and the path towards rewards passes through the fulfillment of the Copenhagen political criteria applied on an equal basis with previous and future candidate states.

To illustrate, the EU confirmed the equal status of all candidate states subjected to the same criteria and conditional rewards in many instances: "Turkey is a candidate state destined to join the Union on the basis of the same criteria as applied to the other candidate countries" (European Commission 2001: 6; European

Council 1999: 11). Moreover, the Accession Partnership with Turkey (European Council 2001) stressed conditional financial assistance strictly referring to the Copenhagen criteria: "Community assistance is conditional on the fulfillment of essential elements, and in particular on progress towards fulfillment of the Copenhagen criteria".

As seen, rather than using conditionality as a political tool, the EU applied its conditionality in a technical style, linking the accession to the Copenhagen criteria strictly, in 1999–2002. Such an exercise led to a significant increase in the credibility of EU conditionality. Therefore, EU's conditionality was highly credible in this era and was further strengthened in the upcoming years.

Domestic dynamics: no pull

In 1999–2002, like the EU level, the domestic-level developments signify a transition period from cautious governance for minority reforms to a pro-minority and pro-reformist platform. The period also lacks any significant improvement in minority rights, not because of the EU push, but because of the inner dynamics of the coalition government of DSP-MHP-ANAP (Narbone and Tocci 2007: 238).

The two parties of the coalition, the left-wing DSP and the right-wing MHP, represented the nationalist outlook of the coalition, while the ANAP, a center-right party, constituted the liberal wing of the coalition (Keyman and Öniş 2007: 41). Again the two dominant parties, the DSP and MHP, of the coalition government constituted a Euro-skeptic wing in the Parliament, although they were not principally opposed to the accession process to the EU, and only the ANAP in the government adopted a pro-EU agent and pro-reformist approach (Öniş 2003: 17). To clarify further, the coalition government adopted a moderated hard-Euroskeptic approach, keeping its critiques against the EU, but not the accession process (Yılmaz 2011: 186, 195). At the end, the government demonstrated a vague and limited commitment to EU membership, and its agenda continued to be dominated by a nationalist outlook (Keyman and Öniş 2007: 41).

Most importantly, the MHP and DSP were resistant to political reforms – especially to the extension of minority protection – conditioned by the EU for Turkey's accession process through the launch of candidate country status in 1999 (Keyman and Öniş 2007: 41). No signal of failure-diagnosis and aspirations for change by the coalition government existed in any policy area in this era, which, in turn, signify the satisfaction of the government with the status quo and, thereby, its inaction. Furthermore, as Öniş (2003: 17) stresses:

> Indeed, none of the major political parties were able to or willing to challenge the fundamental precepts of state ideology on key issues of concern such as "cultural rights" or "the Cyprus problem" – issues which appeared to lie beyond the parameters of the normal political debate.

Consequently, the coalition parties – even the pro-reformist ANAP – were cautious to launch minority-right reforms, especially any related to cultural rights, such as promoting broadcasting and teaching in Kurdish (Avcı 2003: 198; Öniş 2003: 18). The very resistance of the coalition government to reforms in minority rights stemmed from the idea that the reforms would have posed a threat to national security and sovereignty (Hale 2003: 109; Rumford 2001: 58). The nationalist ideology of the dominant parties in the coalition was the primary reason for this perception, which was clarified in Bahçeli's words, the leader of the ultra-nationalist MHP: "cultural and ethnic rights can fuel ethnic clashes and division" (Rumford 2001: 58).

The aforementioned understanding, reflected by Bahçeli's words, originates from the Sevrés syndrome, commonly referred by the nationalists, regarding the Sevrés Treaty that led to the partition of the Ottoman Empire (Aydın-Düzgit and Keyman 2007: 80). The political and historical fear among these nationalist groups has been loaded with the fear of separatism and partition of Turkey among various ethnic groups; for example, Kurds that may dismember the country and establish a Kurdish state or Greeks that may revive the Pontus Kingdom (Aydın-Düzgit and Keyman 2007: 80; Oran 2009). It was widely assumed among nationalists, accordingly by the coalition government, that providing rights to ethnic, linguistic and religious groups in the country would fuel Turkey's partition among these minorities supported by foreign countries.

The role of the MHP was critical for minority reforms in this period, since it represented the hyper-nationalist and anti-minority approach within the coalition government. The measures necessitated by the EU accession process in minority rights caused deep resentment within the MHP, especially referring to the struggle with the PKK. The party attributed reforms in minority rights to the Kurdish question and to the struggle between the PKK and the Turkish army (Avcı 2003: 161). Moreover, the capture of the PKK leader, Abdullah Öcalan, in 1999 triggered a more rigid political stance from the MHP on the issue. As a result, the MHP became the representative of both Euro-skeptic and anti-minority groups within the wider society, obstructing political reforms including minority measures (Avcı 2006: 68).

At the end, the years in 1999–2002 signify no dissatisfaction for minority rights by the coalition government. Rather, the government was closer to defend and sustain the status quo. With the pressure of euphoria in these years and the resistance of the coalition government for reforms, the nationalist coalition government came to a breaking point (Müftüler-Baç 2005: 22; Narbone and Tocci 2007: 239).

In conclusion, push without pull of 1999–2002 resulted with a step to minority reforms, but to a very limited degree. Despite the weak commitment of the coalition government to EU membership, nationalist tendencies within the government and low degrees of pull, EU push led to political reforms, including very minor change in minority reforms, in this era, but with "the unconvincing, slightly hollow quality that comes with an 'outside-in' process" (Sugden 2004: 257). This picture changed with the November 2002 elections and the rise of AKP government.

Towards dissatisfaction: failure in politics, policy and economics

Between 1999 and November 2002, Turkey experienced an outburst of long-standing and ignored problems, which caused a series of political and economic crises. As Aydın and Çarkoğlu (2006: 4) emphasize, "the 1999–2002 period prepared the ground for political as well as economic shake up in the whole Turkish politico-economic system". The inability of the coalition government to address these problems led to a boom of political and economic crises. This, in turn, caused societal dissatisfaction in two dimensions: economy and politics – including the inability of governing with a specific focus on EU–Turkey relations – and democratization – including minority policy (Aydın-Düzgit and Keyman 2007: 70).

To start with, Turkey experienced two major economic crises in November 2000 and February 2001. The initial spark for these was a political dispute between Prime Minister Ecevit, and President Ahmet Necdet Sezer, causing a rush in the value of the dollar (Narbone and Tocci 2007: 240). The crises initiated a total collapse in the Turkish economy with devastating impact on the country with soaring unemployment, which led, in turn, to discussions on the necessity of economic reforms (Aydın and Keyman 2004: 11; Narbone and Tocci 2007: 240). The series of economic crises "bore the brunt of voters' dissatisfaction with the austerity measures of the economic reform program" (Sayarı 2007: 200). The economic recession and austerity measures caused a high degree of public discontent with the government and created a strong societal pull for change, demonstrated in the 2002 elections (Narbone and Tocci 2007: 240–1).

The economic crises were closely related to political ones, which were overwhelmingly due to the loose coalition government. The first signs of the failure in political governance emerged when the massive earthquakes in August and November 1999 hit Istanbul, quickly demonstrating the ineffectiveness of the government to respond the needs and demands of the Turkish public (Aydın and Çarkoğlu 2006: 6). Moreover, high levels of corruption among political parties, including one of the coalition parties (i.e. ANAP) and the leaders of some other political parties, caused the public trust to further wither (Sayarı 2007: 199).

Most importantly, the nationalist coalition government came to a breaking point when the EU-candidacy process pressed for domestic reforms (Narbone and Tocci 2007: 239). Especially the reforms in minority rights led to increasing tension among coalition parties. While the prospect of EU membership was promising for improvement in the economy and democracy, the inability of the government to launch democratic reforms, including minority ones, necessary for the EU reform process caused resentment in the public area (Narbone and Tocci 2007: 238).

Aydın and Çarkoğlu (2006: 81) summarize the causes of such increase in societal dissatisfaction in the wider public that was reflected in the 2002 elections:

> The election results demonstrated the popular feeling in Turkey that the ineffective and undemocratic governing structure based on economic populism, clientalism, corruption and democratic deficiencies had run its course and that a strong single-party government with institutional and societal support could make Turkey a democratic and economically stable country.

As a result, the long-sensed failure in politics, policy, and economy by Turkish society led to the collapse of the old order by the November 2002 elections with an extraordinary defeat of the coalition government, which failed to recognize the failure (Sayarı 2007: 197–9). The AKP, which was formed only 18 months prior to the elections, won a crushing victory, and the elections dramatically transformed the political landscape as none of the parties in the previous parliament won seats in the new Parliament (Ifantis 2007: 225).

As seen, the 2002 elections constitute an example of the tremendous reaction of voters against the inability of a government, which was ineffective in solving the problematic issues of the country. Therefore, the elections "symbolized the deep anger that the voters felt about the existing authoritarian, corrupt, and clientalist (coalitions) government" (Aydın-Düzgit and Keyman 2007: 70). Aydın and Çarkoğlu (2006: 7) precisely underline the developments behind the 2002 elections:

> The ruling coalition of DSP, MHP and ANAP survived immense economic difficulties, which seem to have exhausted public trust in the future of the country. It was time for the ultimate political punishment associated with this failure.

The AKP was established against this background of failure in various areas. Therefore, the party was aware of the dissatisfaction arising within the wider public and "held out to voters the promise of clean, competent government – a promise that was lent credibility by Erdoğan's widely admired reformist administration of Istanbul – and was duly rewarded by the electorate" (Bahcheli and Noel 2011: 104). Therefore, the AKP was well aware the necessity of change to sustain its victory in the elections; the voters believed that the AKP would be decisive in response to the deep-rooted economic, political and policy problems of the country (Bahcheli and Noel 2011: 104).

From satisfaction to dissatisfaction: diagnosis of failure

The AKP started to rule under the pressure of failure in various areas necessitating urgent action. Yet, unlike the previous period, failure existing in different areas began to be diagnosed by the AKP leaders. A wide range of deep-rooted problems in the country that needed to be urgently tackled were outlined in the speeches and documents of the party in detail, such as governance and financial problems demonstrated by the economic crises; democratization problems including the problems in the area of fundamental rights and freedoms; cultural and social problems, including the Kurdish problem; and the Cyprus problem. To illustrate this, in one of AKP meetings (AKP Political Group 2004a), it was emphasized that "From democratization to economic structure, from urbanization to structural problems of the sector of agriculture, from problems in judicial arena to rationalization of public management a wide range of problems will remain in our agenda." Moreover, it is argued that the problems Turkey faced were interconnected and troublesome to solve at once (e.g. AKP Political Group 2003a).

Past failure – including problems experienced and mistakes made by the previous governments – has been the issue most referred to in the speeches of AKP leaders. First of all, the party leaders put heavy emphasis on the economic and political crises in the past (e.g. AKP Political Group 2002a, 2007a). Second, another stressed issue to a great extent was the inability of previous governments to provide solutions to Turkey's problems (e.g. Address to the Nation 2008a; AKP Political Group 2002b, 2004b, 2006a). Third, the leader of the party diagnosed systemic problems in a number of areas – justice and development, political and economic governance, bureaucracy – leading to the loss of political trust on policymakers in the wider society (e.g. Address to the Nation 2007a; AKP Political Group 2003b, 2004c).

Interestingly, AKP leaders' speeches and party documents did not focus much on minority issues until 2008. This is primarily due to the urgency of dealing with other issues, such as pressing economic and governance failure, and the strong EU push driving political reforms, including the ones related to minority protection. However, a gradually increasing trend in the AKP's diagnosis of minority-related policy failure is observed from 2002 to 2008 with a surge occurring by 2008.

The attention of the AKP, mainly between 2002 and 2004 and to a lesser extent by 2005, was devoted to preventing an increase in tension and polarization in the wider society – including minority groups and nationalist forces – and also to eliminating the political manipulations triggering tension among different groups in society (e.g. AKP Political Group 2002c, 2003c, 2008a). For instance, the party highlighted the use of Newroz as a means of increasing tension between Kurds and other groups in the country: "They aim to turn the feast of Newroz into a social area of tension" (AKP Political Group 2006b).

Specific problems of minorities were also diagnosed. For instance, the problems in the Foundations Law, directly related to the problems of minority foundations, were recognized: "We already believed that the Foundations Law of 1935 was inadequate to solve today's problems and there was a need of new law" (AKP Political Group 2006c).

Most importantly, the party (especially by 2008) explicitly recognized specific problems of ethnic, linguistic and religious minority groups, such as the problems of Kurds, Alevis and Roma (e.g. AKP Political Group 2009a, 2010a). Recognizing these was a departure from the previous policy of denial. Yet, naming these minorities and recognizing their existence do not mean a change in the official minority policy relying on the Lausanne Treaty. Therefore, minorities were still referred as non-Muslims in the country not including Muslim groups.

AKP leaders refrained from using the term 'ethnic groups' to signify ethnic minorities, such as Kurds. In contrast, they use the concept 'ethnic elements' to refer to ethnic groups. This indicated that the groups were components of one inclusive nation rather than being minority groups. The following quotes illustrate this:

> I (Erdoğan) have expressed that there is the reality of the Kurdish problem in this country. By saying this, I do not accept that other ethnic elements do not have any problems; they do have problems. Every region has its own problems.
>
> (AKP Political Group 2006d)

In this country, the problems of my Kurdish and Roma sisters and brothers, of Albanian, Bosnian, Abkhazian, Georgian and my other sisters and brothers with different ethnic backgrounds were ignored and denied for years. The problems of my Sunni and Alevi sisters and brothers were denied. The problems of minorities and my non-Muslim citizens were denied.

(AKP Political Group 2010b)

The party also differentiated the problems of ordinary Kurdish citizens from the terror problem, mostly associated with the PKK. The speeches of AKP leaders lay emphasis on terrorism and the PKK as crucial problems, while isolating these issues from the problems of Kurds related to democratic governance, such as broadcasting and teaching in Kurdish (e.g. AKP Political Group 2007b, 2008b).

In conclusion, the previous coalition government neglected failure, but the AKP government by 2002 started to contend with a number of problematic issues in the country, including minority problems. Between 2002 and 2007, the AKP diagnosed failure in various areas – though to a lesser extent in minority issues – which could be linked to the AKP's prioritizing urgent economic and political problems to deal with in the first years of their government. After tackling these issues, by 2008, minority issues were at the top of the AKP's agenda. However, it has to be kept in mind that minority rights as a sensitive issue touches on a number of areas, such as democratization and social and security problems including the Kurdish issue. Though there was little exclusive and explicit mention of minority rights in the first years of its rule, the AKP recognized failure in the noted wider areas, and those indirectly affect minority problems.

2002–2004: push without pull

The period in 2002–2004 signifies an acceleration of reforms including minority reforms and seen as the Golden age of Turkish Europeanization. As the previous section demonstrated, reforms on minority reforms were shallow in 2002–2004, and the following focuses on the why question through employing the pull-and-push model.

Golden age of Europeanization: EU conditionality triggering the reforms

In 2002–2004, the strong trigger of EU push provided a source of legitimacy to the AKP at a time of powerful domestic consensus on the EU accession process and democratic reform, including minority reform (Aydın-Düzgit and Keyman 2007: 75; Sayarı 2007: 201). Moreover, the AKP's victory in the 2002 elections and continuing support by the electorate demonstrated by the 2004 elections provided strong legitimacy to the party and its reforms. Yet, the AKP did not explicitly and exclusively focus on minority problems in this era, which in turn suggests minority reforms were a result of pressure by EU conditionality.

Launching candidate country status in 1999 with the Helsinki Summit, later in 2002 stating that the membership conditions for Turkey depended solely on the Copenhagen criteria with a possible date for opening accession negotiations and giving a possible date for the launch of accession negotiations at the 2002 Copenhagen Summit in the case of compliance with the Copenhagen criteria, the EU exercised a technical conditionality and immensely strengthened its credibility (European Commission 2003: 15). Such remarks delivered a certain signal that Turkey was on the track towards accession negotiations when the country fulfilled the Copenhagen criteria (Keyman and Öniş 2007: 176). Moreover, giving a specific date for the launch of accession negotiations brought a 'sense of certainty' to Turkey's accession process (Aydın and Keyman 2004: 16).

It is widely confirmed by the literature that working via reinforcement by rewards highly credible EU conditionality provided a strong trigger to the reforms in this period (e.g. Aydın-Düzgit and Keyman 2007; Müftüler-Baç 2005; Narbone and Tocci 2007). Even Öniş (2008) calls this period a "golden age of Europeanization" for Turkey. Using the membership carrot, like in the previous enlargement rounds, the EU successfully put pressure on Turkey to launch reforms, including minority rights (Engert *et al.* 2003: 507).

Notably, the 1999 Helsinki decision led to the development of a powerful pro-EU coalition in Turkey, which was determined to push reforms for the fulfillment of the Copenhagen criteria (Eylemer and Taş 2007: 572; Keyman and Öniş 2007: 40; Tocci 2005: 78). The AKP, the Republican People's Party (*Cumhuriyet Halk Partisi* – CHP), NGOs, and the military established a pro-EU coalition in the post-2002 period (Keyman and Öniş 2007: 64–5; Öniş 2010: 12). Not only the AKP strongly committed to the EU accession process, but also the CHP was supportive of the process, despite its reservations on the conditions related to monolithic national identity and secularism (Öniş 2010: 12).

NGOs like the Turkish Industrialists' and Businessmen's Association (*Türk Sanayicileri ve İşadamları Derneği* – TÜSIAD), the Turkish Economic and Social Studies Foundation (*Türkiye Ekonomik ve Sosyal Etüdler Vakfı* – TESEV) and the Economic Development Foundation (*İktisadi Kalkınma Vakfı* – IKV) were also among the active actors within the pro-EU coalition (Eylemer and Taş 2007: 564). For instance, 175 Turkish NGOs formed the European Movement in order to push political reforms to fulfill the criteria for EU membership (Kubicek 2011: 916).

To illustrate the perceptions of NGOs further, TÜSIAD, as an active pro-EU business interest group, perceived the EU as an anchor to promote domestic reform (Uğur 2003; Uğur and Yankaya 2008) and put special emphasis on the EU accession process in order to promote democracy and the market economy:

> Since its foundation in 1971, TÜSIAD has aspired and worked for Turkey's achievement of the standards of a European democracy and a globally competitive economy. To achieve this goal, TÜSIAD has put special emphasis on improving Turkey's relations with the EU and assuring its compliance with the Copenhagen political criteria.
>
> (TÜSIAD 2004)

72 Push without pull in 1999–2004

Additionally, in the early years of the accession process TÜSIAD clearly defined its perceptions on the role of the EU in the reform process as providing legal and political justification or a 'sense of legitimacy' to the legal and political reforms in the country (TÜSIAD 2001: 9). It is important to note that these NGOs played an important role in the mobilization of public support for reforms (Eylemer and Taş 2007: 564). Most importantly, the EU accession process enabled Turkish civil society to fulfill this role via providing standing and legitimacy to NGOs, especially in their relations with political elites (Kubicek 2011: 916).

The EU accession process is supported also by the military (particularly under former Chief of Staff General Hilmi Özkök until his retirement from the office in 2006) (Heper 2005: 40–1; Narbone and Tocci 2007: 244). However, the military had some reservations concerning the EU accession process. It was believed that the reform process could weaken Turkey's hand in its struggle against political Islam and Kurdish separatism (Heper 2005: 38). Nevertheless, Özkök displayed the enthusiasm of the military for Turkey's EU membership and several times stated its support for the process (Heper 2005: 41). For instance, stating: "The European Council in December is vital for Turkey's next 10 years" (Radikal 2004).

In addition to the pro-EU coalition, public support for EU membership was high and consistently increased until the autumn of 2004 (see Figure 4.1). Consistent with credible EU conditionality in 2002–2004, public support reached its peak level in the spring of 2004 and started to decrease by late 2004 (Eurobarometer 2002, 2003, 2004) Surveys (Eurobarometer 2002, 2003, 2004) also demonstrate low levels in the societal perception of EU membership as 'a bad thing' in 2002–2004.

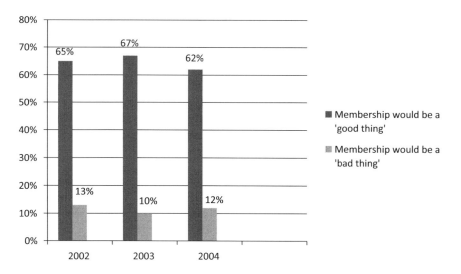

Figure 4.1 Turkish public support for EU membership in 2002–2004
Source: Eurobarometer (2002, 2003, 2004)

No need for the pull: popular support to the AKP government

The landslide victory of the AKP in the 2002 elections significantly strengthened the power of pro-EU reformists (Tocci 2004: 194). The AKP, promoted itself as a pro-reformist and pro-EU actor, came to power in 2002 having a 34 per cent share of the vote, which was the first time in 15 years that one party won a majority of seats in the Turkish parliament (see Figure 4.2) (Mecham 2004: 340).

Notably in the 2002 elections, the AKP received considerable number of protest votes from various fronts against the inability of the previous coalition government to manage the economic and political crises (Başlevent et al. 2004: 308). As Mecham (2004: 340) stresses, the success of the AKP as a new and untested party can be explained by widespread dissatisfaction and protest:

> Many factors relevant to the success of the AKP reflect sources of dissatisfaction with Turkish politics and the Turkish economy that became channeled into the AKP as protest against an ineffective governmental system. Rapid inflation in 2001, coupled with a profound economic recession in 2001–02 created widespread unemployment and consumer desperation among many of those living on and beyond the margins of the Turkish economy. Public perceptions of parliamentary deadlock, embedded inequitable patronage networks, and desperate personalized political battles among incumbents provided strong incentives to vote for change. These perceptions, coupled with the AKP's formidable grassroots organizational strength and the continued public legal persecution of the party's populist leader made it appear the most promising of the potential agents of change.

The failure in a number of areas, as mentioned before, fuelled the voter sanction of the previous coalition government parties. Yet, the AKP as a new party provided hope to the electorate to solve the endemic problems faced by the country. Therefore, the AKP's success in 2002 depended on presenting itself as a clean, democratic and reformist party – an alternative to the discredited political parties (Bahcheli and Noel 2011: 105).

Moreover, an analysis of the 2002 election results shows that the AKP received substantial support from Kurdish voters and won a majority of the seats in the regions highly populated by the Kurds, keeping in mind the 10 per cent election threshold (See Table 4.1). The pro-Kurdish party, the Democratic People's

Table 4.1 Eastern region votes to the AKP and pro-Kurdish DEHAP in the 2002 elections

Region / Political Party	Eastern Anatolia	Southeastern Anatolia
AKP	32.231 %	26.568 %
DEHAP	21.403 %	27.735 %

Source: Author's own elaboration

Party (*Demokratik Halk Partisi* – DEHAP), remained under the threshold despite receiving the majority of the votes in the region (Bahcheli and Noel 2011: 105–6). In this context, the appointment of Dengir Mir Fırat, the Kurdish AKP Member of Parliament (MP) as deputy leader of the party was remarkable, signaling a gesture to Kurdish voters (Bahcheli and Noel 2011: 106; Hürriyet 2002).

Besides, the AKP strengthened its electoral base even further receiving a 41.6 per cent share of the votes cast in 2004 local elections, which brought a victory through winning 57 of the 81 mayoral contests (Sayarı 2007: 202). Moreover, the pro-Kurdish DEHAP, which participated in the elections with an election alliance of various political parties, suffered a considerable loss of support in the 2004 elections (Çarkoğlu 2004: 6). The AKP, on the other hand, further increased its electoral support from the region in the 2004 elections (Kumbaracıbaşı 2009: 103).

In addition to EU conditionality, strong public support for the AKP, demonstrated by election results, provided further legitimacy to political reforms, including minority rights, in this period. However, the priority of the AKP government, in this era, was not minority rights. According to research by Çarkoğlu and Kalaycıoğlu (2007: 51), both prior to and in the aftermath of the 2002 elections, economic problems were at the top of the voters' agenda. As a result, by 2002, the most pressing issue for the AKP government were economic problems, due to the financial crises in 2000 and 2001. Moreover, Eurobarometer Surveys (2003, 2004) reveal that public opinion perceived unemployment and the economic situation as the most important problems for Turkey in this period.

In turn, as was mentioned previously, the AKP devoted its attention to the failure in the economy and the political sphere and the possible solutions to these problems. The early government agenda was dominated by economic reforms, anti-corruption measures, educational reforms and Turkey's accession process to the EU (Mecham 2004: 254). The urgency to tackle these problematic areas, also considering the electorates' expectations, dominated this period. Although the AKP framed its political stance on minority issues referring to the principle of non-discrimination and comprehensive citizenship of the Republic (AKP Party Program 2001), the issues and problems related to minority rights received less attention from the party in this period and AKP's aspirations regarding the issue remained limited. This conclusion suggests the heavy influence of EU push in the strategic calculations of the AKP government providing strong legitimacy to minority reforms for the fulfillment of the Copenhagen criteria.

In the name of the Copenhagen criteria: it is the push not the pull

The discourse of the AKP on EU accession between 2002 and 2004 reveals the dominant pressure of the EU push to launch domestic reforms, including minority rights, to fulfill the Copenhagen criteria for EU membership. Speeches of AKP leaders, as the representatives of the AKP government, demonstrated a sense of optimism about the EU accession process, explicitly stressing the commitment of the government to the process and the necessity of Turkish compliance with the Copenhagen criteria. However, starting by 2004, the discourse of the AKP leaders on the EU accession process relied less on EU membership, consistent with the decrease in the credibility of EU conditionality.

To start with, AKP leaders stressed through all their speeches from 2002 to 2004 that they supported EU membership for Turkey as a national goal (e.g. AKP Political Group 2002d, 2003d). Moreover, they emphasized the consensus among domestic actors on the accession prospects of Turkey to the EU. For instance, stating:

> [I]n Turkey, there is a broad consensus among the government, opposition party, public agencies, civil society organizations, media and intelligentsia on the issue of the EU.
> (Address to the Nation 2004)

Second, AKP leaders put heavy emphasis on the necessity of domestic reforms to comply with the Copenhagen and Maastricht criteria for accession to the Union (e.g. AKP Political Group 2002e, 2003e). Therefore, prominent figures of the AKP stress both the awareness of the AKP government about the necessity of compliance with the specific requirements for membership to the Union and the measures taken to this end (e.g. Address to the Nation 2004). In this context, the explicit impact of the EU on reforms launched in the country is evident. Such statements reveal the trigger of the credible reward of EU membership on domestic reforms.

Third, AKP leaders increasingly stressed that Turkey would not accept any other option than unconditional membership to the Union (e.g. AKP Political Group 2004a, 2004d). The significant rise in the emphasis of this particular issue was due to the increasing application of politicized conditionality by the Union. Therefore, the transition from technical conditionality to politicized conditionality by the EU starting in late 2004 was well translated to the domestic arena, reducing the impact by push of conditionality on the government.

Last, starting at the end of 2003 through 2004, the AKP demonstrated signs of a fever for the EU decision about launching negotiations at the end of 2004 (e.g. AKP Political Group 2003f, 2004e). The party showed strong optimism about the positive decision of the EU to launch negotiations, for instance stating: "We are optimistic but also realistic about the launch of accession negotiations with the EU in December 2004" (AKP Political Group 2004f). Yet, the party leaders also gave signals in 2004 of a possibly negative response from the EU concerning Turkey's accession process:

> In December 2004, the Copenhagen criteria give the result we want or not. What happens If not? We call them Ankara criteria and maintain path.
> (AKP Political Group 2004f)

76 *Push without pull in 1999–2004*

Although this statement can be perceived as a strategic move on the part of the AKP before the decision date of the EU on the launch of accession negotiations in 2004, it signalled a change in the AKP's discourse on domestic reforms presenting them on the grounds of domestic utility irrespective of Turkey's accession perspective. The stress by the AKP on unconditional and full EU membership for Turkey and domestic utility of reforms, especially by 2004, needs to be evaluated within the framework of decreasing credibility of EU conditionality starting by 2004.

Conclusions: shallow change in minority protection through push without pull

In 2002–2004, the strong trigger of the EU push, leading powerful domestic consensus on the EU accession process and democratic reforms (including minority reforms) provided strong legitimacy to the AKP (Aydın-Düzgit and Keyman 2007: 75; Kulahci 2005: 400; Narbone and Tocci 2007: 239). Moreover, the launch of reforms in various areas, including minority reforms, satisfied the reformist, pro-minority and minority electorates of the AKP. Yet, failure in minority protection was not at the top of the AKP's agenda due to low levels of the threat of sanctions by the electorate against the party on this issue. Rather, urgency to deal with failure in other areas, such as economic or governing problems, was pressing in this period. Therefore, the AKP government was primarily motivated to satisfy the Copenhagen criteria rather than deal with failure in minority rights. As a result, the expected outcome from the pull-and-push model for the existence of push without pull, shallow policy change, is confirmed by the actual minority-related policy change in Turkey in 2002–2004 (see Table 4.2). In this early reform phase, policy change remained shallow due to the low levels of implementation in minority rights.

Table 4.2 2002–2004: push without pull

Pull and Push / Time Period	Pull	Push	Pull-and-Push
2002–2004	Low	High	High degree of push without pull Push > Pull
Expected outcome			**Shallow policy change**
Actual outcome			**Shallow policy change**

Source: Author's own elaboration

5 Transition to pull without push in 2005–2007
From the EU to the 'domestic'

In 2005–2007, the legitimacy of the AKP government itself and its policies was significantly questioned. A series of political crises between the AKP and Kemalist and nationalist elites in various state institutions, such as the military and the presidency, threatened stability of the country (Avcı 2011a: 413; Ifantis 2007: 229). Meanwhile, the AKP lost a powerful source of legitimacy with the weakened credibility of EU conditionality and began to rely on public support by the electorate as the primary source for legitimacy for its rule and the guarantee of its political survival.

Pull without push: from the EU push to the domestic pull

In spite of the 2005 EU decision to launch accession negotiations with Turkey that considerably strengthened the credibility of EU conditionality, developments following the decision dragged EU conditionality into a politicized, indecisive and less credible status. To begin with, although accession negotiations with Turkey opened in 2005, references to the open-ended nature of the negotiations and EU's non-Copenhagen-related considerations of Turkey's accession (e.g. EU's absorption capacity, public support for enlargement within the EU's borders, Turkey's size and demographic growth) influenced the credibility of EU conditionality negatively (European Commission 2005b: 2–4; European Commission 2005c; Tocci 2005: 77). For instance, the Negotiating Framework for Turkey (European Commission 2005c) referred to the negotiations as an open-ended process: "these negotiations are an open-ended process, the outcome of which cannot be guaranteed beforehand." Besides, the same document referred the absorption capacity of the EU as a Copenhagen criterion: "While having full regard to all Copenhagen criteria, including absorption capacity of the Union". At the end, the EU overemphasized the open-ended nature and the possibility of a halt of/in the accession process and pushed EU conditionality towards a more politicized level, though recommending the launch of accession negotiations (Tocci 2005: 77).

Furthermore, increasing stress by the Commission (e.g. 2006: 5, 16) on the necessity of public support for the enlargement process constituted another challenge against Turkey's accession process. Such an increasing emphasis can be linked to the downward or negative trend of European public support for Turkey's possible membership to the Union in the concerned period (Transatlantic Trends 2006: 21). The report of Transatlantic Trends (2006: 21) illustrates this by stating that

> there has been a reversal in the percentages who see Turkey's membership as a good or bad thing – those who see Turkey's membership as a good thing have fallen each year from 30% in 2004 to 21% in 2006, and those who see Turkey's membership as a bad thing have grown from 20% in 2004 to 32% in 2006.

In turn, taking into account public support within member states, the Commission primarily reflected that downward trend in public support for Turkey's membership and such an emphasis within the enlargement process had a negative impact on Turkey's accession process through implying that no public support for enlargement means no more enlargement.

In addition to the aforementioned issues, debates among EU member states in 2005 following the decision to launch accession negotiations influenced the credibility of EU conditionality negatively. During 2005, Germany, France and Austria proposed a 'privileged partnership' to Turkey rather than full membership, stressing open-ended accession negotiations, and the debate added further ambiguity and uncertainty to the accession process. It is vital to note that the debate was partly a result of the change of relatively Turkey-friendly leaders of France and Germany with Turkey-skeptics (Göksel 2009: 34).

The debate among EU member states focused on the absorption capacity of the Union, in which the ability of the EU to absorb Turkey with its size, population and culture was discussed (Öniş 2010: 365). As Narbone and Tocci (2007: 238) emphasize, "Other 'non-Copenhagen criteria' reasons started to be aired openly, summed up in the heightened concern about the EU's 'absorption capacity'". Besides, the arguments of member states found a place in the 2005 accession framework of Turkey with reference to the EU's absorption capacity as one of the Copenhagen criteria (Aydın-Düzgit 2006: 6). Even though absorption capacity – mentioned in the 1993 Copenhagen Summit – was not a new argument and previously considered as part of the Copenhagen criteria, it had rarely been applied until the Turkish accession process (Kirişçi 2007: 8). After all, the 'privileged partnership' debate, open-ended negotiations and absorption capacity discussions added to the Turkish accession process further ambiguity and uncertainty on the grounds that the EU may refuse Turkish membership and alternative outcomes of the accession process were possible rather than EU membership and further weakened the credibility of EU conditionality (Aydın-Düzgit 2006: 6; Najslova 2008: 51; Öniş 2010: 364–5; Schimmelfennig 2009: 418).

In addition to the hesitancy within the EU and among its member states on Turkish accession process, in the post-2004 period, the dispute over Turkey's recognition of the Republic of Cyprus (RoC) and implementation of the Additional Protocol to the Ankara Agreement, which extended the Customs Union to all new member states, including the RoC, led to serious repercussions to Turkey's accession process (Aybet 2006: 532–4; International Crisis Group 2007: 17).

Cyprus issue in Turkey's accession process came to direct attention with the Turkish government's signature of the Additional Protocol to the Ankara Agreement in July 2005, which extended the Customs Union to all new member states, including a certain new member state, the RoC (Açıkmeşe and Aydın 2009: 57). Tension between the parties arose when Turkey issued a unilateral declaration stating that its signature did not mean a formal recognition of the RoC (i.e. recognition of the Greek Cypriot government as the legitimate representative of all Cyprus) (Aybet 2006: 532; International Crisis Group 2007: 20). In response, the EU declared in September 2005 that recognition of all member states is an integral part of accession negotiations and urged Turkey to recognize the RoC, implement Customs Union covering the RoC and develop good neighborly relations (Schimmelfennig 2008: 931; Ulusoy 2009: 401). However, Ankara refused to do so unless the EU lifted the isolation of the Northern Turkish part of Cyprus, which was undertaken by the EU in 2004 (Müftüler-Baç 2008: 208).

The reluctance of Turkey to implement the Additional Protocol, fully comprising all new member states including the RoC, led to a freeze in negotiations on eight chapters and restriction on the closure of any chapter in 2006 (Schimmelfennig 2009: 428). Moreover, in 2009 the RoC blocked the opening of a further five chapters on the basis of non-implementation of Additional Protocol and France also declared that it would block the opening of five chapters directly related to free movement of goods and people (Oğuzlu 2012: 230). All in all, the dispute over Turkey's recognition of the RoC and implementation of the Additional Protocol created obstacles for Turkey's accession process and the credibility of EU conditionality in this period (Narbone and Tocci 2007: 236).

The situation, in turn, was translated to the Turkish domestic arena as an instance of EU's unfair approach for Turkey's accession process relying on double standards employed for the RoC and Turkey, due to the Union's acceptance of the divided island as a member state without conditioning the resolution of the conflict, but demanding a resolution from Turkey for its accession, and its failed promises to Turkish Cypriots in response to their cooperation for the resolution of the Cyprus problem on the basis of the 2004 UN plan to reunite the island (Öniş 2010: 7; Tocci 2008: 887). At the end, EU's approach on Cyprus issue created a popular sense of European hypocrisy and unfair treatment on Turkey-related issues among Turkish elites and the public (Göksel 2009: 36; Öniş 2009: 26). Therefore, the Cyprus issue has become a key challenge for Turkey's accession negotiations that was translated to the domestic arena as an issue weakening the credibility of EU conditionality (Najslova 2008: 52).

In turn, Turkish public support for EU membership started to fall by 2005 (see Figure 5.1). Surveys (Eurobarometer 2005, 2006, 2007) demonstrated a steady decrease in public support for EU membership between 2005 and 2007, while showing an increase in the public perception of EU membership as 'a bad thing'. This trend highlights a loss of public enthusiasm for Turkey's accession process and a growing public disenchantment with the EU.

Within the negative atmosphere in the domestic arena regarding the accession process, pro-EU NGOs continued their spirited support to the EU accession

80 *Transition to pull without push*

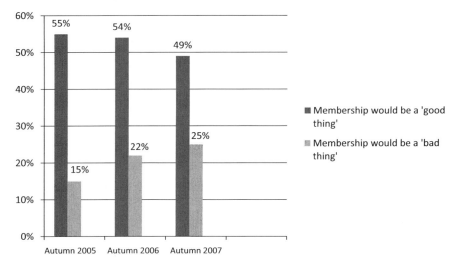

Figure 5.1 Turkish public support for EU membership in 2005–2007
Source: Eurobarometer (2005, 2006, 2007)

process despite stating their disappointment and discontent on the stalemate. To illustrate the disappointment, IKV made a statement after the decision by the European Council on 14–15 December 2006 on partial suspension of accession negotiations:

> After the launch of accession negotiations . . . the EU's sincerity was compromised by the still ongoing debate about Turkey's accession prospects and by its attempts to create stumbling blocks for country's accession.
> (AB Haber 2006)

The Executive Board Chairman of TÜSIAD, Ömer Sabancı, also made a statement about the EU's decision, in which he described the decision as unjust and not compatible with EU norms and called the EU to be "rational and farsighted in its negotiations with Turkey and avoid vicious circles" (Turkishpress 2006). These statements from the pro-EU NGOs revealed the disappointment with the direction of EU negotiations.

At the end, the hesitant signals from the EU and its member states and 'privileged partnership' debate stressing EU's absorption capacity, open-ended nature of accession negotiations and alternative outcomes rather than EU membership in addition to the suspension of negotiations in a number of chapters had a significantly negative effect on Turkey's accession process. After all, in 2005–2007, as Aydın-Düzgit (2006: 5) emphasizes, "The credibility of EU commitments toward Turkey have been characterized by mixed messages, contradiction of commitments, and opposition to the principle of accession on the basis of constructed borders that the country itself could do nothing about", and all mentioned denotes the application of a politicized conditionality, which contributed to the significant weakening in the credibility of EU conditionality.

The rise of reactionary nationalism and domestic crises: AKP's legitimacy challenged

When the credibility of EU conditionality waned by late 2004, a nationalist and Kemalist Euro-skeptic coalition became vocal expressing concerns about EU demands on highly sensitive issues (e.g. Cyprus problem) and stressing that the EU treated Turkey unfairly in its accession process (Öniş 2007: 253; Patton 2007: 345–7). As Öniş (2007: 253) stresses, the pendulum started to swing in the direction of the nationalist and Kemalist Euro-skeptics after 2005.

Eventually, the loss of credibility in EU conditionality strengthened the hand of the Euro-skeptic and nationalist groups to promote anti-EU discourse. As Patton (2007: 345) emphasizes:

> EU finger shaking, negative criticisms and nonreciprocal EU demands have given Turks the impression that their country is a supplicant at Europe's door, generating feelings of humiliation and indignation which nationalist hardliners have been quick to turn to their advantage, placing the spotlight of blame on the AKP for its government's pro-EU policies.

At the end, previous members of the pro-EU coalition, the military and the CHP and the office of the president built an alliance relying on a nationalist Euro-skeptic perspective and Kemalist principles of monolithic national identity and secularism (Uğur and Yankaya 2008: 595).

The rise of reactionary nationalism in the country was not a coincidence, since a number of sensitive issues, such as the Cyprus settlement or the extension of minority rights to Kurds, demanded by the EU were at the top of the Turkish agenda without any tangible promise by the Union (Patton 2007: 345). For instance, the Cyprus problem significantly empowered nationalist and Euroskeptic groups. The general sense of the Turkish public was that Turkey was being treated unfairly by the EU despite both Turkey's and Turkish Cypriots' support for the Annan Plan for a solution to the Cyprus problem (Öniş 2007: 254). The freeze of various chapters in accession negotiations due to the Cyprus problem further strengthened the perception of EU double standards in the wider Turkish public, which, in turn, contributed to the nationalist and Euro-skeptic discourse (Aybet 2006: 532–3). Besides, the failure of the EU to deliver its promise of financial aid to Turkish Cypriots and to lift the embargo further decreased the popularity of the EU among the Turkish public (Grigoriadis 2006: 11). As Grigoriadis (2006: 11–12) emphasizes, the wider Turkish public perception of the issue was one of disappointment:

> that the European Union did not remain neutral in the Cyprus dispute but took the Greek Cypriot side. While the Greek Cypriots were responsible for

the lack of the solution in the Cyprus issue, it was not them but the Turkish Cypriots who were penalized for that.

The nationalist and Kemalist Euro-skeptic wing quickly capitalized on decreasing public support for EU membership and promoted strong opposition to the EU's policy on Cyprus and Kurdish issue, and to the AKP on the basis of secularism (Ifantis 2007: 228; Uğur and Yankaya 2008: 595). In 2005–2007, an atmosphere of fear emerged and fuelled public frustration against the AKP, the EU and the West in general, referring to the Sevrés syndrome (Ifantis 2007: 229).

An illustration of public discontent framed by the Sevrés syndrome and the rise of nationalism in the wider public is the publication of the book called the Metal Storm (*Metal Fırtına*), which became a bestseller and went through 10 editions between 2004 and 2006 (Grigoriadis 2006: 13–14). The book narrates a fictitious war between the United States (US) and Turkey in the near future with a secret military operation called 'Operation Sevrés', which intends to divide Turkey between Greece and Armenia, while allowing the establishment of a Kurdish state within Turkish territory (Yanık 2008: 13). Giving one of the best examples of Sevrés syndrome, the partition of Turkey by a Western country, this book represents how Turkey witnessed the rise of nationalism with specific emphasis on anti-Americanism and anti-Europeanism in 2005–2007 (Visier 2006: 47). Notably, the ultra-nationalist reaction demonstrated itself not only with symbolic politics, but also with violent assassinations (e.g. the murder of a Catholic priest in Trabzon in 2006; the murder of Hrant Dink in 2007) (Freedom House 2008: 15; Grigiriadis 2006: 15; Human Rights Watch 2007: 12; Ifantis 2007: 229).

The nationalist and Euro-skeptic movement soon turned into a polarization of domestic actors, mainly between Kemalist actors and the AKP, referring primarily to the unitary and secular character of the state (Avcı 2011a: 413; Ifantis 2007: 229). To start with, relations between the senior military and the AKP government deteriorated with the retirement of General Özkök and the appointment of General Büyükanıt as chief of staff in 2006 (Bahcheli and Noel 2011: 110). Since Büyükanıt succeeded Özkök, military's influence over domestic politics and critiques against the AKP government and EU officials regarding the reforms increased; the main argument behind this was that reforms would handicap the military in protecting the regime and defending the founding principles of the Republic (Patton 2007: 354). Moreover, Büyükanıt did not shy away, openly criticizing the EU on a number of issues, such as in minority rights. For instance, in a speech in 2007, Büyükanıt accused the EU of creating new minorities in Turkey by reference to calling some groups in Turkey as minorities in its reports on Turkey (Radikal 2007). This reaction by Büyükanıt revealed the discontent of senior generals of the Turkish Armed Forces (TAF) towards the promotion of minority rights demanded by the EU, which were perceived as a threat to the monolithic national identity of Turkey. The change in attitude of the key leadership of the military on the EU accession process by 2005 portrays the uncomfortable position of the military vis-à-vis the political reforms sponsored by the EU (Öniş 2007: 251).

Like the military, the CHP also adopted an explicit anti-EU discourse, primarily accusing the AKP of giving concessions to every EU demand and framing these demands as being detrimental to the national interests of Turkey (Celep 2011: 430–1; Yılmaz 2011: 196). Moreover, the party adopted a nationalist discourse on a number of issues, such as the Cyprus and Kurdish problems (Yılmaz 2011: 196). As Öniş (2007: 257) emphasizes, the CHP became

> virtually indistinguishable from Turkey's major ultra-nationalist party, the MHP . . . established itself as one of the strongest elements of the defensive nationalist bloc and is clearly trying to extend its electoral base by capitalizing on the rising nationalist and Euro-skeptic mood in the country.

Together with the military and the president (i.e. Ahmet Necdet Sezer) to some extent, the CHP formed a hard-line opposition to the AKP government and the EU accession process. As a result, a series of political crises between the AKP and Kemalist elites started with the presidential crisis (Kumbaracıbaşı 2009: 59). The crisis surfaced even before the announcement of the candidates for presidency. The military announced its concerns about the presidential elections with a press conference on 12 April 2007 by the Chief of Staff, Yaşar Büyükanıt, and stressed the importance of secularism and the ideals of the Republic to which the future President should be bound by heart (NTVMSNBC 2007). The next day, the president, Sezer, made a speech stating, "Internal and external forces had joined together in their shared interest in questioning the basic values of the secular republic" (Polat 2009: 137). These statements led to a series of nationwide protests (i.e. Republican rallies) against the government to demonstrate support for secularism (Polat 2009: 137). At the end, Abdullah Gül was announced as the AKP's candidate for the President of the Republic and secularists resentment burst further in response to the announcement (Keyman and Gümüşçü 2014: 33).

The sharp reaction of Kemalists against the election of Gül as President was followed by TAF's post of a statement on its official website (i.e. e-memorandum) on 27 April 2007, criticizing AKP policies and increasing attention to secularism and national identity (Polat 2009: 137; Posch 2007: 23). Most importantly, the memorandum raised the issue of the PKK and stressed the ethnic definition of the nation on the basis of Kemalist ideals: "anybody who is against the motto of 'Happy is who calls himself/herself a Turk' is and will be the enemy of the Republic of Turkey" (Turkish Armed Forces Press Release 2007). Importantly, the e-memorandum raised the concerns of the military not only on the issue of secularism, but also minority reforms that challenge the definition of national identity.

In this process, Euro-skeptic Kemalist NGOs also became vocal in their criticisms of the AKP government on the basis of secularism and unity of state referring to PKK activities together with the EU accession process. A number of demonstrations, called Republican rallies, were organized by these organizations (e.g. Association for Kemalist Thought (*Atatürkçü Düşünce Derneği* – ADD) and Association for the Support of Modern Life (*Çağdaş Yaşamı Destekleme Derneği* – ÇYDD) in a number of cities by 2007 (Posch 2007: 28). Despite including different factions, the mass demonstrations were dominated by nationalist and Kemalist speeches and slogans with emphasis on secularism, terrorism, unity of state and, in some cases, even accusing the EU and the US of tolerating separatism regarding PKK activities (Posch 2007: 28–9). To illustrate, some of the slogans in the Istanbul demonstration on 29 April 2007 were: "All of us are Kemalists, all of us are Turkish"; "Turkey is secular and will remain secular"; "Neither the US nor the EU, but independent Turkey" (Milliyet 2007).

As seen, in 2005–2007, the AKP faced incremental criticism about its pro-EU policies and, therefore, adopted more qualified support for the EU accession process (Öniş 2010: 12). As Bardakçı (2010: 32) emphasizes, "at the end of the day as the AKP's electoral fortunes rely on the support of the people, the AKP has quietly shelved the EU issue and has committed its attention to domestic challenges". No EU push and no legitimacy provided by the EU push anymore led the increase of pull's influence on the AKP's strategic calculations, since popular support demonstrated in the elections would provide legitimacy to its rule and policies and, therefore, guarantee party's survival in a highly polarized and conflictual era.

Pull on the rise: dissatisfaction with the status quo

In an era, in which its rule was increasingly questioned by secular actors accusing the party being a center of anti-secular activities, the AKP focused on its struggle for survival in a hyper- secularist and Kemalist state (Çınar 2011: 111). To clarify it further, with the loss of the dynamism in EU accession process by 2005, the AKP lost a powerful source of legitimacy to its rule and reforms. In the previous period, the accession process provided strong legitimacy to the AKP, especially in its first years of rule, to counteract secular segments concerned about the Islamist roots of the party (Aydın-Düzgit and Keyman 2007: 75). When such an important source for legitimacy was lost, the popularity of the AKP displayed via elections has become a valuable asset in the quest of the party to gain recognition from secularists. Receiving a considerable number of protest and minority votes in the elections against the poor performance of previous governments on several issues, including democratic development, the AKP found its political fate bound to democratic reforms, particularly minority reforms. At the end of the day "democracy has turned into be a matter of survival" for the AKP (Dağı 2006: 96).

Confirming the aforementioned discussion, the 2005–2007 period reflects a change of AKP focus from EU accession reforms to increasingly addressing policy failure in minority protection. This was done to increase further public support from pro-reformist and pro-minority groups that would contribute to the increasing share of the votes in the elections and, in turn, legitimize the AKP's rule, especially in an era with several political crises. Because a high degree of support in the elections would mean that the AKP government rules by the will of people and would thereby legitimize its position. At the end, the challenge from various fronts against the AKP led the party adopt an electoral strategy to legitimize and later consolidate its rule and policies.

It is very important to note that some minority groups like Kurds have enough population that could affect the outcome of an election (Liaras 2009: 8). Besides, high electoral volatility of the Turkish party system and therefore high threat of sanctions by the electorate, which was demonstrated by the AKP's own rise in the 2002 elections, put the performance of the AKP in government to the upfront for re-election (Çarkoğlu and Kalaycıoğlu 2007: 34–5). As a result, the AKP continued its reformist approach in minority rights that gradually relied on selective approximation of minority rules with EU rules – depending on its problem-solving approach in failed areas and its agenda. This, in response, demonstrates the change of push to pull in the strategic calculations of the AKP driving its minority policies.

Exploring the upward trend in the pull, first of all, failure in minority protection and solutions offered and already provided by the AKP found an increasing place in the AKP leaders' discourse starting by 2005. AKP leaders exclusively and explicitly started to diagnose problems of minorities more than the previous and less than the next period. For instance, the Kurdish problem as well as the problems in the Foundations Law, directly related to the problems of minority foundations, were often recognized by the AKP leader as follows:

> We already believed that the Foundations Law of 1935 was inadequate to solve today's problems and there was a need of new law.
> (AKP Political Group 2006c)

> I (Erdoğan) have expressed that there is the reality of the Kurdish problem in this country. By saying this, I do not accept that other ethnic elements do not have any problems; they do have problems. Every region has its own problems.
> (AKP Political Group 2006d)

Second, regarding policy aspirations of the AKP on minority rights, in 2005–2007, AKP leaders put heavy emphasis on the unity of the nation to include each citizen without regard to his or her ethnicity, religion, sect and class. The following words by the Prime Minister and the leader of the AKP, Erdoğan, illustrate this:

> The people who live in Turkey and bound to the Republic of Turkey via citizenship bonds ... need to behave in a consciousness of being a nation ... The base of being a nation is having a common history and common will for the future. In this sense, nation is not an integrity that is constituted by uniform individuals in all manners and excludes differences.
> (AKP Political Group 2005a)

What is more was the increasing emphasis on fraternity, solidarity, non-discrimination and the co-existence of different religions throughout the Turkish history in order to unite different groups (including minorities such as Kurds, Alevis and Armenians) in the country (e.g. AKP Political Group 2005b, 2006b, 2007c, 2007d). Therefore, an inclusive definition of the nation was determined as the baseline for the AKP regarding minorities and their problems. Most importantly, the main endeavor of the party seemed to unite everyone in the country under the framework of a territorially defined supra-identity and inclusive citizenship of the Turkish Republic. The following words exemplify this:

> [T]he citizenship of the Turkish Republic is insurance for 73 million and a sufficient assurance for all of us. The common power of the people who live in this country is constitutional citizenship. . . . We are a mosaic. We know that this mosaic has different elements. You cannot find this richness if you leave out one or the other. But if you integrate this with supra-nationality, which is the citizenship of the Turkish Republic, you have this [richness].
> (AKP Political Group 2005c)

As the gap in the failure and discursive recognition of it and aspirations of the party regarding minority protection demonstrate, AKP's dissatisfaction with the status quo regarding minority rights was increasing by 2005. Party leaders increasingly diagnosed failure in the area, offered solutions to the failed issues and put the suggestions into action in line with their dissatisfaction. Yet, both AKP's discourse and policies regarding minority rights was not that assertive in 2005–2007. Rather, this period signifies an increasing gap between failure and aspirations of the AKP in minority protection and a transition from the push to pull in AKP's strategic calculations.

The 2007 elections: legitimacy through popular support

The AKP government was forced to call early parliamentary elections in 2007, facing enormous pressure from various fronts (Çarkoğlu 2008: 3). The results of the 2007 elections confirmed the legitimacy of the AKP by a 47 per cent vote share of the total votes and to some extent ended political uncertainties about the power of the AKP. The results represent a significant increase in the AKP's share of the national vote from 34 per cent in the 2002 elections to 47 per cent in the 2007 elections.

A number of factors brought about AKP's victory in the 2007 elections: economic growth and low inflation; the party's approach of social justice backed with charity-based redistribution; lack of effective opposition parties; and, most important among these influences, support of the party by various fronts due to its reformist agenda, including protest and pro-minority votes (Öniş 2009: 23).

Contributing of popular support to the AKP exemplifying some of minority votes in the elections, the Kurdish vote to the party in the elections is critical.[1] Notably, the AKP raised its share of the vote in the predominantly Kurdish Eastern and Southeastern regions and even surpassed the share of pro-Kurdish DTP in many parts of the region (Çarkoğlu 2007: 514; Polat 2009: 137). Such a result demonstrated that the AKP seems to have persuaded the Kurds with its problem-solving approach and willingness to solve the Kurdish problem by clearly stating the existence of the problem – differing from the previous official denial of the problem – and adopting an approach to solve it via the improvement of democracy, human and minority rights (Polat 2009: 137).

Most importantly, Kurdish support for the AKP indicates that many moderate Kurds were uncomfortable with the revival of violence due to the end of the ceasefire by the PKK and gave credit to the AKP in its political approach to the Kurdish problem (Bahcheli and Noel 2011: 112). Therefore, the 2007 elections demonstrated that the AKP's reformist approach including minority rights yielded results via the reward of an increase in votes. As Öniş (2009: 29) emphasizes, for the first time in history, a mainstream political party received more votes than the pro-Kurdish party in the region (see Table 5.1).

Apart from the minority votes, the political crises between the Kemalist powers and the AKP enlarged the electoral base of the AKP in the 2007 elections as a reaction of voters against top-down interventionist frequent tendencies among Kemalist elites in various institutions on the democratic process, such as the e-memorandum by the TAF (Öniş 2009: 25). As Grigoriadis (2009: 182) points out, "The triumphant victory of the AKP in the elections of July 22, 2007, was the amplest manifestation that the Turkish people opposed bureaucratic tutelage and favored democratic government".

The AKP government successfully instrumentalized election results to prove that it ruled the country by the will of people, reflecting a will for further democratic development, and this was a signal of AKP's majoritarian understanding of democracy as well as its electoral strategy to legitimize its rule and policies. The following statement of an AKP MP in a personal interview, on 30 March 2010, supports this argument:

> The July 22, 2007 election results demonstrated the demand of the people for democracy. . . . The AKP carries this mission and plays a vital role in the consolidation of civilian rule and providing solutions to the structural problems.[2]

Two other factors were also effective in the AKP's strategic calculations regarding the threat of sanctions by the electorate: the nationalist upsurge by 2005 and the disappointment of pro-Islamic voters. The threat of sanctions in the forthcoming elections by these two groups affected the assertive reform agenda of the AKP, especially regarding minority rights. As Patton (2007: 355) explains:

Table 5.1 Eastern region votes to the AKP and pro-Kurdish DTP in the 2007 elections

Region / Political Party	Eastern Anatolia	Southeastern Anatolia
AKP	54.64 %	53.14 %
DTP	19.42 %	24.40 %

Source: Author's own elaboration

Election politics have intersected with the rise in Turkish nationalism and with the disappointment of pro-Islamic voters that the EU process has not produced tangible gains in religious freedom influencing the AKP's strategic calculations for holding onto power. It has redirected its priorities towards short-term electoral concerns (winning votes).

The 2005 ECHR decision on a case brought by a Turkish university student, Leyla Şahin, which found the headscarf ban not in violation of the freedom of religion and education, was a clear disappointment for the pro-Islamic AKP voters (Saatçioğlu 2011: 33). With this decision, holding on to Islamic voters by the AKP became challenging in a period with strong backlash from Kemalists and nationalists (Patton 2007: 348). The AKP's attempt to remove the ban on the headscarf in public institutions in 2008, which led to a harsh backlash from Kemalist secularists, needs to be considered with this background of appeasing the Islamic electorate.

The rise of nationalism also manifested itself as a challenge to the AKP in the elections, which brought the possibility of nationalist parties' empowerment in the next elections. To balance the reformist and nationalist voters was a challenging issue for the AKP, which was one of the reasons why the AKP was not very assertive in its minority policy in 2005–2007 (Patton 2007: 348). However, the 2007 elections demonstrated that the rise of nationalism and the nationalist and Kemalist parties capitalizing on this process was counterproductive contributing to the electoral success of the AKP via fueling protest votes to the AKP (Öniş 2009: 22). Nevertheless, these two issues influenced the election calculations of the AKP to balance the reformist and pro-minority voters, on the one hand, and the Islamic and nationalist voters, on the other (Patton 2007: 347–8; Saatçioğlu 2011: 34).

From the Copenhagen criteria to the Ankara criteria

The shift in the AKP's position from an exclusive focus on the EU accession process to the 'domestic' was best reflected in its discourse. Despite expressing the continuing commitment of Turkey to the EU accession process (e.g. Address to the Nation 2007b; AKP Political Group 2005d), AKP leaders put heavy emphasis on unconditional full membership of Turkey to the EU in response to the alternative prospects offered for Turkey by some circles in the EU (e.g. privileged membership discussions for Turkey among EU member states) (e.g. AKP Political Group 2005e). Moreover, speeches by AKP leaders increasingly expressed discontent with the EU's conditionality focusing on criteria other than Copenhagen, which started to be felt more by 2005 (Address to the Nation 2007b; AKP Political Group 2005e).

Most importantly, AKP leaders often expressed their discontent with the Cyprus issue, which was translated as EU's unfair treatment against Turkey because resolution of the issue had become a precondition for Turkish accession (e.g. AKP Political Group 2005e). Because the AKP government had adopted a policy separating the EU accession process from the Cyprus issue, the EU's agenda regarding the membership of the RoC created a reactive approach by the AKP towards the EU (e.g. Address to the Nation 2006).

By 2005, a remarkable transition in the AKP's discourse, in which the dominance of EU push gave a way to the domestic choice for change, was evident. Due to the decline in the credible commitments of the EU, the AKP started to rely on the 'domestic' by portraying domestic change as a necessity and an essential component of primary ideals of the Republic to reach the standards the Turkish people deserve to have. In this context, EU reforms started to be instrumentally framed by the AKP as solutions to domestic problems and as a means of achieving better standards for Turkish people. Some of the statements of AKP leaders in this context are:

> Our people demand a freer and more prosperous country respected in the international arena. This demand is in accordance with the full membership ideal of the EU. In the following days, negotiations with the EU will start and the standards our people deserve will be brought into action.
> (AKP Political Group 2005f)

> If we support freedom of speech, freedom of religion and conscious, freedom of enterprise, freedom of association and want a free and democratic life, it does not matter what the EU decides. We call the Copenhagen Criteria the Ankara Criteria instead and maintain our path.
> (AKP Political Group 2005g)

> Full membership to the EU is not a periodic or tactical political matter. First, the goal of EU membership is the necessity of the foundation ideals of the Turkish Republic. Second, the prospective membership of Turkey to the EU is in the interests of both the EU and Turkey. Third, membership to the EU is not a choice imposed to Turkey from outside; on the contrary it is one of the principal choices of Turkish foreign policy. Fourth, at the basis of this choice, there is the will of Turkey to be more democratic, freer, fairer, and more prosperous; there is the will of our nation for change and evolution.
> (AKP Political Group 2006e)

Conclusions: selective change in minority protection through pull without push

The period between 2005 and 2007 represents a transition period from the trigger of push to arising pull. The period endured a series of both EU-related and domestic crises leading to questioning legitimacy of the AKP regarding its reforms and most importantly its rule. Losing the push of conditionality that provided legitimacy to the AKP government and reform process and the accelerating conflict

Table 5.2 2005–2007: pull without push

Pull and Push / Time Period	Pull	Push	Pull-and-Push
2005–2007	Medium	Low	Medium degree of pull without push Pull > Push
Expected Outcome			Selective policy change
Actual Outcome			Selective policy change

Source: Author's own elaboration

with secular Kemalists and nationalists led to an increase in the AKP's dissatisfaction – considering the threat of sanctions from many sides. In turn, the AKP pursued its reformist agenda, including minority rights such as addressing the Kurdish problem, in order to gain and keep votes from different segments of the society, reformists and Kurds.

The AKP adopted a selective approach regarding minority rights in this period due to the loss of momentum in the EU accession process and rather addressed minority-related policy failure, leaving behind the EU priorities that were not helpful for its strategic calculations. As a result, the period ended with selective policy change, though still limited in scope, confirming the expected outcome of selective policy change by the pull-and-push model (see Table 5.2). It is vital to note that the outcome of selective change that remained limited in scope is caused by the medium degree of pull by dissatisfaction.

Notes

1 Here the share of Kurdish votes in the elections is used to exemplify minority voting, because Kurdish votes can be clearly enumerated through analyzing regional distribution of votes, considering that the East and Southeast Turkey are highly populated by Kurds.
2 Zeynep Dağı, personal interview, March 30, 2010, Grand National Assembly Turkey, Ankara.

6 Pull without push in 2008–2014

Drift from the EU and rule by the 'domestic'

Granted a high degree of popular support in the 2007 elections, the AKP government adopted a more assertive reform agenda in the years following the elections. The AKP focused on consolidating the support of the electorate in the 2007 elections and capitalizing on the support of people to legitimize its rule and policies.

Despite the AKP's victory in the 2007 elections, polarization both within the society and political elites accelerated and, accordingly, AKP's reliance on electoral strategy based on its electoral popularity has become more apparent. Yet, especially after 2010, internal and international critiques increased on AKP's rule stressing the AKP's approach regarding democracy. Different ideas emerged on the new approach, although all united on the conclusion that the democratic stance of the AKP was determined by new understandings of democracy that led to a different kind of exercises in the area like majoritarian democracy through electoral hegemony (Keyman and Gümüşçü 2014; Öniş 2013; Özsel *et al.* 2013) or delegative or plebiscitarian democracy (Özbudun 2014). Interestingly, despite criticized on the halt and even worsening of democratic reforms and policies in the country, the government continued its minority reforms in this period, which was determined by the pull by dissatisfaction due to the significant weakening of the EU push.

No credible conditionality for Turkey! Towards a drift from Europe

EU's conditionality remained less credible and even weaker, in this era, when compared to the other periods. Cyprus issue continued to be the main stumbling block in the Turkish accession process regarding the implementation of Additional Protocol and peaceful settlement of disputes (European Commission 2010: 47–95; European Council 2008: 5). Moreover, in the following years, proposals for alternative partnership ideas with Turkey continued to be expressed by some member states. For instance, the French Secretary of State for European Matters Pierre Lellouche stated in 2009: "Realizing that it (Turkey) is a friendly and important country, we wonder whether it is not time to begin reflecting on alternative paths without interrupting the negotiation" (TurkishNY 2009). Again in the same year, the RoC vetoed the opening of a further five chapters in the negotiations on the basis of non-implementation of Additional Protocol by Turkey (Tocci 2010: 28). At the end, such developments were translated into the domestic arena as an increasingly limited EU push, accordingly, with limited influence on reforms.

The decrease in the Turkish public support for EU membership (see Figure 6.1) also supported this picture and signalled that the EU accession process of Turkey had become a low denominator in domestic politics. According to the surveys by Eurobarometer (2008, 2009, 2010, 2011, 2012, 2013, 2014), Turkish public support for Turkey's membership to the EU had a significant decreasing trend from 49 per cent to 38 per cent between 2008 and 2014. Most importantly, the surveys show an increasing trend in the group who perceives EU membership as 'a bad thing', reaching 33 per cent in 2014.

Considering the opposition in the Parliament after the 2007 elections, the elections brought two Euro-skeptic political parties, the CHP and the MHP, into the Parliament and both parties increasingly pursued a Euro-skeptic perspective. Notably, the re-entrance of the MHP to the Parliament, who was ousted from power in the previous elections, shows the ultra-nationalist and anti-EU party benefited from rising nationalism and Euro-skepticism in previous years (Avcı 2011b: 443).

Ironically, opposition of the MHP to EU accession was not to the idea per se, but to the conditions for the accession touching on several sensitive issues, such as the national unity of the state, specifically related to the Kurdish problem (Öniş 2010: 12). The opposition of the MHP to the EU accession process was framed

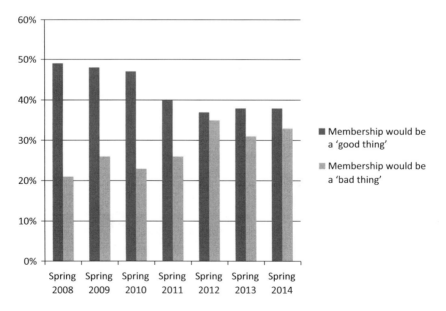

Figure 6.1 Turkish public support for EU membership in 2008–2014
Source: Eurobarometer (2008, 2009, 2010, 2011, 2012, 2013, 2014)

by describing the EU roadmap for accession as being a minefield including unfair and unacceptable conditions like Cyprus issue, Armenian problem and minority rights (MHP ARGE 2009, 2010). Specifically related to minorities in Turkey, the MHP accused the EU of referring groups like the Kurds as minorities in its annual reports (MHP ARGE 2009). With or without the EU reference, at the end, the MHP has strictly been against minority-related reforms due to its ultra-nationalist stance.

The CHP opposed both to the AKP government and the EU accession process in even harsher terms after the 2007 elections. For instance, after the murder of Armenian journalist Hrant Dink, a debate emerged about the abolition of Article 301 of the Constitution,[1] which was used to prosecute Dink, claimed by many to have made him a target for ultra-nationalists (Avcı 2011a: 418). Yet, the most vocal opposition to the abolition of the Article came from the CHP (Avcı 2011a: 418). The deputy Chairman of the CHP, Onur Öymen, made a statement about the views of the CHP on the issue, emphasizing that the AKP government brought the revision of Article 301 into the agenda in order to win the EU's praise, which would in turn harm the national independence of Turkey (Haber3 2008). The CHP and MHP built an alliance to hinder the revision of the Article, especially opposing the replacement of the term 'Turkishness', implying an ethnic definition of national identity, with Turkish nation in the amendment of Article 301 (Radikal 2008). Yet, the amendment was adopted with the support of pro-EU actors, the AKP, and the pro-Kurdish DTP (Avcı 2011a: 418).

The DTP, entered into the Parliament in the 2007 elections through bypassing the 10 per cent threshold indirectly, emerged as a key actor in Turkish politics after the elections. The DTP as a pro-Kurdish party supported the solution of the Kurdish problem through democratization measures and, therefore, located itself as a pro-reformist and pro-EU actor in the political spectrum (Saylan 2012: 192). Besides, pro-Kurdish parties have traditionally been supportive of Turkey's membership to the EU, since the reforms in the accession process would strengthen democratic rights for Kurds and contribute to the solution of the Kurdish problem (Bardakçı 2010: 34).

In the meantime, the pro-EU and pro-reform NGOs continued to declare their support on both the EU accession and the reform process, in spite of the weakened EU push, harsh criticism by the opposition and decreased Turkish public support to the accession process. For instance, TÜSİAD consistently and repeatedly called for the revival of the accession process as well as the launch of reforms for the democratization of Turkey (Hürriyet 2013). Yet, it is important to note that the impact of Turkey's civil society, including a high number of NGOs, on policy-making remained limited in this era, as was the case previously (Kubicek 2011).

Most importantly, the EU has become less attractive to many, including the Turkish government after the Eurozone crisis. While the Turkish economy was robust without any major economic crisis, Greece was pretty much devastated economically despite being a EU member state (Öniş 2013: 110). This, in turn, led to a weakened image of the EU in the minds of the Turkish political elites with a strong and self-confident Turkish image. For instance, Prime Minister Erdoğan often stressed that the global economic crisis had a devastating impact on many powers like the US and the EU, while "the crisis was slightly touched to the Turkish economy" (e.g. Address to the Nation 2012). At the end, the EU's magnetic impact was significantly reduced, due to the Eurozone crisis, and the EU affairs lost its priority at the government's agenda even more.

In line with the loss of momentum in the EU push, the AKP presented qualified support to the EU accession process in this period (Öniş 2010: 12). Even more, the changing direction of AKP's foreign policy towards the East, particularly the Middle East, in the recent years demonstrates a further estrangement from the EU (Oğuzlu 2012: 236). Various statements by the AKP representatives confirmed this changing balance, such as Erdoğan's statement in November 2013 expressing the will of Turkey for a free trade agreement with Eurasian states and calling the concerned states to accept Turkey as a member of the Shanghai Cooperation Organization (Radikal 2013a). Additionally, Erdoğan's statement of not recognizing the European Parliament decision on Turkey on June 12, 2013 that criticized the AKP government's policies specifically regarding the Taksim *Gezi* Park protests[2] demonstrates even an apparent drift from the EU (Radikal 2013b). At the end, all demonstrates the Turkish disappointment with the EU–Turkey relations, which proceeded step by step towards a Turkish drift from the EU path (Öniş 2013: 111).

Towards the 2009 elections: the rise of domestic polarization and no push, increasing pull for survival

Following the 2007 elections, the CHP, the MHP, the military and the Constitutional Court quickly formed a nationalist-Kemalist and Euro-skeptic opposition against the AKP, and political crises between these continued and even accelerated later on as mentioned before, despite the 2007 elections that appeased domestic polarization for some time. The crises were again concentrated on the issues of secularism and political reforms demanded by the EU on sensitive issues, such as the Kurdish issue, which is closely related to the unity of state, considering the PKK problem and monolithic identity of Turkey (Gençkaya and Özbudun 2009: 107; Kumbaracıbaşı 2009: 59; Somer 2011: 30). Besides, the further weakened credibility of EU conditionality strengthened the opposition against the AKP government and its reforms.

Starting with the headscarf issue, the tension in the domestic arena raised day by day. When the removal of headscarf ban as a part of the constitutional amendments proposed by the AKP in early 2008, the proposition fuelled contention between the AKP and primarily the Kemalists (i.e. CHP, military, and the Constitutional Court) (Gençkaya and Özbudun 2009: 107). Nevertheless, collaborating with the MHP, the AKP abolished the ban on wearing headscarves in public and specifically universities through amending the Articles in the Constitution related to equality and education (Gençkaya and Özbudun 2009: 107; Toktaş and Kurt 2010: 397). Yet, the Kemalist opposition harshly criticized this on the basis of secularism as the foundational principle of the Republic, and the CHP took the issue to the Constitutional Court, which annulled the amendments in June 2008 (Toktaş and Kurt 2010: 397).

The headscarf issue was accompanied by the closure case against the AKP charging the party of being a center for anti-secular activities in March 2008. The Constitutional Court, in the end, decided against the closure of the party, yet ruled only to deprive the AKP of treasury aid on the grounds that the party was becoming a center for anti-secular activities (Somer 2011: 30). No matter what the conclusion was, the very existence of the party was significantly threatened by the case and the survival of the AKP in the hyper-secular Republic was once again tested, this time by the Constitutional Court, which became a vocal point within the opposition against the AKP.

While domestic polarization deepened over the issues of secularism and political reforms demanded by the EU on sensitive issues, such as the Kurdish issue after the elections, the 2008 *Ergenekon* case, charging military officials and civilians for plotting military intervention against the AKP government, and the reforms strengthening civilian control over the military led to a shift in the balance of power between the AKP government and the military in favour of the government (Cengiz and Hoffmann 2013: 12; Kumbaracıbaşı 2009: 59). *Ergenekon* case was a turning point for the role of military in the Republic, which was traditionally acting as the guardian of the foundational principles of the Republic (e.g. secularism) and, therefore, involved in politics.

Ergenekon case was followed by the 2010 *Balyoz* (Sledgehammer) case that charged around 200 military officers for coup plots against the AKP government. Most importantly, the *Ergenekon* case with later the *Balyoz* case signify the beginning of an era with the civilianization of politics as well as political delegitimization and criminalization of military interventions (Keyman and Gümüşcü 2014: 46). While the cases built an image for the AKP as the "protector of civic democracy against military tutelage raised the popularity of the party even more", they had an opposite effect on the military's image and reputation (Özsel *et al.* 2013: 563).

As a matter of course, the cases against the military had a dramatic effect on its relations with the government. Although the appointment of Ilker Başbuğ as the Chief of General Staff in August 2008, who adopted a non-interventionist position of the military on domestic politics and refrained public declarations in conflict with the AKP government, softened the domestic turmoil of the previous years, the launch of the *Ergenekon* case caused a more reactive discourse by Başbuğ (Heper 2011: 244–6). Accordingly, a more polarized picture emerged in the domestic politics with the sharpened Kemalist opposition against the AKP government focusing on the *Ergenekon* and *Balyoz* cases (Gürsoy 2011: 298). Most importantly, the revelations of *Ergenekon* and *Balyoz* acted as a catalyst to popular support for reforms promoting civilian control of military and reducing the power of the military to intervene in politics (Cizre 2011: 66; Gürsoy 2011: 298). Yet, despite started as an attempt to challenge the Turkish 'deep state', the trials faced both domestic and international critiques due to long detention periods and charging many with vague connections to the alleged coup plots (Öniş 2013: 107).

Linked to the domestic crises, polarization and, therefore, AKP's survival anxiety, a significant change in the push-pull balance within the strategic calculations of the AKP in favour of the pull emerged in this era. Accession remained low and later even non-existent on the agenda of the AKP government, with the increasing impact of Euro-skeptic tendencies among domestic actors and in the wider public. Rather, domestic politics overweighed the EU accession process at a time without the support of credible rewards from the EU. This, in turn, compelled the AKP government to rely on public support to legitimize its rule and survive in the conflictual political arena, which significantly required sustaining political reforms (especially minority reforms) to attract and consolidate the pro-reformist, pro-minority, and minority electorates. However, such survival considerations were replaced by extreme-confidence, yet still in need of electoral support, later especially after the 2011 elections.

In line with the domestic polarization, the rise of the pull within the AKP strategic calculations became more explicit. First of all, the change in the AKP discourse on the EU accession process reveals the decreasing focus of the AKP government on the issue and increasing emphasis on reforms as a domestic choice in response to domestic problems. Although AKP leaders stated, in some instances, the commitment of the AKP government to the accession process (e.g. Address to the Nation 2008b; AKP Political Group 2009b, 2010b), the focus of the party shifted from accession and remained superficial. Moreover, by 2008, AKP leaders increasingly stressed the necessity for the EU to keep its commitments – referring to the privileged partnership debates and the Cyprus issue (Address to the Nation 2009; AKP Political Group 2008c, 2009c). This reflects a loss of trust in the EU delivering its commitments or rewards.

In turn, the leaders of the AKP explicitly shifted their emphasis from EU membership to the domestic utility of reforms and the necessity of EU standards for the future of the country, irrespective of accession. This signifies the transition of the AKP's perspective on political reforms, including minority rights, from the EU push to domestic choice, referring to the utility of reforms for the sake of Turkey, which is explicitly illustrated as follows:

> We maintain our path by replacing the Maastricht Criteria with the Istanbul Criteria and the Copenhagen Criteria with Ankara Criteria. . . . Despite all the obstacles and unfair treatment . . . we are committed to the accession process to the EU.
>
> (AKP Political Group 2009d)

Confirming the transition to pull, AKP's survival and electoral considerations, the bursting aspirations of the AKP regarding minority protection constituted a vital indicator for the primacy of pull in AKP's strategic considerations. The all-embracing and inclusive approach of the party regarding minorities and their rights even with explicitly referring to the concept of 'minority' and their rights as was not the case previously demonstrates AKP's increasing minority aspirations.

Besides emphases by AKP leaders on the problems of minorities and solutions offered by the government, also specifically the Kurdish problem and the solution process, the principle of non-discrimination, the refusal of the previous perception of minorities as second-class citizens, the national unity and fraternity among different groups tied to each other with common historical experience and common ideals, the inclusive territorially defined supra-identity and citizenship of the Republic were even more perceived in this era (e.g. Address to the Nation 2013, 2014; AKP Political Group 2008d, 2009a, 2009d, 2009e, 2009f, 2010b, 2010c, 2010d). Some of the illustrative statements are the following:

> We have to rapidly improve an atmosphere in which all feel first class citizens without any discrimination on the basis of ethnicity, religion or sect; an atmosphere in which we consider our differences as our richness and we strengthen our fraternity.
> (AKP Political Group 2008b)

> It is becoming clear that every ethnic origin and sect are not matters of disintegrating and all this diversity is richness under the framework of the citizenship of the Turkish Republic.
> (AKP Political Group 2010e)

> Nobody can be accused for being an imperfect and second-class citizen due to having his/her mother's or father's ethnic origins, belief, sect, color, culture, language.
> (AKP Political Group 2010f)

> Being a nation, overarching ethnic belonging is about common history and ideals. . . . Regardless of their ethnicity, all living in this land, all of our citizens are equal members of the same nation and civilization and are siblings. . . . Our equality and fraternity is not only a result of the law of citizenship; but at the same time it is a natural consequence of common history and civilization.
> (AKP Political Group 2008e)

As a conclusion, just after the 2007 elections, domestic politics demonstrated a new phase of polarization among Turkish political elites that gave signals of upcoming further polarization within the society. Until the next elections, political crises became a daily routine and the legitimacy of the AKP, and its policies were increasingly questioned in this process. In this conflictual domestic environment, the AKP relied on the pull rather than the weakened push for its fate, for its survival.

2009 elections: the AKP monopolizing the reform process

After the profound developments of previous years, the year of 2009 was a wake-up call to the AKP. When the local elections resulted in March 2009, it demonstrated a significant loss of votes for the AKP, with a 39 per cent share of the total. Compared to the 2004 local elections and to the 2009 parliamentary elections, support to the AKP was 3 per cent down for the former and 8 per cent down for the latter (see Table 6.1) (Çarkoğlu 2009: 2). Yet, it is necessary to keep in mind that different dynamics shaped the general and local voting decisions (Çarkoğlu 2009: 2).

Most importantly, the 2009 elections demonstrated the AKP's loss of votes in the Kurdish Eastern and Southeastern regions to the DTP (Larrabee and Tol 2011: 147) (See Table 6.2). Even though support from these regions diverted from the AKP, the party still managed to keep its voting share in most of the provinces in Eastern and Southeastern Anatolia (Çarkoğlu 2009: 12). However, as Larrabee and Tol (2011: 147) emphasize, "The AKP's poor showing in Kurdish areas served as an important wake-up call and underscored the need to address Kurdish concerns and grievances more seriously". In this context, the launch of the Kurdish initiative after the 2009 elections is remarkable in that it implies the AKP's tendency to fulfill the expectations of Kurdish voters.

The decrease in the AKP's share of vote in the Eastern and Southeastern Anatolia can be linked to the nationalist discourse adopted by the AKP leaders after the 2007 elections, and also the rise of PKK activity and the government's military response that alienated some in the region (Özsel *et al.* 2013: 565). Despite the AKP later tried to present its rule attractive to the Kurdish population through its pro-Kurdish approach and policies, the party, at the same time, alienated some nationalist-conservative voters (Eligür 2009: 472). Promoting pro-Kurdish policies, the party took "the risk of alienating large segments of the Turkish public

Table 6.1 Comparing local elections of 2004 and 2009

Political Party	2004 Local Elections Vote Share %	2007 General Elections Vote Share %	2009 Local Elections Vote Share %
AKP	41.7	46.6	38.8
CHP	18.2	20.9	23.1
MHP	10.5	14.3	16.1
DTP	5.2	–	5.6

Source: Çarkoğlu (2009: 3)

Table 6.2 Eastern region votes to the AKP and pro-Kurdish DTP in the 2009 elections

Region / Political Party	Eastern Anatolia	Southeastern Anatolia
AKP	39.2 %	39.2 %
DTP	29.7 %	25.3 %

Source: Author's own elaboration

and its own electoral base" (Bahcheli and Noel 2011: 117). However, it is hard to determine the extent of the distance that emerged from these groups regarding the AKP's pro-Kurdish approach (Çarkoğlu 2009: 15).

Although the AKP preserved popular support by the wider society in the elections, the volatility of the electoral base of the party was demonstrated in each election, either with a rise or fall in votes for the party. As Bahcheli and Noel (2011: 116) emphasize, the AKP, as a party having support from various fronts, needed to be mindful to maintain the support of its electorate whom among many would be difficult to convince of the need for further reforms in the existence of the PKK violence. At the same time, to keep and increase the reformist, reactionary and minority votes (such as Kurds or Alevis), the AKP had to satisfy the demands of these groups, which was demonstrated in recent reforms.

To keep and consolidate the popular support, the AKP government continued its reforms and, most interestingly, began to promote itself as the sole democratizing or pro-reform actor (not anymore a pro-EU reformist due to the weakened EU push across time) in the domestic arena without cooperating other political and civil actors. Consequently, its reform process was criticized due to the lack of dialogue and compromise among political parties, insufficient consultation to the parties within the parliament, civil society and other stakeholders (European Commission 2012, 2013).

2010 Constitutional change: further polarization and legitimacy through the referendum

In 2010, the AKP adopted Constitutional amendments touching several issues such as human rights, but most importantly providing increased civilian control of the military and reforming judicial system (Alessandri 2010: 23). However, the civilian control of the military and restructuring the judiciary seen by the Kemalists as the last pillar of the older system led to further polarization (Alessandri 2010: 26).

In an attempt to gain legitimacy to the amendments, the AKP scheduled a national referendum on September 12, 2010, but the referendum campaign also demonstrated an increasing level of polarization within both the society and political elites (Alessandri 2010: 25). As Öniş (2013: 106) emphasizes, the referendum was both a test case and key step for challenging and eliminating the legacy of the old order established by the military through 1982 Constitution. Even the day the referendum held was meaningful referring to the latest military intervention on September 12, 1980. As this also demonstrates, the AKP strategically positioned itself as the democratizing actor of Turkey in opposition to the old repressive order.

Promoting itself as the primary democratizing force in the country, the AKP gained legitimacy on its amendments through the 58 per cent share of the total votes at the referendum. This strategic move of the AKP clearly shows its reliance on popular support to legitimize its rule and reforms in sensitive areas, such as in civil–military relations.

Most importantly, the referendum demonstrated a highly polarized and divided society over the AKP's policies and reforms. As Keyman and Gümüşcü (2014: 54) stress, the AKP's electoral hegemony creates a tendency for crisis-prone country and leads to a discourse of polarization and 'otherization' by the AKP, which in turn creates tension in the society as well as the alienation of the secular middle class. At the end, the AKP day after day increased the tone of its two-block discourse dividing both the political arena and the society into two spheres: the AKP versus the 'Rest' (Çınar 2011: 122).

The 2010 Referendum was not only a referendum, but also a signal of the upcoming monopolization of power by the AKP. This phase started after the referendum through the elimination of the historical role played by the military and the judiciary as intervening governments' rule and policies. First, the political influence of the military was significantly weakened by the Constitutional amendments, and military interventions were both delegitimized and later criminalized (Kuru 2012: 51). Second, the power of judiciary was also reduced through the Constitutional amendments, which redesigned higher courts as well as the Higher Council of Judges and Prosecutors (*Hakimler ve Savcılar Yüksek Kurulu* – HSYK) (Keyman and Gümüşcü 2014: 48). The amendments "led to a process that eventually ended the pro-military, especially assertive secularist, domination in the HSYK" (Kuru 2012: 51). Besides, the key positions in several important institutions has gradually been dominated by the pro-government figures like the presidency of High Education Council with a crucial role in monitoring the universities and appointing the rectors (Çınar 2011: 112).

To conclude, while eliminating interventions over its rule, the AKP government did not provide any other institutional arrangement for checks and balances over its rule and "the AKP has established control over the parliament, government, and the presidency, creating considerable monopolization of power at the hands of the party leadership" (Keyman and Gümüşcü 2014: 50).

Towards a new style of politics: authoritarian, majoritarian or what?

In the road to one and only hegemonic power of the Republic, the AKP faced increasing domestic and international critiques due to its controversial policies. Besides, any critique or opposition to the policies of the AKP was translated by the key AKP cadre as a declaration against 'the will of nation', which was delegated to the AKP in the elections (Özsel *et al.* 2013: 564).

Electoral strategy of the AKP, which dominated the previous periods of its rule, turned into an 'electoral hegemony', as Keyman and Gümüşcü (2014) put it, or "unbalanced and lop-sided political structure", as Öniş (2013: 113) stresses. However, even within this framework the support of minority and pro-minority groups to the AKP was necessary to keep and consolidate its electoral hegemony, and therefore, the AKP was in need to continue minority reforms, despite not for its survival like the previous period, but for the consolidation and legitimacy of its rule.

While monopolizing the political arena, the AKP also monopolized the reform process, presented it as the single-handed delivery of the AKP – as the main democratizing force of the country – without the contribution of any other actor and claimed that reforms were launched in spite of the opposition to the reforms, as also argued in the AKP's 2011 election campaign (Çınar 2011: 110, 118). As seen, the AKP reserved the pro-reformist, democratizing status for only itself, but no other actor in the domestic arena.

In the 2011 elections, the victory of the AKP receiving the 50 per cent share of total votes doubled the legitimacy of the AKP government, its reforms and granted the public approval to the AKP as the primary democratizing actor of the country. In the meantime, the support to the opposition – constituted primarily by the CHP (26 per cent) and MHP (13 per cent) – remained more or less the same compared to the previous elections (Hürriyet 2011).

The election campaign of the AKP focused on its service-delivery approach in the past 9 years and the inability of the 'Rest' to govern and provide what the nation wants (Çınar 2011: 123). Therefore, the divisive discourse of the AKP relying on 'us and others' or 'the AKP and the Rest' was further sharpened through the election campaign. Importantly, political and cultural populism were also dominant in the AKP's election discourse (Çınar 2011: 123).

Despite the AKP's assertive election campaign, the vote share of the part, on one side, dropped in the Eastern and Southeastern regions. On the other side, the Labour, Democracy and Freedom Bloc (*Emek, Demokrasi ve Özgürlük Bloğu* – EDÖB) formed by minor left-wing parties and the successor of the pro-Kurdish DTP (i.e. Peace and Democracy Party (*Barış ve Demokrasi Partisi* – BDP)) received 6.58 per cent of the total votes and demonstrated a significant success.

When compared to the 2007 general elections, the numbers, as mentioned, show a decrease in the vote share of the AKP in the Eastern and Southeastern regions and an increase in the bloc the pro-Kurdish BDP involved (BBC 2011) (see Table 6.3). In spite of the effort by the AKP to sideline the BDP as its competitor for the Kurdish votes, which determined the AKP's approach in the Kurdish issue, the AKP was not that successful about this in the 2011 elections (Çınar 2011: 120).

Table 6.3 Eastern region votes to the AKP and pro-Kurdish Party in the 2007 and 2011 elections

Region / Political Party	Eastern Anatolia 2007	Eastern Anatolia 2011	Southeastern Anatolia 2007	Southeastern Anatolia 2011
AKP	54.64 %	51.8 %	53.14 %	51.38 %
Pro-Kurdish Party	19.42 %	26.71 %	24.40 %	32.37 %

Source: Author's own elaboration

The loss of votes by the AKP and the success of the BDP-led bloc are closely related to the developments before the elections and AKP's approach regarding these developments. The ban of the DTP, predecessor of the BDP, in 2009, the arrests of hundreds for their membership to an organization (i.e. KCK) affiliated with the PKK, the failure of the Kurdish opening, the exclusionary approach of the AKP regarding the DTP and later the BDP, and the rise of nationalist-conservative discourse of Erdoğan influenced the election results in the Eastern and Southeastern regions (Satana 2012: 176).

To attract the Kurdish voters after the loss of votes in the 2011 elections, Erdoğan announced that negotiations were held to solve the Kurdish problem in 2012. The Kurdish Peace Process followed the announcement and was launched in March 2013 through the PKK leader Öcalan's letter calling an end to the armed struggle. The timing of the peace process is noteworthy, as it was just after the 2011 elections, and confirms the electoral strategy of the AKP considering minority votes as vital regarding the electoral support to the party.

Considering the opposition at the Parliament, the CHP entered to the Parliament with a 26 per cent of the total vote in the elections. Interestingly, this period signifies a change in the policies and discourse of the CHP, primarily due to the resignation of the party leader, Deniz Baykal, and the election of Kemal Kılıçdaroğlu as the new Party Chairman in 2010. Kılıçdaroğlu represented a symbol of change in the CHP and "The 'New CHP' materialized as a response to criticisms leveled at the CHP concerning Deniz Baykal's nationalistic leanings, the party's ambivalence on the Kurdish issue, opposition to EU accession" (Uysal 2011: 132, 134).

Through the 'New CHP', Kılıçdaroğlu changed CHP's elitist discourse based on secularism; emphasized the poverty and corruption as two important problems of the country; embraced different segments of the society; adopted a softer rather than Euro-skeptic stance towards the EU; stressed pluralistic and democratic society, changed its focus regarding the Kurdish issue from counterterrorism to democratization (Gülmez 2013: 316; Uysal 2011: 134–5). However, the actions of the 'New CHP' demonstrated rather more of a rhetorical change than a change in practice. For instance, as Gülmez (2013: 321) notes, in the Constitutional Referendum the CHP advocated a 'no' to the amendments and accused the EU for supporting a 'yes' to the Constitutional Referendum. Moreover, the party advocated that the *Ergenekon* trials are entirely political and put names prosecuted in the *Ergenekon* case on their 2011 election list (Gülmez 2013: 321; Uysal 2011: 137). At the end, the 'New CHP' pursued its old-style approach despite changing its rhetoric by 2010.

The MHP, on the other hand, received 13 per cent of the total votes in the 2011 elections. The party positioned itself within the opposition and kept its Euro-skeptic outlook. For instance, the electoral strategy of the party in the 2011 elections was primarily based on an anti-AKP one, criticizing the AKP government in various issues for leading to a disintegration of Turkey's unity; weakening the nationalist character of the country; establishing a new and rich class of people by means of corruption and political protection (Bacık 2011: 178–9). Regarding the EU accession process, the party strictly preserved its red lines (e.g. on Armenian issue), and only confirms Turkey's accession perspective if the EU's approach does not harm national interests in various issues, such as terrorism or the Cyprus issue (MHP 2011: 188–9). It is important to note that the Euro-skeptic alliance of the CHP and MHP broke in this period due to the change in CHP's approach.

What is more is the inability of the opposition at the Parliament to provide powerful, meaningful and effective checks and balances to the government's rule and policies. While these parties struggle internally with issues like leadership contests, the AKP did not face any strong and challenging opposition against its rule and policies, which has further contributed to the monopolization of power in the hands of the AKP (Keyman and Gümüscü 2014: 56).

At the end, despite increasing polarization among domestic actors and society on several issues, the AKP gained more room for maneuver for its policies, which are selected and pursued in line with its political preferences, comparing to the previous period. The "excessive concentration of political power" within the AKP's hands brought "an unusual degree of over-confidence" to the party and intolerance to the opposition (Öniş 2013: 113).

With such over-confidence, the AKP started to implement policies of its preference that triggered domestic and international critiques. For instance, in 2012 Prime Minister Erdoğan announced that the AKP government was in preparation of a law banning abortion and cesarean (Radikal 2012). Erdoğan declared their decisiveness on the issue and portrayed abortion as murder and the cesarean operations as a tool to prevent the increase of Turkey's population because "there can be no children more than two if the birth is with cesarean" (Radikal 2012). However, such statements and propositions were translated in the domestic arena as the violation of fundamental rights and freedoms, protested widely by women and various activists. At the end, the anti-abortion law was dropped by the AKP government, and instead a law on cesarean operations was adopted that limits the operations only if it is essential (Aljazeera 2012; Haber3 2012).

AKP's criticized policies continued in 2013 through a series of regulations on alcohol sales, which were translated by the domestic elites and society as an 'alcohol ban' (Ozbilgin 2013). Although the regulations did not ban alcohol, they tightened the alcohol sales and banned alcohol advertisements, which, in turn, drew criticism from the political actors, society and brewing industry (Ozbilgin 2013).

Most importantly, deterioration in the freedom of press and expression in the second half of this period led to increasing attention and criticism internationally. As Freedom House (2013, 2014) stresses, Turkish media is lively, but does not demonstrate signs of high quality: many journalists have been incarcerated; almost all media institutions have been belong to giant holding companies having ties to political parties; many journalists have lost their jobs when they seem critical of the government; and, therefore, self-censorship has become a common phenomenon in the country. Moreover, the AKP government was highly criticized both domestically and internationally, when a ban on public statement by academicians outside the academic discussions or statements was introduced in January 2014, which was limiting academic freedom as well (Freedom House 2013).

Notably, censorship has also been imposed on the internet, yet, gradually: various web sites are blocked by Turkish cyber police at different times; a filtration system for the internet was introduced in 2011; and a law on the internet use was adopted in 2014, which brought many restrictions on the internet, such as ceasing the access on certain web sites that are violating the right of privacy (Eldem 2013; Freedom House 2013, 2014; Milliyet 2014; Yilmaz 2016).

While the above-mentioned developments were drawn criticism from wide segments of the society and international actors, the AKP launched a discussion on adopting a presidential system in the country (ahaber 2012). Such a proposition increased concerns stressing that too much power concentrated in the hands of one man as an all-powerful president might significantly harm the Turkish democracy (Aydınlı 2012; Kılıç 2013). All these debates gave signals of the AKP's will to increase and consolidate its power as well as to achieve a hegemonic position through the electoral support.

2013 Taksim *Gezi* Park Protests and beyond: the burst by the 'rest'

The year of 2013 was remarkable for Turkish politics regarding critical developments like the launch of Kurdish peace process and the Taksim *Gezi* Park Protests. Sparked by few environmentalists in May 2013 to preserve the Taksim *Gezi* Park in Istanbul from the authorities, who decided to reconstruct Taksim military barracks with a shopping mall inside the new building, the protests spread all over Turkey (e.g. Ankara, Izmir and Hatay) and gained an anti-government character over a short time. In the protests, many were injured, and six people died due to the excessive use of force by the police (European Commission 2013: 5).

During the protests, the AKP government censored the media broadcasting the events; took harsh measures against the protestors; and blamed the protestors being tools of external forces, such as the Jewish diaspora (Amnesty International 2013: 6; European Commission 2013: 5–6; Freedom House 2014). Yet, government's response to the protests signified the recent controversial process in the country including the "the denial of the right to peaceful assembly, excessive use of force by police officers and the prosecution of legitimate dissenting opinions while allowing police abuses go unchecked" (Amnesty International 2013: 7).

In addition to the aforementioned issues, media as the fourth estate of democracy faced major pressure from the government during and after the protests: censorship and self-censorship were common; many media workers, who seemed sympathetic to the protestors lost their jobs; TV stations, who aired the protests, were fined on the basis of inciting violence; social-media platforms, such as Twitter, were declared as a 'menace' due to their usage by the protestors to organize the protests (Freedom House 2014).

During the demonstrations, the AKP government internationally and internally faced incremental criticism due to its response to the protests. Yet, the intolerance of the government against the opposition and critiques over its policies became quite visible in this process. For instance, the European Parliament (EP) issued a resolution on Taksim *Gezi* Park protests expressing concerns over the response of the police and the government to the protestors and criticized the government for its policies during the demonstrations (European Parliament 2013). Prime Minister Erdoğan swiftly responded that he did not recognize the EP's decision, which, in turn, clearly reflects the estrangement of Turkey from the EU in the recent years (Radikal 2013b).

During the protests, the AKP government did not approach for any negotiations to appease the protestors, rather its leaders' discourse (e.g. calling the protesters 'looters') further polarized the bursting society. AKP's refusal to engage with the protestors was mainly based on the majoritarian understanding of democracy, relying on the electoral participation as the only meaningful type of political participation (Keyman and Gümüşcü 2014: 58).

While the protests signalled the reaction of all the 'Rest' other than the AKP's supporters, the end of AKP's collaboration with the Gülen movement surfaced at the end of 2013. Despite the cool off in the relations began in 2012, it was only publicized through the December 2013 criminal investigations charging government members (even the Prime Minister and his family) for corruption-related cases (Özbudun 2014: 159).

After that, a serious conflict between the members of the Gülen movement and the AKP cracked open and, as Özbudun (2014: 160) stresses, "the AKP government chose a policy of confrontation by galvanising and mobilising its core supporters around charges of a foreign conspiracy".

After the burst of polarization from many fronts in the domestic arena, the 2014 local elections demonstrated a war-like struggle between the AKP and the 'Rest' including the Gülen supporters later on. Yet, in March 2014, the elections resulted with another victory of the AKP getting 43.1 per cent of the total votes and again no striking change in the share of the CHP (26.6 per cent), the MHP (17.6 per cent) and the BDP (4.2 per cent) (Haber Türk 2014). The results also suggest that the changing direction of AKP's policies, the corruption charges and popular unrest, as well as the response of the government to the protests, did not prevent the governing party to win the elections with a significant victory. Although there were some allegations on the counting of votes in favour of the AKP, these did not influence the announced victory of the AKP (Letsch 2014).

Very important to note during this process is Erdoğan's emphasis in his election rallies linking the halt of the peace process to the Gülen Movement and signals on the decisiveness of the AKP to continue the Kurdish peace process after the elections (Dalay 2014). Besides, the release of 37 activists charged through the KCK case just on the eve of the elections demonstrates a last move to attract Kurdish votes by the AKP (Dalay 2014).

The election results show that AKP's efforts were successful enough to attract a high number of votes from both the Eastern and Southeastern Anatolia. Comparing the results with the ones in the previous 2009 elections. the AKP significantly raised its share of votes in the Eastern Anatolia from 39.2 per cent to 47.2 per cent and in the Southeastern Anatolia from 39.2 per cent to 44.2 per cent; the BDP, on the other hand, lost significant share of votes in the Eastern Anatolia from 29.7

Table 6.4 Eastern region votes to the AKP and pro-Kurdish DTP in the 2014 elections

Region / Political Party	Eastern Anatolia	Southeastern Anatolia
AKP	47.2 %	44.2 %
DTP	23.1 %	32.3%

Source: Author's own elaboration

per cent to 23.1 per cent and increased its share of the votes from 25.3 per cent to 32.3 per cent in the Southeastern Anatolia (see Table 6.4) (Haber Türk 2014). The numbers signified that while the AKP preserved its superiority in the regions and even further increased its share of votes denoting a positive feedback from the Kurdish electorate, the BDP lost significant support from the Eastern part to the AKP, while it increased its votes in the Southeastern Anatolia.

Whatever the results of the 2014 local elections, the political and societal arena continued to be dominated by striking polarization, and this was again demonstrated in the 2014 Presidential elections, which was held within the Parliament in the previous decades, yet in 2014 through direct vote. In spite of the low turnout, Erdoğan won the elections by taking the 51.95 per cent of the total votes, while the CHP-supported candidate Ekmeleddin İhsanoğlu had 38.34 per cent and the co-chair of the Kurdish People's Democratic Party (*Halkların Demokrasi Partisi* – HDP), which was merged with the BDP in 2014, Selahaddin Demirtaş got 9.71 per cent of the total votes (Letsch 2014).

The presidential elections notably revealed the increasing role of the pro-Kurdish party as nominating a presidential candidate for the first time in the Republican history (Bakeer 2014). In spite of the loss of Presidential race, Demirtaş's share of votes in the elections was seen as a considerable success, due to the increase of his party's votes from 2.7 million to around 3.9 million (Kızılkaya 2014).

As seen, the AKP consolidated its rule through the legitimacy granted by popular support in the elections, despite the opposition, despite the unrest, despite the domestic and international critiques. From survival to consolidation considerations in the strategic calculations of the AKP, elections continued to be the key component, in which the support by minorities as well as pro-minority groups remained a vital element. At the end, this period demonstrates a transformation of the AKP's electoral strategy towards a more kind of an electoral hegemony.

Conclusion: from survival to hegemony

The years between 2008 and 2014 demonstrate a critical transformation from push to pull and from Europeanization to a more controversial phase of domestic change in Turkey. Yet, in contrast to the general trend, the reforms in minority rights continued in these years without any break in the process through the strong pull without push.

While the EU accession process granted legitimacy to the AKP's rule and policies in the first half of the 2000s, the loss of momentum in the EU accession

Table 6.5 2008 and 2014: pull without push

Pull and Push / Time Period	Pull	Push	Pull and Push
2008–2014	High	Low	High degree of pull without push Pull > Push
Expected Outcome			**Selective policy change**
Actual Outcome			**Selective policy change**

Source: Author's own elaboration

process, especially to a higher extent by 2008, mostly contributed to the pressure on the AKP to keep its reformist agenda and the increasing reliance on the pull. As also seen, the domestic arena was transformed from a polarized political arena to a highly polarized political and societal arena in 2008–2014. In such a conflictual era, though with changing actors in the clashes, the AKP pursued, to an increasing trend, an electoral strategy for its survival, relying on the popular support in the elections that legitimizes its rule and policies. However, this electoral strategy turned into one with hegemonic tendencies. Besides, while the motivation of the AKP was primarily its survival in the first years of the period, it turned into the consolidation of its rule after eliminating the prominent opposition in the political area.

In short, the 2008–2014 period witnessed a series of both EU-related and domestic crises leading to a series of legitimacy crises for the AKP in terms of justifying its rule and reforms. Due to the weakened EU push that provided legitimacy to the reform process previously and the accelerating opposition from various sides, the period reveals the dominance of pull in the AKP's strategic calculations, demonstrated through the increasing focus on attracting and keeping the support of the pro-minority and minority electorates. This, in turn, resulted in selective policy change regarding the AKP's failure-oriented and pragmatic approach that relied on providing solutions to minority problems with the aim of further attracting and keeping public support for its reformist rule. As a result, the period of 2008–2014 represents a high degree of pull without push, and the expected outcome by the pull-and-push model corresponds with the actual policy change: selective policy change (see Table 6.5).

Notes

1 Article 301 has been used to restrict freedom of speech on the basis of insulting Turkishness, the Republic and the organs and institutions of state. For instance, to charge Nobel laureate Orhan Pamuk and Hrant Dink (Avcı 2011a: 418; European Commission 2007: 14–15).
2 *Gezi* Park protests will be further detailed later.

7 Alternative explanations

While the pull-and-push model accounts for the variation in minority-related change in Turkey, the question of whether other approaches can explain the puzzle remains. This section explores the explanatory power of different perspectives existed in the external Europeanization literature regarding the minority puzzle of Turkey.

The section starts with examining one of the most influential frameworks in the literature: the social learning model. Next, it focuses on the 'domestic' and explores the role of veto players incurring domestic adoption costs and the impact of pull via societal mobilization (i.e. civil society, business interest groups, media and political parties) on Turkey's minority policy.

Social learning model

As explained in the theoretical part, the social learning model is based on three factors: resonance with the EU norms, values and rules; legitimacy of the EU rules; and the identity. To what extent these factors play a role in the variation of change in Turkish minority rights is, though, questionable as the following analysis demonstrates.

First of all, when the reforms kicked off in the country in the first half of the 2000s, the EU and Turkey had significant difference in their minority approach. As explored in the previous sections, the concept of minority in Turkey is derived from the Lausanne Treaty, which is still in force and cited by many as the official policy regarding minority rights (Nas 1998). Yet, the limited interpretation of the Treaty with restricted policies in the past reveals Turkey's historically negative approach to minorities and minority rights (Çapar 2006; Oran 2004).

The Kemalist narrow definition of national identity on the grounds of homogeneity and indivisibility of the state and nation, both excluding minorities and denying their rights, was mostly the primary reason behind Turkey's restrictive minority approach (Engert 2010: 110; Toktaş 2006: 489–90). Strengthened by Sevrés syndrome, minorities were historically considered as threats to the "indivisible unity of the state and of the nation" (Oran 2009). Promoting minority rights, in turn, was considered as a threat to the national unity that might lead to social fragmentation on the basis of demands for autonomy and secession by minorities, especially referring to the Kurdish problem (Engert 2010: 111).

Although the AKP brought relative openness to the Turkish political arena regarding minority rights, the government promoted a careful approach relying on official state policy rather than de jure recognition of minorities other than interpreted by the previous authorities (Engert 2010: 118). Therefore, the AKP has not radically changed the rhetoric of official minority policy; rather, it adopts a pro-minority rhetoric relying on non-discrimination and cultural rights. For instance, Erdoğan clarified the AKP's position in regard to preserving official state policy on minorities: "Minorities in our country are evident and they are defined by the Lausanne Treaty. There are no other minorities than these in our country" (AKP Political Group 2007b). Therefore, as Aras and Toktaş (2010: 716) emphasize:

> [T]he Turkish state does not seem willing to extend minority rights beyond the Lausanne regime and has made it clear that it will handle this issue through improvements in three realms: elimination of discrimination, cultural rights, and religious freedom.

The aforementioned practice in minority rights suggests a low degree of resonance of the EU's norms, values and rules regarding minority rights in the enlargement process demanding an open and advanced framework providing rights and protection for minorities (Duyulmuş 2008: 12–13; Engert 2010: 110). Besides, the norms and values on minority rights remain vague in the Union, and therefore, their impact is expected to be limited. At the end, the lack of resonance between Turkish previous experiences, norms and values and the EU's in minority rights demonstrates limited explanatory power of the resonance-factor for the variation in Turkey's minority policy.

Legitimacy of the EU's minority rules, second, provides another perspective to explain the Turkish minority puzzle, although it again remains limited. As mentioned before, the EU has not adequately institutionalized a minority regime, not one like its human rights regime. Besides, the legitimacy of EU rules for minority protection in the enlargement process remains weak due to a number of reasons. To begin with, the EU, as explored previously, does not have a clear minority standard at the internal *acquis*, which is applicable to all member and candidate states (Schwellnus *et al*. 2009; Toggenburg 2000). Thereby, the lack of standards limits the clarity of EU demands for minority reforms in spite of the priorities stressed in EU's specific reports on the concerned candidate state (Schwellnus 2005: 51). Besides, some of these priorities cause tension as they form double standards for member and candidate states in such a sensitive area.

Since minority rights still constitute a problematic area within the member states, the EU does not urge its members to adhere the same legal norms as it urges candidate states, and problematic actions of some EU member states, such as the French dismantling of Roma camps and deportation of Roma, further harm EU's legitimacy regarding minority rules for candidate states (BBC News Europe 2010; Rechel 2008: 181).

Most importantly, the exclusive focus by the EU on only some minorities weakens the legitimacy of the EU on the grounds of whether its minority rules are legitimate in providing rights for some minorities, but not for others. For instance, all progress and regular reports by the European Commission for Turkey address issues related to Armenians, Greeks, Jews, Kurds, Alevis and Roma (Yilmaz 2011). Non-Muslim minorities are mentioned in almost all progress and regular reports, while the Kurdish problem in three-quarters of the progress and regular reports, and Alevis and Roma in half of the progress and regular reports (Yilmaz 2011). However, the Commission rarely mentions other minorities, such as Arabs or Bosnians in its reports. This, in turn, leads to questions about the EU's approach on minority rights in the enlargement process, in that there is no fair and equal rapprochement for all minorities.

In short, aforementioned problematic aspects indicate that the legitimacy of EU's minority rules remains weak for all candidate states. Turkey is not an exception in this sense, thus, the legitimacy condition of the social learning model does not account for variation in minority-related change of Turkey (see also Duyulmuş 2008).

Third, the identity factor within the social learning model begs for an answer to the question of to what extent Turkish government and society feel European and identify itself with the EU. In 2002–2014, the identification of Turkish government itself with the EU was constant, due to continuing single-party government of the AKP in the whole time period. However, to what extent the AKP government identified itself with the EU was not clear because of the mixed conceptualization of its identity.

The identity of the AKP and its leader, Erdoğan, has been a concern for many since the 2002 electoral victory of the party (Bilge Criss 2010: 46). In the first half of 2000s, Erdoğan defined his worldview by referencing religious points, his economic view by referring to liberal ideas and his political view by calling himself a conservative democrat (Akdoğan 2006: 49–52; Bilge Criss 2010: 46).

Despite its pro-Islamic roots, the AKP adopted a pro-reformist and pro-EU stance in the first half of 2000s and enthusiastically supported Turkey's EU membership and reforms required for accession (Dağı 2006: 92; Duyulmuş 2008: 20). Referring to the Islamic roots of the AKP, Dağı (2006: 92) emphasizes with the establishment of the AKP it has become clear that:

> Integration into the West and maintaining Islamic identity are no longer seen as mutually exclusives choices; one can remain attached to an Islamic identity yet advocate integration with the West as in the case of Turkey's EU membership bid.

Yet, the conservative element of AKP's ideology combining cultural conservatism with political reformism does not let the party identify itself with the EU entirely (Taşkın 2008: 61). Moreover, the decreased credibility of EU conditionality by 2004 affected the pro-EU course of the AKP negatively, and rather a drift has emerged in the recent years between the EU and the AKP. In this regard, the identification of the government with the EU and its norms and values was quite limited in the years under investigation.

Considering the identification of Turkish society with the EU, it is necessary to refer to the Kemalist modernization and Westernization project. The primary aim of the Kemalist elite in its early nation-building process was to reach the 'contemporary level of civilization' referring to the Western modernity as the way to build modern Turkey (Keyman and Öniş 2007: 295). Thus, European standards constituted the main reference point driving Turkey's modernization regarding political, economic, social and cultural life (Rumelili 2011: 244). However, the Kemalist project also constructed Europe as the 'other' in framing Turkish national identity (Büyükbay and Merdzanovic 2012: 10; Lazarou 2007: 15).

Built on hyper-nationalism and hyper-secularism, the Kemalist approach has still shaped more or less the Turkish attitude to Europe as both a reference point for imitation of modernism and a threat to the national values by being Turkey's 'other' (Büyükbay and Merdzanovic 2012: 10; Keyman and Öniş 2007: 60; Lazarou 2007: 15).

The conflictual construction of Turkish national identity was in line with the rise of nationalist and Euro-skeptic views among Turkish society after the decrease in credibility of EU conditionality in the post-2004 period, thus, limiting the entire identification of Turkey with the EU. As a result, the identity hypothesis of the social learning model remains limited in explaining the variation in Turkey's minority policy due to the low levels of Turkish identification with the EU.

To conclude, both the identification of the Turkish government and society remained limited in the period under consideration. Together with resonance and legitimacy hypotheses, the identity hypothesis also signifies limited capability of the social learning model to explain the variation in Turkish minority-related change.

Veto points incurred domestic adoption costs: no, not halted the minority reforms!

In 1999–2002, two parties of the coalition government, the DSP and the MHP, acted as veto points with their cautious approach to the accession process and the reforms it entailed, especially the reforms in sensitive areas like minority rights (Keyman and Öniş 2007: 41, 65). The primary reason behind their approach was the inclination to resist the reforms that are hyper-costly to adopt (e.g. civil–military relations, human and minority rights). However, regarding minority rights, the arrest of Öcalan and the ceasefire with the PKK that came along with it reduced the adoption costs to a greater extent (Bahcheli and Noel 2011: 108).

With a highly credible EU push of the era put significant pressure on the coalition government, though, only a minor development was observed in minority rights. Besides, the coalition government could not have resisted the strength of EU push and the pressure of euphoria in the society, and it collapsed in 2002 (Narbone and Tocci 2007: 238–9). Highly credible EU conditionality stronger than domestic adoption costs led to reforms, yet, not exactly to minority protection measures.

At the end, the transition period of 1999–2002 demonstrates a problematic phase, in which the empowerment of the pro-EU actors and the disempowerment of the Euro-skeptic actors emerged. While pro-EU actors triumphed considering credible EU conditionality, the Euro-skeptic coalition government failed. Even though this time period is not included to the analysis due to its nature for preparation to the reforms, if it would be included, it would represent the failure of the external incentives model due to highly credible conditionality with low degrees of domestic adoption costs veto points incurred with the end result of inertia in minority-related change.

When the AKP came to power in 2002, the picture of the previous period changed regarding both the government and the opposition. The AKP promoted itself as a pro-reformist and pro-EU actor in the domestic arena and primarily Kemalists and nationalists were the resistant veto points against the AKP government and its reforms, especially against minority reforms.

To begin with, by 2002 Kemalist elites concentrated on key state institutions (the CHP in the Parliament, the president, the military and the judicial elites) acted as the main veto players (Çınar 2011: 13). Kemalism as the state ideology of Turkey was significantly challenged by the whole reform process and especially by minority reforms. Kemalist ideology, as mentioned, has two important characteristics: secularism, which adheres to strict separation of religion and state, and reinforcement of a single Turkish identity causing problems of allegiance with other ethnicities (Posch 2007: 10). As Ulusoy (2007: 477) notes, the reforms challenge "the whole political project upon which the Republic was established in 1923".

Kemalist elites acting as veto players were incurred with high degree of adoption costs, particularly regarding minority rights. First of all, the reforms broke many taboos (e.g. acknowledging the existence of Muslim minorities – mainly Kurds) regarding one of the core principles of Kemalism, the single and uniformed Turkish identity. Moreover, the PKK was considered the main reference point in dealing with minorities by the veto players, who argued that minority reforms endangered the indivisible unity of the state and the nation (Oran 2009). Second, the secular character of Turkey constituted an even more problematic area for veto players regarding the Islamist roots of the ruling party, the AKP. Through time, the reaction of veto players increased against AKP's policies on the basis that the Islamic roots of the party created a danger against the secular state.

Since the AKP formed the majority in the Parliament, in the time period under consideration, the impact of the CHP, MHP and DTP (later BDP) as the main opposition parties remained limited (Kumbaracıbaşı 2009: 76). Therefore, veto players with actual influence were the President, the military and the Constitutional Court, representing the judicial veto players: the President with veto powers; the military as the 'guardian' of Kemalist ideals with popular support from the wider public to that end; and the Constitutional Court with the power of jurisdiction as final decisions over constitutionality of laws, governmental decrees and rules for parliamentary procedures (Çınar 2011: 13; Kumbaracıbaşı 2009: 76).

All had immense powers to veto the whole reform process including minority measures (Kumbaracıbaşı 2009: 62–70). It is important to note that the power and influence of these actors vary across time, as the significant influence by the military as a veto point was effective in 2005–2010, the role of the Constitutional Court as a veto player was by 2007.

In 2002–2004, domestic actors reached a consensus to launch reforms comprising minority-protection measures within the EU accession process (Aydın and Çarkoğlu 2006: 73). Besides, the arrest of Abdullah Öcalan, the leader of the PKK, in 1999 and the ceasefire with the PKK significantly decreasing adoption costs eased the pressure on the government to launch minority reforms with the decreasing public anger and the change in attitude in which minority issues are perceived as concessions to the PKK (Bahcheli and Noel 2011: 108; Öniş 2003: 14). As a result, domestic adoption costs triggering the reaction of veto players regarding minority rights were at a low degree, while the credibility of EU conditionality was firmly high, as explored previously (Aydın-Düzgit and Keyman 2007: 75; Saatçioğlu 2010: 10). This, in turn, demonstrates the explanatory power of the external incentives model regarding change in minority rights for the period of 2002–2004.

Starting by late 2004, as explained in detail before, a number of events stirred nationalist sentiments in Turkey leading to reactionary nationalism caused by EU demands concerning sensitive issues such as the Cyprus problem, cultural rights to the minorities (especially Kurds are the subject of the reaction), and the Armenian issue (Patton 2007: 345). With the EU's privileged partnership debate, reactions from domestic actors against any European demand boomed dramatically.

The case of the Minority Report released in 2004 by Working Group on Minority Rights and Cultural Rights, a committee working under the Office of Prime Minister, illustrates the rise of reactionary nationalism, which acted as a catalyst to the launch of a debate on national identity and the widespread reaction against it (Grigoriadis 2009: 143; Oran 2007: 6). The report stressed contradictions in Turkish national identity, combining territorial and ethnic nationalist definitions, and advocated a civic national identity and replacement of ethno-territorial definition of *Türk* ('Turkish') with *Türkiyeli* ('a person from Turkey') (Oran 2007: 74–5). The report put also heavy stress on the definition of the 'minority' concept and treatment of minorities by emphasizing the limited interpretation and implementation of the Lausanne Treaty (Oran 2007: 68–9).

The release of the report, touching highly sensitive issue of national identity, sparked a widespread reaction from Kemalist and nationalist fronts (e.g. members of Parliament, military, some NGOs) (Grigoriadis 2009: 146). The reaction against the report relying on the argument of a monolithic national identity put immense pressure on the AKP government, although it also represented a milestone in the debate of Turkish national identity (Grigoriadis 2009: 148). As Aydın-Düzgit and Keyman (2007: 82) point out:

> This picture shows that the shift from the traditional interpretation of the Turkish nation to a redefined notion of political community, which requires

114 *Alternative explanations*

a more inclusive concept of citizenship and the recognition of cultural and ethnic pluralism in the country, is proving to be a painful process in Turkey.

Moreover, the end of the ceasefire with the PKK in 2004 and the PKK's renewed violence later, which fuelled nationalist sentiments further in the country, had particular importance for increasing domestic adoption costs regarding minority reforms (Aydın and Çarkoğlu 2006: 61–4; Bahcheli and Noel 2011: 108).

The period after 2005 also witnessed a series of political crises between the AKP government and veto players, primarily Kemalist opposition led by the CHP, the military, the president, Ahmet Necdet Sezer, and the Constitutional Court, as was explored in the previous sections. This group became active in vetoing the reforms through the direct veto of the president or the indirect submission of cases to the Constitutional Court.

Although appeased for some time after the 2007 elections, the contention between the Kemalists and the AKP intensified, later, on issues like the presidential elections, e-memorandum, headscarf issue, nationwide protests for defending secularism and closure case against the AKP, as detailed previously. In addition to the Kemalist opposition to minority reforms, domestic adoption costs further increased due to the struggle with the PKK mostly continued in the whole period by 2005 to 2014, despite the back-and-forth ceasefire launched from time to time.

The 2007 elections also brought two further actors to the political scene: the MHP and the DTP. While the MHP acted as a solid veto player against any reforms regarding minorities, the DTP and its successors with a pro-Kurdish approach had always a supportive manner of minority reforms. At the end, both Kemalists and nationalists were incurred high adoption costs for minority reforms and acted as veto players regarding the issue.

In sum, the impact of veto players and adoption costs on minority-related policy change is self-evident, though it varies through time. Although veto players incurred a low degree of adoption costs and strong credibility of EU conditionality accounts for the minority-related change in 2002–2004, the increasing adoption costs veto players incurred with the weakened credibility of EU conditionality did not hamper minority-related change in 2005–2014, as expected by the external incentives model and, accordingly, did not account for the differentiated change in minority rights through time.

Pull via societal mobilization

The original version of the push-and-pull model for EU member states focuses on societal mobilization from the different actors like the NGOs and media triggering dissatisfaction of policymakers with the status quo, as stressed previously. Yet, this study argues that the societal impact would be weak in the transition countries to effectively put pressure on the government alone as the case of Turkey demonstrates.

Besides, societal dissatisfaction still needs to be clearly demonstrated through the threat by the electorate at the elections to trigger dissatisfaction and action of policymakers. Although the support of reforms from the societal arena strongly influences the Europeanization process in favour of pro-reform government, in cases like the weakened EU push, all-alone societal mobilization is unlikely to drive reforms in highly sensitive areas, which are also prone to create controversy among societal actors.

The following explores the indirect pull through societal mobilization to explain minority-related change in Turkey in 1999–2014. The focus is on the prominent societal actors: civil society, business interest groups exemplified with the most powerful ones in the domestic arena (i.e. TÜSİAD and MÜSİAD), the media and political parties in Turkey.

Civil society in Turkey: still in transition

Civil society in Turkey was historically weak due to the state-centric ideology granting the state a sovereign role in societal affairs and prioritizing collective interest over the individual (Grigoriadis 2009: 44; Keyman and Öniş 2007: 275). During the 1990s, the number and activities of civil society organizations and citizen participation significantly grew due to various dynamics, such as the increasing impact of globalization (Grigoriadis 2009: 46–51).

With the 1999 Helsinki decision, the EU accession process further contributed to the Turkish civil society in a number of ways. First, the EU provided credibility and legitimacy to the demands of civil society concerning democratization (Tocci 2005: 81). A credible EU accession perspective allowed pro-reformist domestic actors – including civil society – actively support and also justify reforms. Second, the EU accession process empowered civil society actors and enabled them to flourish via facilitating Turkey's reform process concerning the freedom of associations (Tocci 2005: 81). However, the decreasing credibility of EU conditionality by late 2004 weakened both the empowerment of civil society organizations and their reform demands. Third, EU's financial support on the development of Turkish civil society organizations is critical. The Union provides significant amounts of funding to Turkish civil society via different programs (e.g. Civil Society Development Program) (Kubicek 2011: 916). Therefore, the EU accession process has a more concrete bolstering impact on the development of Turkish civil society.

Another development that contributed positively to Turkish civil society was the AKP government's more receptive approach in its relations with civil society in the first half of the 2000s (Göksel and Güneş 2005: 63). With the AKP's more positive approach, Turkish civil society was incorporated in the formulation of laws and policies, and accepted by the government as a legitimate social actor, providing consultancy to the process of policy-making (Göksel and Güneş 2005: 63; Grigoriadis 2009: 63). Yet, the AKP's positive approach faded in time and besides the party did not consistently consult civil society organizations in each and every issue, as was the case in designing a strategic action plan in 2010 for the fight against corruption (Yilmaz and Soyaltin 2014: 18).

Although the aforementioned dynamics still enabled civil society organizations to shift from being loose and informal groups to more structured and organized ones, the impact of civil society on policy-making has remained limited in the concerned time period (see Bertelsmann Stiftung 2006, 2008, 2010, 2012, 2014; CIVICUS 2005, 2010). Additionally, low levels of citizen participation and weak organizational structures in civil society organizations remain among the most important challenges for development of Turkish civil society (CIVICUS 2010: 14; İçduygu 2011: 390).

Besides, civil society in Turkey is highly heterogeneous and fragmented, which, in turn, restricts its autonomous power to drive domestic change (Diez *et al.* 2005: 10; Şimşek 2004: 62). Notably, political positions of civil society organizations determine the support of these organizations on particular issues. For instance, it is difficult to imagine a pro-Kemalist civil society organization vigorously supporting all democratization reforms, some which touch upon Kemalist principles (e.g. national unity, secularism) (Diez *et al.* 2005: 10). Political fragmentation becomes even more interesting in human rights being as universally accepted norms and values (Şimşek 2004: 62). There are a number of human rights associations in Turkey with different political stances, such as the Solidarity Association of the Families of the Prisoners and the Sentenced (*Tutuklu ve Hükümlü Aileleri Dayanışma Derneği* – TAYAD) adopting a radical position on the left and the Association for Human Rights and Solidarity with the Oppressed (*İnsan Hakları ve Mazlumlar İçin Dayanışma Derneği* – Mazlum-Der) adopting a pro-Islamic political view (Şimşek 2004: 62). However, on certain issues with common goals civil society organizations may act together, such as in gender issues. For instance, the Women's Platform on the Turkish Penal Code is an example of a joint initiative by various civil society actors aiming at a comprehensive change in the Turkish Penal Code from a gender perspective (Özdemir 2014: 128).

Despite significantly growing in recent years, Turkish civil society remains weak, politically oriented and fragmented. Although the accession process empowered civil society organizations via legal, financial and technical support, Turkish civil society has not been able to exert considerable pressure on policy-making (Börzel and Soyaltin 2012: 15; Diez *et al.* 2005; Grigoriadis 2009; Heper and Yıldırım 2011; İçduygu 2011; Kubicek 2011). Therefore, the impact of organized societal pressure via civil society in Turkey is still in the making and needs time to accomplish its transition.

Business interest groups in Turkey: cases of TÜSIAD and MÜSIAD

The positive and growing role of business interest groups on pushing democratic development in Turkey became remarkable by the 1990s (Grigoriadis 2009: 61). Especially with the acceleration of Turkey's accession process by 1999, business interest groups and organizations related to the private sector, such as the TÜSIAD, Independent Industrialists' and Businessmen' Association (*Müstakil Sanayici ve İşadamları Derneği* – MÜSIAD) and the IKV, have extensively and exclusively become dominant in supporting domestic reforms (Diez *et al.* 2005: 9; Yankaya 2009: 3–4). TÜSIAD and MÜSIAD as the most active, prominent and influential business interest groups illustrate the impact of the big business groups on Turkey's reform process, and their role is explored next.

TÜSIAD: the support to the EU accession process from the liberals

In the 1990s, TÜSIAD emerged as a pro-democratizing force, promptly demonstrating its determination to support the improvement of democracy in Turkey (Öniş and Türem 2001: 98). In this regard, TÜSİAD presented itself as a member of civil society with a special role of supporting the process of Turkey's democratization (Grigoriadis 2009: 62; TÜSIAD 1997). The 1997 TÜSIAD report on democratization, called Perspectives on Democratization in Turkey, was a clear demonstration of TÜSIAD's determination to push democratic rule in Turkey. The report touched on a variety of sensitive and controversial issues, such as the freedom of expression, cultural rights for the Kurds and civil–military relations (Öniş and Türem 2001: 100; TÜSIAD 1997).

With the launch of EU candidate country status for Turkey in 1999, TÜSIAD perceived the EU as an anchor for political reforms in Turkey, providing legitimacy to the reform process (Uğur and Yankaya 2008: 589). Therefore, EU membership and political reforms were put at the top of TÜSIAD's agenda (Visier 2009: 104). Although the credibility of EU conditionality significantly weakened by late 2004, TÜSIAD continued to emphasize the importance of EU accession for Turkey's reform process and the necessity of reviving the process (TÜSIAD 2008).

TÜSIAD started to act as a pressure group for democratic reforms in Turkey, including sensitive issues such as the Kurdish problem, long before the momentum of the 1999 Helsinki decision (Visier 2009: 111). Therefore, its support for Turkey's democratization was intact after the loss of momentum in Turkey's accession process to the EU. The 2007 TÜSIAD report on democratization, published on the 10th anniversary of the 1997 report, was critical in this context. The report demonstrated the continuing commitment of TÜSIAD to democratic reforms in Turkey. From freedom of speech to minority rights, the report diagnosed a number of problems in the country and provided proposals for change (TÜSIAD 2007).

TÜSIAD also called for further democratization in a number of public statements and criticized the Turkish government for the problems of Turkish democracy. For example, the association called the government to lower the 10 per cent election threshold to allow minority parties to enter the Parliament before the 2007 elections and in 2008 for taking action against the increasing human rights violations (Hürriyet 2008; Minority Rights Group International 2007: 25).

Regarding its relations with the government, TÜSIAD had cooperative relationship with the AKP government in 2002–2006, despite its increasing criticism of the government in the post-2006 period, urging the government to maintain the reform and EU accession processes (Yavuz 2010: 83–8). By 2006, the domestic crises between the AKP and Kemalists also affected the position of TÜSIAD (Yavuz 2010: 85). Although some tension within the association emerged due to various members situating themselves on different points of the political spectrum regarding their attitude towards the AKP government, the association continued to

118 *Alternative explanations*

support political reforms promoted by the government, such as the Constitutional reform after the 2007 elections (Yavuz 2010: 87–8).

In conclusion, TÜSIAD has played an active role in putting pressure on Turkish governments to launch domestic reforms and consistently supported the democratic reform process (Öner 2012: 106). However, the association's impact on accelerating reforms by 2002 is still questionable. For instance, the speed of reforms in 2002–2004 cannot be due to the pressure from business interest groups, most notably from TÜSIAD. As Kubicek (2005: 266) argues,

> [T]he speed with which these reforms were initially proposed may give one pause, given the fact that many of these measures (especially on rights for the Kurdish language) were deemed impolitic or impossible literally months before they were put on the table.

Moreover, in the last decade, TÜSIAD has extensively relied on the EU accession process for domestic reforms and for the revival of the process (Uğur and Yankaya 2008: 589; Visier 2009: 104). Portraying the accession process as an anchor providing legitimacy to sensitive reforms, TÜSIAD lost a strong ally with the weakened EU push for reforms by late 2004. At a time of decreased credibility of EU conditionality and Turkish public support for EU membership, heavy emphasis on EU membership did not have the necessary solid ground to have an impact on domestic change. Nevertheless, the association, as the most influential among business interest groups, played an active role supporting political reforms and successfully put pressure on Turkish government for Europeanization, including Europeanization of minority rights.

MÜSIAD: the support to the EU accession process from the conservatives

MÜSIAD was established in 1990 as an association with pro-Islamist orientation for small and medium-sized firms in widespread Anatolian towns (Öniş and Türem 2001: 100). While the association had strong attachment to Islamic and communitarian values, it was also supporting the integration of its members with the global markets (Keyman and Gümüşcü 2014: 32).

MÜSIAD aimed a redefinition of business and state relations to access state resources in favour of its members with a "qualified commitment to the optimal state" (Öniş and Türem 2001: 107). As Keyman and Gümüşcü (2014: 32) emphasize rightfully, MÜSIAD represented a

> new class of entrepreneurs with distinct social and political preferences and its relative autonomy from the state presented a serious challenge to the state-centric modernization and its allies among the secular upper and middle class . . . a strong alternative to Turkish assertive secular modernity.

While adopting more of an anti-European stance in the first half of the 1990s (e.g. direct opposition to the CU with the EU), the association adopted a pro-EU approach later on (Öniş and Türem 2001: 101). Interestingly, MÜSIAD strongly supported democratic reforms in the second half of the 1990s and 2000s, with special emphases on social rights and freedom of religion (Eligür 2010: 205; Öniş and Türem 2001: 107).

The association adopted a solid pro-EU stance from the launch of candidate country status for Turkey in 1999 until the beginning of accession negotiation with the EU in 2005, though still stressing the risky issues like the Cyprus issue for the Turkish national interest within the accession process (Yankaya 2009: 10). After 2005, the association approached to the accession process with an increasing critical stance towards the EU, due to the hesitation within the EU for Turkish possible membership (Yankaya 2009: 11). In spite of such Euro-skeptic stance by 2005, MÜSIAD, nevertheless, declared its support for democratic reforms, including the sensitive areas like minority rights, as the AKP, within the framework of the 'Ankara criteria' for the sake of the Turkish people (MÜSIAD 2007: 91; Yankaya 2009: 10, 13).

Relations between the AKP and MÜSIAD dated back to the chair-elections in the Virtue Party as the successor of the banned Welfare Party, when the association supported Abdullah Gül as the representative of the reformist branch within the pro-Islamist movement (Özsel *et al.* 2013: 556). When the Virtue Party was also banned, the reformists established the AKP with a strong support by the MÜSIAD, in which many members joined the AKP, and they were even elected as MPs of the AKP (Özsel *et al.* 2013: 556). Therefore, a strong bond between the AKP government and MÜSIAD existed by the establishment of the party and the two had a good working relations in all governing eras of the AKP government. At the end, while challenging the strong state, as Gümüşçü and Sert (2009: 966) stress, the AKP's "liberal economic orientation and its ideology on democracy, human rights and freedoms have provided MÜSIAD members . . . the political base that they were looking for".

Despite MÜSİAD's strong support to the democratic reforms, it is important to note that the association approached to the issue of minority rights selectively in line with their political preferences and prioritized religious freedom and rights, such as the headscarf ban in the universities and public offices (MÜSIAD 2005: 98; Yankaya 2009: 13). At the end, despite its support of the EU accession process and reforms in 2002–2004, the weakened credibility of EU conditionality negatively affected MÜSIAD's enthusiastic support by 2005, and the association pursued a very much parallel approach with the AKP government emphasizing the importance of reforms with or without the EU membership. Most importantly, due to both the speed of reforms in 2002–2004, like in the case of TÜSIAD, and selective approach of MÜSIAD regarding minority rights, the association's impact on minority reforms remains highly questionable.

Media and politics in Turkey: far from being a watchdog, civic forum and mobilizing agent!

The role of media on Europeanization is vital considering its influence on societal mobilization by being a civic forum in which pluralistic debates are fostered; a watchdog guarding the public interest; a mobilizing agent, which encourages public learning (Çarkoğlu and Yavuz 2010: 613). Yet, the impact of media as a civic forum, watchdog and mobilizing agent on Europeanization and minority reforms remains limited in Turkey.

By the 1980s, the media landscape had radically changed through the shift in media ownership – a shift from family-owned media outlets to media holdings (Christensen 2007: 186). The 1990s brought an acceleration of this process and by 1995 five business groups (*Doğan, Bilgin, Aksoy, İhlas* and *Uzan* Groups) already dominated the Turkish media landscape (Sümer 2011: 56). In the meantime, the shift from the traditional ownership to a new conglomerate ownership brought a competitive corporate mentality to the media (Christensen 2007: 187).

The 1999 banking crisis and 2000 and 2001 economic crises led to an extended restructuring of media ownership, though this time a compulsory one. Operating in many areas including the banking sector, some holdings lost their banking licenses, and their debts led to the confiscation of their media assets (e.g. *Aksoy* Group, *Uzan* Group) (Sümer 2011: 57). Those media assets were transferred to the Savings Deposit Insurance Funds (*Tasarruf Mevduatı Sigorta Fornu* – TMSF) and later sold through tenders (Sözeri 2015: 11).

By 2004, media ownership was quite different than before and it was to be further restructured in the following years. In those years and after, Turkish media was dominated by four major players (*Doğan* Group, *Merkez* Group, *Çukurova* Group and Star [*Uzan*] Group) and four smaller ones (*İhlas* Group, *Doğuş* Group, *Samanyolu* Group and *Aksoy* Group) (Gül 2011: 35). Notably, these media outlets were divided along diverse political orientations, and their business interests in other areas, such as in construction, compelled them to have good relations with the government (Elmas and Kurban 2011: 24; Somer 2010: 557).

By mid-2007 new business groups, known as pro-government circles, began to enter the media landscape. *Merkez* Group's media assets were confiscated and later sold to the *Çalık* Group (*Turkuvaz* Media Group), which is known to have closer ties with the government (Sümer 2011: 57). In turn, this media group was sold to pro-government *Zirve* Holding in 2014 (Sözeri 2015: 12).

In 2013, Ethem Sancak, a businessman who openly supports the government and Prime Minister Erdoğan, bought *Çukurova's* media properties after another confiscation due to the debt of *Çukurova* Group to the state (Corke *et al.* 2014: 13). Ultimately, a pro-government media has become increasingly vocal across time. Notably, this becomes obvious when multiple newspapers run the same headline in cases of pro-government political stakes. For instance, when Prime Minister Erdoğan and Deputy Prime Minister Bülent Arınç disagreed on using the police to investigate co-ed student houses, six newspapers ran the headline "We will solve it amongst ourselves" (Corke *et al.* 2014: 13).

The developments outside the reconfiguration of the media towards a more pro-government orientation also contributed to the change of balance in the media landscape. Most importantly, fines against media outlets that are critical of the government have become more common in recent years. The case of *Doğan* Media Group's dispute with the government in 2008 illustrates this.

Alternative explanations 121

An open conflict between *Doğan* Group and Prime Minister Erdoğan emerged when the AKP-led municipality refused to grant a property demanded by *Doğan* holdings (Kaya and Çakmur 2010: 532). In response, *Doğan* Media Group began to voice criticisms against the AKP government (Kaya and Çakmur 2010: 532). After Erdoğan publicly instructed the authorities to fine *Doğan* Media Group for alleged tax irregularities, a fine of 3.75 billion Turkish Lira was issued in 2009 (Çarkoğlu and Yavuz 2010: 618). After the fine in 2011, *Doğan* Group sold two newspapers (i.e. *Milliyet* and *Vatan*) to another holding, *Demirören* Group, which has a pro-government orientation (Corke *et al.* 2014: 7).

The outcome was that media holdings with different political orientations either chose to sell some of their media outlets and downsized their operations in the media or adopt a more pro-government approach (Sözeri 2015: 15). While *Doğan* Group, mostly associated with secularists, was among the first group downsize media outlets, *Doğuş* Group adopted a pro-government orientation (Sözeri 2015: 15).

Moreover, the holdings that own media outlets benefit from government contracts (e.g. *Doğuş* Holding's gain of a $702 million bid for the operation of Istanbul's Galataport in Karaköy in 2013) and such contracts have led to an increasing atmosphere of censorship and self-censorship in large part of the Turkish media (Çarkoğlu and Yavuz 2010: 618; Corke *et al.* 2014: 12–13). Most recently, in October 2015 government-chosen trustees were appointed to the *Koza İpek* Holding, known to have close ties with the Gülen Movement; and the administration of the media outlets owned by the *İpek* Group, *Kanal Türk* television as well as *Bugün* and *Millet* newspapers, was transferred to a pro-government trustee (Srivastava and Güler 2015). In the end, pro-government media groups have become increasingly dominant in the Turkish media.

Most of all, the independence, impartiality and quality of media in Turkey still remains low (Çarkoğlu and Yavuz 2010: 618; Freedom House 2015b). On one hand, the divisions within the Turkish media along political orientations and, on the other, problems in freedom of expression and freedom of press (e.g. imprisonment of journalists and media workers) raise serious questions regarding the independence and maneuverability of the media (European Commission 2012: 21; Somer 2010: 557). Notably, both government censorship, which was explicitly demonstrated in the 2013 Taksim Gezi Park protests not broadcasted by the mainstream media, and self-censorship become common phenomena in Turkey (European Commission 2012: 21; Martinez 2013). Moreover, many journalists, such as *Hürriyet's* columnist Bekir Coşkun, had to resign due to their critiques against the government (Martinez 2013).

It is important to note that outside the mainstream media formed mainly by big media corporations, there is an alternative media in Turkey composed of various outlets of limited financial means such as *Agos* (a minority newspaper) or *Bianet* (an online news portal established with EU support), and also new social media such as Facebook and Twitter (Elmas and Kurban 2011: 9; Kaya and Çakmur 2010: 533).

To summarize, the media landscape is quite fragmented in Turkey and ownership is fluid, changing hands quickly. With regard to political orientations, the

122 *Alternative explanations*

Turkish media landscape covers a wide and diverse spectrum (e.g. secularists, *Gülenists*, pro-government groups, minority groups). Dominated by the big corporations, which have affiliated business in many different areas such as energy or construction, the Turkish media have become vulnerable to pressures from the authorities and open to instrumentalization by the state (Çarkoğlu and Yavuz 2010: 618; European Commission 2015: 24). Most importantly, the lack of transparency in media ownership has led to suspicions concerning the independence of editorial policies and, therefore, the media as a whole (European Commission 2015: 24). At the end, Turkish media, except the limited alternative media, is far from being a watchdog, civic forum and mobilizing agent and its impact is, therefore, restricted. In that regard, it is questionable to assert that Turkish media as a whole puts immense pressure for Turkey's Europeanization.

Political parties and their influence for the pull

Turkish political parties have not presented a monolithic support for Turkey's Europeanization and minority reforms. While the AKP and the pro-Kurdish parties (i.e. DEHAP, DTP and currently BDP as successors of each other across time) have been on the reformist side on the spectrum until the recent years, the CHP and the MHP have positioned themselves as Euro-skeptics in many areas of Europeanization (e.g. Kurdish issue). However, since the AKP formed a majority in Parliament in the last decade, the negative impact of the CHP and MHP on the reform process has remained limited.[1]

The CHP adopted a Euro-skeptic approach, increasingly by 2004, regarding the Europeanization process and more explicitly the minority measures. Although the party declares its support to the EU accession process perceiving it as the extension of Atatürk's modernization project, it has kept its reservations on conditions related to monolithic national identity and secularism (Başkan-Canyaş and Gümrükçü 2015: 156). In spite of the change in leadership, the CHP preserved the red lines of its previous leader, Deniz Baykal, in many issues, though, with a relatively positive approach on the EU and Turkey's accession (Gülmez 2013).

The MHP as an ultra-nationalist party has always been critical of the Europeanization process and mostly the minority reforms. Although the MHP has not opposed the EU membership possibility in principle, it has opposed the conditions the accession process entails (e.g. Kurdish problem) and the sacrifices regarding these conditions (Avcı 2011b: 442; Başkan-Canyaş and Gümrükçü 2015: 152). At the end, the MHP opposed to the Europeanization process on the grounds of political reforms clarified by the EU's roadmap for accession, which was described by the party as being a minefield including unfair and unacceptable conditions regarding minority rights, the Armenian question and Turkey–Armenia relations (MHP ARGE 2009).

On the other spectrum, the pro-Kurdish parties have traditionally adopted a pro-EU stance. They have been supportive of Turkey's membership to the EU since the reforms in the accession process would strengthen democratic rights for Kurds and contribute to the solution of the Kurdish problem (Başkan-Canyaş and

Gümrükçü 2015: 149; Oğuzlu 2012: 223). The BDP as the current pro-Kurdish party, for instance, emphasizes in its party program that the party is supportive of Turkey's accession process with special references to the democratization (BDP Party Program 2009).

The AKP has also established itself as a pro-reformist and pro-EU party. Since its establishment, the AKP has consistently declared that it is not an Islamist party despite its key cadre's affiliation with previous Islamist movements (Doğan 2005: 429). Rather, the AKP defines itself as 'Conservative Democrat' – a combination of cultural conservatism and political reformism with neoliberal economic views, and a pro-globalization and pro-EU manner (Taşkın 2008: 61). Although the reformist approach of the AKP has had its ups and downs across time, the AKP as the government party constituting the majority in Parliament launched a number of democratic reforms regarding minority protection by 2002.

A number of scholars (e.g. Doğan 2005: 430; Narbone and Tocci 2007: 239; Patton 2007: 343; Tocci 2005: 80) explore the AKP's commitment to the EU accession process and political reforms through employing interest- and ideology-based approaches. Interest-based explanations assert that the AKP's commitment to the EU accession process and political reforms stems from the legitimacy provided by the accession process as a valuable asset to overcome the suspicion in the wider domestic and international arena about the Islamic background of the party and its possible hidden Islamic agenda (Narbone and Tocci 2007: 239; Tocci 2005: 80). Ideology-based approaches suggest that the political values of the AKP are coherent with the values of the EU and the requirements of the accession process (Doğan 2005: 430; Narbone and Tocci 2007: 239).

In essence, the AKP's commitment to the reforms is primarily due to its strategic calculations influenced by a sequential impact of EU conditionality for the pre-2005 period and popular elections for the latter period. While the EU accession process provided a strong sense of legitimacy to the rule of the AKP, this has been replaced by the legitimacy provided by popular support in the elections across time. In this interest-based perspective, considering the ban of its predecessors (i.e. Welfare Party) from political life after the 1997 'soft' military coup, survival and later rule-consolidation considerations of the AKP in a hyper-nationalist and secular state tradition have motivated the party to continue its reformist path (Dağı 2006: 56).

Keeping the reform pace alive, the AKP gained legitimacy through the EU accession process in the eyes of the nationalists and secularists until late 2004, and by 2005 through the elections that confirmed popular support to the party itself and its policies. Attracting protest, reformist and minority votes in the elections in response to the poor performance of previous governments and being aware of its popularity in the elections providing a valuable asset for the party to gain further recognition from the secularists, by 2005 the AKP found itself in a situation, in which its political fate was bound to the continuing democratic reforms and later its rule-consolidation was either (Dağı 2006: 96; Kumbaracıbaşı 2009: 78). Therefore, both EU-related and domestic dynamics have shaped the preferences of the AKP pushing Turkey's Europeanization. In turn, the preferences of the AKP lead to selective Europeanization due to loss of momentum in the EU accession process, and strategic and problem-solving approach of the AKP, focusing on problematic issues that would keep and further attract votes to the party at the elections and leaving behind the EU priorities that are not helpful in providing solutions to domestic problems.

In conclusion, among the most influential political parties in Turkey in the last decade, the CHP, the MHP, the pro-Kurdish parties and the AKP, demonstrated differentiated support for Turkey's Europeanization in general and regarding specifically minority rights. On one side of the spectrum, the CHP, to a lesser extent recently, and the MHP have established themselves as Euro-skeptics in the process. On the other, the pro-Kurdish parties and the AKP positioned themselves as pro-EU actors until the recent years. Most importantly, the AKP acted as a driver of change in Turkey, though adopting a selective approach, due to its strategic considerations.

Conclusions: it is not 'others', but direct pull!

Exploring alternative approaches to explain the variation in minority-related change in Turkey, the previous analyses demonstrate the limited explanatory power of various perspectives that may drive Europeanizing reforms in minority rights. Social learning, veto points and adoption costs, societal or indirect pull – all of these approaches remained limited in explaining the puzzle.

Rather, as a sequential path the EU push working via conditionality of credible rewards and sanctions and the direct pull operating through threat of sanctions account for the variation of minority reforms across time. Most importantly, their interplay at the decision-making level is the key that drives or hinders change in such a sensitive area for reforms.

Note

1 Because explored before, this part explores the impact of the political parties on minority reforms briefly.

Conclusions and prospects

External Europeanization has attracted wide attention by scholars and practitioners in recent decades. This book contributed to the external Europeanization literature by specifically focusing on the conditions that influence minority-related policy change in Turkey. This concluding chapter summarizes the endeavor by discussing the research findings, implications and limitations of the present research, and avenues for further research in regard to external Europeanization and the case of Turkey.

Summarizing the research findings

> It is for sure that the EU has an impact on the process (minority rights). However, reforms were not launched because the EU wanted. Rather the people of Turkey want this (reforms). Yet, the EU accelerated the process.
> AKP Member of Parliament Orhan Yıldız 2007[1]

This book started with an empirical puzzle of differentiated minority-related change in 1999–2014. Considering this puzzle, the book provided an account of how external Europeanization can be explained from an interactive theoretical perspective through specifically focusing on Turkey's differentiated policy change in minority rights. The above-mentioned quote from Yıldız summarizes the main argument of the book: policy change is a combination and interaction of EU-related and domestic factors. It is argued in the book that effective policy change in a candidate state depends on an interactive process of push by EU conditionality and pull by dissatisfaction of the government. The empirical analysis confirmed this argument by demonstrating an interactive and sequential path of push by EU conditionality and pull by dissatisfaction that influenced minority-related policy change in 1999–2014.

Summarizing the research findings, Chapter 1 established the theoretical and analytical framework of the book, starting with a literature review providing a theoretical background. The review revealed the heavy reliance of research in Europeanization of candidate states on EU conditionality. In this context, the chapter emphasized the danger of neglecting possible explanatory factors in the domestic arena due to prejudging the impact of EU conditionality on domestic

126 *Conclusions and prospects*

change and interventions by elite-level domestic opposition without tracing the internal pressure for change.

In an attempt to prevent over-determination of the EU factor, the book adopted an approach relying on the interplay of domestic and EU-related factors. Although the existing theoretical frameworks of external Europeanization did not fully account for the empirical puzzle, the partial and complementary explanations from the external incentives and lesson-drawing models directed the research to combine these models via adjusting the pull-and-push framework of Börzel (2000) for external Europeanization and the case of Turkey. The pull-and-push model is operationalized in Chapter 1 through exploring the push factor (credibility of EU conditionality) and the pull factor (dissatisfaction of the government with status quo). Last, the theoretical framework proposed interactive combinations of pull and push that influence the strategic calculations of the government to explain the variation in minority-related change in Turkey.

Chapter 2 started with an overview of the EU's minority rights regime, minority-related change and EU's policy in the 2004 enlargement process, Turkey's minorities and minority rights prior to the launch of reforms and EU's demands from Turkey regarding minority rights. First, lack of minority standards within the EU has been complicating the transformation of minority protection in candidate states. Yet, the 2004 enlargement demonstrated the relative success of the EU transforming the CEECs regarding minority protection, although exclusively in legal adoption, not exactly in the implementation. Second, Turkey's cautious approach in minority rights was detailed starting by the Ottoman era and a very limited, and restrictive minority policy in the country prior to the launch of reforms was clearly seen.

Considering the underdevelopment of the EU's minority rights regime, EU's demands from Turkey were explored via analyzing the country-specific measures specified in the EU's regular and progress reports, as well as the Council decisions for Turkey. The analysis revealed that the EU consistently: insisted on the solution of Turkey's basic problems in minority rights, such as eliminating the restrictive definition of minorities; detailed its priorities over time providing a roadmap for minority reforms; and increasingly put emphasis on the problems of implementing minority rights.

Chapter 3 mapped the dependent variable of the research: minority-related change in Turkey. The analysis demonstrated that minority-related policy change, signified by legal adoption and implementation, varied in 2002–2014. According to different degrees and coupling/decoupling of two forms of rule adoption, minority-related policy change was indicated as preparation period in 1999–2002; shallow policy change in 2002–2004; selective policy change, though limited, in 2005–2007; and selective policy change in 2008–2014.

Chapters 4, 5 and 6 mapped pull and push across time to explain the variation of minority-related change and provided an analysis of the interplay between the pull and push in the strategic calculations of the Turkish government in the period under consideration. The chapters revealed a sequential path from the trigger of EU push to the pull of dissatisfaction and an interactive process of the pull and push within the realm of strategic calculations of the government, motivated by, first, the considerations of survival in a hyper-secular Republic and, later, the rule-consolidation considerations. Providing legitimacy to the rule and policies of the AKP, both the credibility of EU conditionality and public support (demonstrated via national and local elections) for the AKP empowered the EU push and pull by dissatisfaction and interacted through time.

Demonstrating the changing balance of the pull and push between 2002 and 2014 in the strategic calculations of the AKP government, the analysis showed the loss of momentum in EU push due to the decline in the EU's credibility to deliver the membership reward and the increasing impact of pull by dissatisfaction imposing threat of sanctions in case of the AKP losing the reformist agenda over time. Interacting at the decision-making process, varying degrees of pull and push led to different policy outcomes in 2002–2014. Most importantly, change in minority rights became selective over time due to the increasing reliance of the AKP on its dissatisfaction, in which the AKP was motivated to address minority-related policy failure to attract, keep and consolidate the support by minority and pro-minority groups and leave out all other EU rules that were not helpful in dealing with minority problems.

Next, the empirical analysis was concluded by alternative explanations to the variation in minority-related change. Exploring the social learning model, veto points and adoption costs and societal pull for change, the section demonstrated the limited capability of all to account for the empirical puzzle.

To conclude, this book showed that different combinations of pull and push led to the variation of minority-related change in Turkey. The analysis revealed that change in minority rights was due to the rationalist calculations of the government, in which pull and push factors interacted and followed a sequential path due to the variation in their degree over time. Yet, the analysis confirmed that effective policy change necessitates a high degree of pull and push together.

Implications and limitations

Investigating how and under which conditions domestic change is promoted and constrained by focusing on the case of minority rights in Turkey, this book enhances the theoretical understanding in external Europeanization and empirical knowledge regarding the case of Turkey and its minority policy. It has also important implications for the external Europeanization literature and specifically Turkish studies.

Starting with theoretical implications, the book has a threefold contribution to the external Europeanization literature. First, it offers new insights into the literature by shifting the focus away from EU conditionality, which has heavily dominated the research. Demonstrating that policy change in one of the most sensitive issue areas is possible even if the EU push is weak, the book moves the literature beyond the EU's impact on domestic change, especially in the transformation process of candidate states.

Revealing the importance of domestic drivers of policy change, in one of the least likely area for reforms, the book also put forward voluntary and domestically

128 Conclusions and prospects

driven change by emphasizing the independent impact of domestic choice within the framework of the lesson-drawing model, which is usually neglected and not entirely developed within the literature. Therefore, the book contributes to the literature through further elaboration of the lesson-drawing model, as a neglected theoretical framework of external Europeanization.

Second, the book draws attention to the implementation process in addition to legal adoption regarding Turkey's minority rights. Considering the heavy emphasis on legal adoption and rather mostly neglected implementation process in the literature, the book includes the implementation process in the research, operationalizes policy change by coupling/decoupling of legal adoption and implementation and provides theoretical explanation for both implementation and legal adoption to have a broad understanding of transformation in candidate states.

Third, and most importantly, the book provides a testable interaction-oriented theoretical framework to external Europeanization, which is hardly explored in the literature. Despite applied in a limited fashion due to focusing on one case and one policy area, the pull-and-push model, adjusted by the book to external Europeanization, provides a comprehensive and interactive framework integrating external and domestic levels, thus giving new interactive insights into the literature rather than treating external and domestic-level mechanisms as alternative explanations.

Regarding the limitations, it is important to recall, first, the close relationship of minority issues with wider issue areas, such as identity, citizenship and national security. Therefore, improvement in this area needs to be evaluated as a strong indicator of the Europeanization process. Second, although it can be argued that Turkey is a *sui generis* case in external Europeanization literature, this book reveals that the theoretical approaches in the research area account for the case of Turkey, though partially, as for the previous candidate states. Despite remaining limited in explanatory power, the external Europeanization theoretical frameworks are not fully ruled out in the case of Turkey. As Börzel and Soyaltin (2012: 13) emphasize, "Approaches to (pre-CEE) Accession Europeanization give rise to a series of hypotheses with regard to the domestic impact on accession countries, which appear to largely hold for Turkey, too".

As a result, still considering room for improvement in the pull-and-push model, the model can be further tested in other issue areas in Turkey and other cases of candidate and neighbourhood states. Yet, it is important to note that the book relies on the direct mechanism of the pull-and-push model. Therefore, this has limited the scope of the book, and there is still room for further improvement in the indirect path of the model, relying on the pull by societal mobilization and the push of EU conditionality on societal actors, such as civil society.

In addition to the theoretical implications, the book has a twofold contribution in the empirical arena. First, it contributes to the empirical knowledge of minority rights in Turkey, which has rarely been explored systematically across time and including practical implementation. In this context, the detailed analysis on the improvement of minority rights across time including both legal adoption and implementation is value added to the literature.

Second, the book includes important insights to EU conditionality in Turkey's accession process, which is usually taken for granted, but has not previously been explored across time, and AKP policy dissatisfaction that has not been investigated at all. Providing a systematic and across-time analysis of EU conditionality in Turkey's accession process and AKP policy dissatisfaction, the book enriches the empirical knowledge on such vital external and domestic factors.

At the end, having theoretical and empirical implications to the literature, the book is a promising starting point for further research in external Europeanization and also the case of Turkey. Therefore, the pull-and-push model needs to be further tested and Turkey's Europeanization researched, as the next sections details.

Further avenues for research

This book provides a vital step for further research to advance the understanding of external Europeanization, in case of Turkey as well as in other cases. First of all, empirical investigation regarding Turkey needs to be extended by testing the theoretical framework developed in this book. Notably, some cases, such as Turkey's asylum policy or civil–military relations, give certain signals of voluntary change, especially in the post-2005 era. For instance, changes in civil–military relations, such as the 2009 amendments to the Turkish Penal Code and other Laws allowing civilian courts to try military personnel for crimes during peace (Haber Türk 2009), suggest voluntary forms of domestic change increasingly by 2008. Thus, future research could explore such case studies via testing the pull-and-push model to explain the puzzling change in these areas referring to weakened EU conditionality by late 2004.

Second, further research is needed to test the interactive pull-and-push model in other cases of candidate states and also the EU's neighbourhood states. The comprehensive model can lead research presenting external- and internal-level factors that influence domestic change in other candidate states, such as Serbia and the former Yugoslav Republic of Macedonia. Therefore, future studies including other cases can provide checks for further improvement in the pull-and-push model.

Moreover, the research needs to be widened to include European neighbourhood states, who are EU's partners within the European Neighbourhood Policy. Especially after the recent Arab Spring, neighborhood countries (such as Tunisia, Egypt and Libya) represent reliable cases for exploring interaction between the impact of the EU and voluntary forms of change. Failed previous regimes and their policies suggest there may be voluntary forms of change in these countries in the coming years in response to previous failure. Therefore, these cases represent viable empirical arenas to test the pull-and-push model.

Third, future studies need to consider indirect paths for domestic change in external Europeanization. Therefore, it is necessary to include pull for change via societal mobilization to the analysis in the cases of accession and neighbourhood states. Exploring different cases than Turkey, indirect mechanism of the pull-and-push model, referring specifically to the indirect impact of EU conditionality and societal pull on domestic change, needs to be closely examined.

130   *Conclusions and prospects*

Last but not least, external Europeanization research needs to move beyond the transformative power of the EU and explore the transformative power of domestic actors and the possible interaction between these two drivers of change in accession and neighbourhood states. Exploring voluntary drivers of change in the case of Turkey in addition to the impact of EU conditionality, this book has provided new insights in respect to domestic drivers of change and the interaction of external and domestic factors. Thus, further research needs to bring the 'domestic' back into the research as a vital factor and focus on the interaction of external and domestic that promotes or constrains domestic change.

Note

1   Orhan Yıldız, personal interview, March 30, 2010, Grand National Assembly of Turkey, Ankara.

Bibliography

AB Haber. 2006. IKV: AB Türkiye Kararı Üzüntü Verici [IKV: The EU Decision on Turkey Is Upsetting], December 15.

Açıkmeşe, Sinem A. and Mustafa Aydın. 2009. "Europeanization through EU Conditionality: Understanding the New Era in Turkish Foreign Policy." In *Turkey's Road to European Union Membership: National Identity and Political Change*, eds. Susannah Verney and Kostas Ifantis. Abingdon, New York: Routledge, 49–60.

Address to the Nation. 2004. Prime Minister's Address to the Nation. May, Ankara. http://www.bbm.gov.tr/ (February 15, 2010).

———. 2006. Prime Minister's Address to the Nation. January, Ankara. http://www.bbm.gov.tr/ (February 15, 2010).

———. 2007a. Prime Minister's Address to the Nation. May, Ankara. http://www.bbm.gov.tr/ (February 17, 2010).

———. 2007b. Prime Minister's Address to the Nation. December, Ankara. http://www.bbm.gov.tr/ (February 17, 2010).

———. 2008a. Prime Minister's Address to the Nation. October, Ankara. http://www.bbm.gov.tr/ (February 20, 2010).

———. 2008b. Prime Minister's Address to the Nation. June, Ankara. http://www.bbm.gov.tr/ (February 20, 2010).

———. 2009. Prime Minister's Address to the Nation. June, Ankara. http://www.bbm.gov.tr/ (February 25, 2010).

———. 2012. Prime Minister's Address to the Nation. May, Ankara. http://www.bbm.gov.tr/ (June 12, 2015).

———. 2013. Prime Minister's Address to the Nation. August, Ankara. http://www.bbm.gov.tr/ (June 12, 2015).

———. 2014. Prime Minister's Address to the Nation. October, Ankara. http://www.bbm.gov.tr/ (June 12, 2015).

ahaber. 2012. Başbakan'dan başkanlık sistemi açıklaması [Statement of the Presidential System by the Prime Minister], May 7.

Akdoğan, Yalçın. 2006. "The Meaning of Conservative Democratic Political Identity." In *The Emergence of a New Turkey Democracy and the AK Parti*, ed. M. Hakan Yavuz. Salt Lake City, UT: The University of Utah Press, 49–65.

AKP Party Program. 2001. http://eng.akparti.org.tr/english/partyprogramme.html (February 12, 2009).

AKP Political Group. 2002a. Chairman of the AKP Political Group Bülent Arınç's Speech to His Political Group. May 16, Ankara. http://www.akparti.org.tr/tbmm/grupkon.asp (March 20, 2010).

——. 2002b. Prime Minister and Chairman of the AKP Recep Tayyip Erdoğan's Speech to His Political Group. May 25, Ankara. http://www.akparti.org.tr/tbmm/grupkon.asp (March 20, 2010).

——. 2002c. Prime Minister and Chairman of the AKP Recep Tayyip Erdoğan's Speech to His Political Group. April 24, Ankara. http://www.akparti.org.tr/tbmm/grupkon.asp (March 20, 2010).

——. 2002d. Prime Minister and Chairman of the AKP Recep Tayyip Erdoğan's Speech to His Political Group. February 13, Ankara. http://www.akparti.org.tr/tbmm/grupkon.asp (March 20, 2010).

——. 2002e. Prime Minister and Chairman of the AKP Recep Tayyip Erdoğan's Speech to His Political Group. June 5, Ankara. http://www.akparti.org.tr/tbmm/grupkon.asp (March 20, 2010).

——. 2003a. Prime Minister and Chairman of the AKP Recep Tayyip Erdoğan's Speech to His Political Group. January 21, Ankara. http://www.akparti.org.tr/tbmm/grupkon.asp (March 21, 2010).

——. 2003b. Prime Minister and Chairman of the AKP Recep Tayyip Erdoğan's Speech to His Political Group. May 6, Ankara. http://www.akparti.org.tr/tbmm/grupkon.asp (March 21, 2010).

——. 2003c. Prime Minister and Chairman of the AKP Recep Tayyip Erdoğan's Speech to His Political Group. March 20, Ankara. http://www.akparti.org.tr/tbmm/grupkon.asp (March 20, 2010).

——. 2003d. Prime Minister and Chairman of the AKP Recep Tayyip Erdoğan's Speech to His Political Group. November 18, Ankara. http://www.akparti.org.tr/tbmm/grupkon.asp (March 21, 2010).

——. 2003e. Prime Minister and Chairman of the AKP Recep Tayyip Erdoğan's Speech to His Political Group. April 29, Ankara. http://www.akparti.org.tr/tbmm/grupkon.asp (March 21, 2010).

——. 2003f. Prime Minister and Chairman of the AKP Recep Tayyip Erdoğan's Speech to His Political Group. December 16, Ankara. http://www.akparti.org.tr/tbmm/grupkon.asp (March 21, 2010).

——. 2004a. Prime Minister and Chairman of the AKP Recep Tayyip Erdoğan's Speech to His Political Group. December 14, Ankara. http://www.akparti.org.tr/tbmm/grupkon.asp (March 21, 2010).

——. 2004b. Prime Minister and Chairman of the AKP Recep Tayyip Erdoğan's Speech to His Political Group. December 14, Ankara. January 13, Ankara. http://www.akparti.org.tr/tbmm/grupkon.asp (March 21, 2010).

——. 2004c. Prime Minister and Chairman of the AKP Recep Tayyip Erdoğan's Speech to His Political Group. January 6, Ankara. http://www.akparti.org.tr/tbmm/grupkon.asp (March 21, 2010).

——. 2004d. Prime Minister and Chairman of the AKP Recep Tayyip Erdoğan's Speech to His Political Group. October 26, Ankara. http://www.akparti.org.tr/tbmm/grupkon.asp (March 21, 2010).

——. 2004e. Prime Minister and Chairman of the AKP Recep Tayyip Erdoğan's Speech to His Political Group. December 14, Ankara. http://www.akparti.org.tr/tbmm/grupkon.asp (March 21, 2010).

——. 2004f. Prime Minister and Chairman of the AKP Recep Tayyip Erdoğan's Speech to His Political Group. May 4, Ankara. http://www.akparti.org.tr/tbmm/grupkon.asp (March 21, 2010).

———. 2005a. Prime Minister and Chairman of the AKP Recep Tayyip Erdoğan's Speech to His Political Group. April 13, Ankara. http://www.akparti.org.tr/tbmm/grupkon.asp (March 22, 2010).

———. 2005b. Deputy Prime Minister and Minister of State Abdüllatif Şener's Speech to His Political Group. December 6, Ankara. http://www.akparti.org.tr/tbmm/grupkon.asp (March 22, 2010).

———. 2005c. Prime Minister and Chairman of the AKP Recep Tayyip Erdoğan's Speech to His Political Group. November 22, Ankara. http://www.akparti.org.tr/tbmm/grupkon.asp (March 22, 2010).

———. 2005d. Prime Minister and Chairman of the AKP Recep Tayyip Erdoğan's Speech to His Political Group. February 23, Ankara. http://www.akparti.org.tr/tbmm/grupkon.asp (March 22, 2010).

———. 2005e. Prime Minister and Chairman of the AKP Recep Tayyip Erdoğan's Speech to His Political Group. April 27, Ankara. http://www.akparti.org.tr/tbmm/grupkon.asp (March 22, 2010).

———. 2005f. Deputy Prime Minister and Minister of State Abdüllatif Şener's Speech to His Political Group. June 7, Ankara. http://www.akparti.org.tr/tbmm/grupkon.asp (March 22, 2010).

———. 2005g. Prime Minister and Chairman of the AKP Recep Tayyip Erdoğan's Speech to His Political Group. June 22, Ankara. http://www.akparti.org.tr/tbmm/grupkon.asp (March 22, 2010).

———. 2006a. Prime Minister and Chairman of the AKP Recep Tayyip Erdoğan's Speech to His Political Group. April 25, Ankara. http://www.akparti.org.tr/tbmm/grupkon.asp (March 22, 2010).

———. 2006b. Prime Minister and Chairman of the AKP Recep Tayyip Erdoğan's Speech to His Political Group. March 21, Ankara. http://www.akparti.org.tr/tbmm/grupkon.asp (March 22, 2010).

———. 2006c. Prime Minister and Chairman of the AKP Recep Tayyip Erdoğan's Speech to His Political Group. September 26, Ankara. http://www.akparti.org.tr/tbmm/grupkon.asp (March 22, 2010).

———. 2006d. Prime Minister and Chairman of the AKP Recep Tayyip Erdoğan's Speech to His Political Group. April 4, Ankara. http://www.akparti.org.tr/tbmm/grupkon.asp (March 22, 2010).

———. 2006e. Prime Minister and Chairman of the AKP Recep Tayyip Erdoğan's Speech to His Political Group. March 14, Ankara. http://www.akparti.org.tr/tbmm/grupkon.asp (March 22, 2010).

———. 2007a. Prime Minister and Chairman of the AKP Recep Tayyip Erdoğan's Speech to His Political Group, October 2, Ankara. http://www.akparti.org.tr/tbmm/grupkon.asp (March 23, 2010).

———. 2007b. Prime Minister and Chairman of the AKP Recep Tayyip Erdoğan's Speech to His Political Group. November 13, Ankara. http://www.akparti.org.tr/tbmm/grupkon.asp (March 23, 2010).

———. 2007c. Prime Minister and Chairman of the AKP Recep Tayyip Erdoğan's Speech to His Political Group. October 16, Ankara. http://www.akparti.org.tr/tbmm/grupkon.asp (March 23, 2010).

———. 2007d. Prime Minister and Chairman of the AKP Recep Tayyip Erdoğan's Speech to His Political Group. October 16, Ankara. http://www.akparti.org.tr/tbmm/grupkon.asp (March 23, 2010).

———. 2008a. Prime Minister and Chairman of the AKP Recep Tayyip Erdoğan's Speech to His Political Group. February 12, Ankara. http://www.akparti.org.tr/tbmm/grupkon.asp (March 23, 2010).

———. 2008b. Prime Minister and Chairman of the AKP Recep Tayyip Erdoğan's Speech to His Political Group. May 6, Ankara. http://www.akparti.org.tr/tbmm/grupkon.asp (March 23, 2010).

———. 2008c. Prime Minister and Chairman of the AKP Recep Tayyip Erdoğan's Speech to His Political Group. November 11, Ankara. http://www.akparti.org.tr/tbmm/grupkon.asp (March 23, 2010).

———. 2008d. Prime Minister and Chairman of the AKP Recep Tayyip Erdoğan's Speech to His Political Group. April 22, Ankara. http://www.akparti.org.tr/tbmm/grupkon.asp (March 23, 2010).

———. 2008e. Prime Minister and Chairman of the AKP Recep Tayyip Erdoğan's Speech to His Political Group. February 26, Ankara. http://www.akparti.org.tr/tbmm/grupkon.asp (March 23, 2010).

———. 2009a. Prime Minister and Chairman of the AKP Recep Tayyip Erdoğan's Speech to His Political Group. June 16, Ankara. http://www.akparti.org.tr/tbmm/grupkon.asp (March 23, 2010).

———. 2009b. Prime Minister and Chairman of the AKP Recep Tayyip Erdoğan's Speech to His Political Group. February 10, Ankara. http://www.akparti.org.tr/tbmm/grupkon.asp (March 23, 2010).

———. 2009c. Prime Minister and Chairman of the AKP Recep Tayyip Erdoğan's Speech to His Political Group. June 9, Ankara. http://www.akparti.org.tr/tbmm/grupkon.asp (March 23, 2010).

———. 2009d. Prime Minister and Chairman of the AKP Recep Tayyip Erdoğan's Speech to His Political Group. November 3, Ankara. http://www.akparti.org.tr/tbmm/grupkon.asp (March 23, 2010).

———. 2009e. Prime Minister and Chairman of the AKP Recep Tayyip Erdoğan's Speech to His Political Group. January 6, Ankara. http://www.akparti.org.tr/tbmm/grupkon.asp (March 23, 2010).

———. 2009f. Prime Minister and Chairman of the AKP Recep Tayyip Erdoğan's Speech to His Political Group. June 16, Ankara. http://www.akparti.org.tr/tbmm/grupkon.asp (March 23, 2010).

———. 2010a. Prime Minister and Chairman of the AKP Recep Tayyip Erdoğan's Speech to His Political Group. January 12, Ankara. http://www.akparti.org.tr/tbmm/grupkon.asp (March 24, 2010).

———. 2010b. Prime Minister and Chairman of the AKP Recep Tayyip Erdoğan's Speech to His Political Group. June 29, Ankara. http://www.akparti.org.tr/tbmm/grupkon.asp (March 24, 2010).

———. 2010c. Prime Minister and Chairman of the AKP Recep Tayyip Erdoğan's Speech to His Political Group. January 26, Ankara. http://www.akparti.org.tr/tbmm/grupkon.asp (March 24, 2010).

———. 2010d. Prime Minister and Chairman of the AKP Recep Tayyip Erdoğan's Speech to His Political Group. February 2, Ankara. http://www.akparti.org.tr/tbmm/grupkon.asp (March 24, 2010).

———. 2010e. Prime Minister and Chairman of the AKP Recep Tayyip Erdoğan's Speech to His Political Group. March 2, Ankara. http://www.akparti.org.tr/tbmm/grupkon.asp (March 24, 2010).

———. 2010f. Prime Minister and Chairman of the AKP Recep Tayyip Erdoğan's Speech to His Political Group. March 23, Ankara. http://www.akparti.org.tr/tbmm/grupkon.asp (March 24, 2010).
Akşam. 2013. THY'den AGOS Sürprizi [AGOS Surprise by THY], February 16.
Alessandri, Emiliano. 2010. "Democratization and Europeanization in Turkey after the September 12 Referandum." *Insight Turkey* 12(4): 23–30.
Aljazeera. 2012. Turkey Drops Anti-Abortion Legislation, June 22.
Alpan, Başak and Thomas Diez. 2014. "The Devil Is in the 'Domestic'? European Integration Studies and the Limits of Europeanization in Turkey." *Journal of Balkan and Near Eastern Studies* 16(1): 1–10.
Amnesty International. 2013. Gezi Park Protests Brutal Denial of the Right to Peaceful Assembly in Turkey. EUR 44/022/2013, October.
Aras, Bülent and Şule Toktaş. 2010. "The EU and Minority Rights in Turkey." *Political Science Quarterly* 124(4): 697–720.
Avcı, Gamze. 2003. "Turkey's Slow EU Candidacy: Insurmountable Hurdles to Membership or Simple Euro-Skepticism?" In *Turkey and the European Union Domestic Politics, Economic Integration and International Dynamics*, eds. Ali Carkoglu and Barry Rubin. London and Portland, OR: Frank Cass, 149–170.
———. 2006. "Turkey's EU Politics: Consolidating Democracy through Enlargement?" In *Questioning EU Enlargement: Europe in Search of Identity*, ed. Helene Sjursen. New York: Routledge, 62–77.
———. 2011a. "The Justice and Development Party and the EU: Political Pragmatism in a Changing Environment." *South European Society and Politics* 16(3): 409–421.
———. 2011b. "The Nationalist Movement Party's Euroscepticism: Party Ideology Meets Strategy." *South European Society and Politics* 16(3): 435–447.
Ayata, Bilgin and Deniz Yükseker. 2005. "A Belated Awakening: National and International Responses to the Internal Displacement of Kurds in Turkey." *New Perspectives on Turkey* 32: 5–42.
Aybet, Gülnur. 2006. "Turkey and the EU after the First Year of Negotiations: Reconciling Internal and External Policy Challenges." *Security Dialogue* 37(4): 529–549.
Aydın-Düzgit, Senem. 2006. *Seeking Kant in the EU's Relations with Turkey*. Istanbul: Turkish Economic and Social Studies Foundation (TESEV) Publications.
Aydın-Düzgit, Senem and Ali Çarkoğlu. 2006. "EU Conditionality and Democratic Rule of Law in Turkey." Prepared for the workshop organized by Sabancı University, Stanford University and Centre of European Excellence – University of Florence on "Europeanisation and Democratisation: The Southern European Experience and the Perspective for New Member States of the Enlarged Europe", December 10–11, Istanbul.
Aydın-Düzgit, Senem and Fuat E. Keyman. 2004. "European Integration and the Transformation of Turkish Democracy." *Centre for European Policy Studies EU-Turkey Working Papers* 2.
Aydın-Düzgit, Senem and Fuat E. Keyman. 2007. "Europeanization, Democratization and Human Rights in Turkey." In *Turkey and the European Union Prospects for a Difficult Encounter*, eds. Esra LaGro and Knud Erik Jorgensen. London: Palgrave Macmillan, 69–89.
Aydınlı, Pınar. 2012. "Turkey's Erdogan has Eye on New, Strong President's Role." *Reuters*, November 6.
Bacık, Gökhan. 2011. "The Nationalist Action Party in the 2011 Elections: The Limits of Oscillating between State and Society." *Insight Turkey* 13(4): 171–187.

136 Bibliography

Bahcheli, Tozun and Sid Noel. 2011. "The Justice and Development Party and the Kurdish Question." In *Nationalisms and Politics in Turkey Political Islam, Kemalism and the Kurdish Issue*, eds. Marlies Casier and Joost Jongerden. London and New York: Routledge, 101–120.

Bakeer, Ali Hussein. 2014. "New Turkey 2014 Presidential Elections and Future Implications." *Aljazeera Reports*, August 27.

Bardakçı, Mehmet. 2010. "Turkish Parties' Positions towards the EU: Between Europhilia and Europhobia." *Romanian Journal of European Studies* 10(4): 26–41.

Barrett, Susan M. 2004. "Implementation Studies: Time for a Revival? Personal Reflections on 20 Years of Implementation Studies." *Public Administration* 82(2): 249–262.

Başkan-Canyaş, Filiz and Selin Bengi Gümrükçü. 2015. "Europeanization and Political Parties." In *Europeanization of Turkey: Polity and Politics*, eds. Aylin Güney and Ali Tekin. Abingdon, Oxon: Routledge, 145–162.

Başlevent, Cem, Hasan Kirmanoğlu, and Burhan Şenatalar. 2004. "Voter Profiles and Fragmentation in the Turkish Party System." *Party Politics* 10(3): 307–324.

Bayır, Derya. 2013. *Minorities and Nationalism in Turkish Law*. Abingdon, Oxon: Routledge.

BBC. 2011. Bölge ve İllere Göre Seçim Sonuçları, June 13.

BBC News Europe. 2010. France Sends Roma Gypsies back to Romania, August 20.

BBC Türkçe. 2009. DTP Kapatıldı [The DTP is Closed down], December 11.

BDP Party Program. 2009. http://www.bdp.org.tr (February 10, 2010).

Bertelsmann Stiftung. 2006. Bertelsmann Transformation Index Turkey Country Report. http://www.bti-project.org (May 13, 2011).

———. 2008. Bertelsmann Transformation Index Turkey Country Report. http://www.bti-project.org (May 13, 2011).

———. 2010. Bertelsmann Transformation Index Turkey Country Report. http://www.bti-project.org (May 13, 2011).

———. 2012. Bertelsmann Transformation Index Turkey Country Report. http://www.bti-project.org (August 18, 2015).

———. 2014. Bertelsmann Transformation Index Turkey Country Report. http://www.bti-project.org (August 18, 2015).

Bora, Tanıl. 2011. "Nationalist Discourses in Turkey." In *Symbiotic Antagonisms Competing Nationalisms in Turkey*, eds. Ayşe Kadıoğlu and E. Fuat Keyman. Salt Lake City, UT: The University of Utah Press, 57–81.

Börzel, Tanja A. 2000. "Why There Is No 'Southern Problem' On Environmental Leaders and Laggards in the European Union." *Journal of European Public Policy* 7(1): 141–162.

Börzel, Tanja A. and Thomas Risse. 2000. "When Europe Hits Home: Europeanization and Domestic Change." *European Integration Online Papers* 4(15), 1–20.

———. 2003. "Conceptualizing the Domestic Impact of Europe." In *The Politics of Europeanization*, eds. Kevin Featherstone and Claudio M. Radaelli. Oxford, New York: Oxford University Press, 57–80.

———. 2009. "The Transformative Power of Europe: The European Union and the Diffusion of Ideas." *KFG Working Paper Series* 1, Freie Universität Berlin.

Börzel, Tanja A. and D. Soyaltın (2012). "Europeanization in Turkey Stretching a Concept to Its Limits." *KFG Working Paper Series* 36, Freie Universität Berlin.

Brosig, Malte. 2010. "The Challenge of Implementing Minority Rights in Central Eastern Europe." *Journal of European Integration* 32(4): 393–411.

Burulday, Remzi. 2010. "PKK'lılar Geri Dönüyor [The PKK Nembers are Returning]." *Ihlas Haber Ajansı (IHA)*, July 19.
Büyükbay, Can and Adis Merdzanovic. 2012. "Euroscepticism in Turkey and Bosnia-Herzegovina." Presented at the 62nd Political Studies Association International Conference, April 3–5, Belfast.
Cagaptay, Soner. 2006. *Islam, Secularism, and Nationalism in Modern Turkey Who Is a Turk?* Abingdon, Oxon: Routledge.
Çapar, Mustafa. 2006. "Tek Parti Donemi: Milli Egitim, Milli Dil ve Türkleştirme Politikaları." In *Tesev Uluslararası Konferans Tebliğleri: Türkiye'de Azınlık Hakları Sorunu: Vatandaşlık ve Demokrasi Eksenli Bir Yaklaşım*. Istanbul: TESEV Publications, 83–93.
Capotorti, Francesco. 1979. Study on the Rights of Persons Belonging to Ethnic, Religious and Linguistic Minorities. United Nations, E/CN4/Sub2/384/Rev1.
Çarkoğlu, Ali. 2004. "Turkish Local Elections of March 28, 2004: A Prospective Evaluation." *TÜSIAD-US*, April 9, Washington.
———. 2007. "A New Electoral Victory for the 'Pro-Islamists' or the 'New Centre-Right'? The Justice and Development Party Phenomenon in the July 2007 Parliamentary Elections in Turkey." *South European Society and Politics* 12(4): 501–519.
———. 2008. *Ideology or Economic Pragmatism: Determinants of Party Choice in Turkey for the July 2007 Elections*. Studies in Public Policy 439, Centre for Public Policy, Aberdeen: University of Aberdeen.
———. 2009. "Turkey's Local Elections of 2009: Winners and Losers." *Insight Turkey* 11(2): 1–18.
Çarkoğlu, Ali and Ersin Kalaycıoğlu. 2007. *Turkish Democracy Today Elections, Protest and Stability in an Islamic Society*. London: I.B.Tauris.
Çarkoğlu, Ali and Gözde Yavuz. 2010. "Press-Party Parallelism in Turkey: An Individual Level Interpretation." *Turkish Studies* 11(4): 613–624.
Celep, Ödül. 2011. "The Republican People's Party and Turkey's EU Membership." *South European Society and Politics* 16(3): 423–434.
Cengiz, F. and L. Hoffmann. 2013. "Rethinking Conditionality: Turkey's European Union Accession and the Kurdish Question." *JCMS: Journal of Common Market Studies* 51(3): 416–432.
Christensen, C. 2007. Breaking the news concentration of ownership, the fall of unions and government legislation in Turkey, *Global Media and Communication, 3*(2), 179–199.
Çınar, Menderes. 2011. "Turkey's Present Ancien Régime and the Justice and Development Party." In *Nationalisms and Politics in Turkey Political Islam, Kemalism and the Kurdish Issue*, eds. Marlies Casier and Joost Jongerden. London and New York: Routledge, 14–27.
CIVICUS. 2005. Civil Society in Turkey: An Era of Transition. CIVICUS Civil Society Index Country Report for Turkey.
———. 2010. Civil Society in Turkey: At a Turning Point. CIVICUS Civil Society Index Project Analytical Country Report for Turkey II.
Cizre, Ümit. 2011. "Disentangling the Threats of Civil-Military Relations in Turkey: Promises and Perils." *Mediterranean Quarterly* 22(2): 57–75.
CNN Türk. 2010. Anayasa Degişikliği Teklifi Kabul Edildi [The Proposal for the Amendment of the Constitution was Accepted], May 7.
Consolidated versions of the Treaty on European Union. 2010. *Official Journal of the European Union* 53.

Bibliography

Corke, Susan, Andrew Finkel, David J. Kramer, Carla Anne Robins, and Nate Schenkkan. 2014. *Democracy in Crises: Corruption, Media, and Power in Turkey*. Freedom House Special Report, Freedom House.

Criss, Nur Bilge. 2010. "Dismantling Turkey: The Will of the People?" *Turkish Studies* 11(1): 45–58.

Dağı, Ihsan, D. 2006. "The Justice and Development Party: Identity, Politics, and Human Rights Discourse in the Search for Security and Legitimacy." In *The Emergence of a New Turkey Democracy and the AK Parti*, ed. M. Hakan Yavuz. Salt Lake City, UT: The University of Utah Press, 88–106.

Dalay, Galip. 2014. "Turkey's Local Elections Context Meaning and Future Scenerios." *Aljazeera Center for Studies*, April 16.

Diez, Thomas, Apostolos Agnantopoulos, and Alper Kaliber. 2005. "File: Turkey, Europeanization and Civil Society: Introduction." *South European Society and Politics* 10(1): 1–15.

Doğan, Erhan. 2005. "The Historical and Discursive Roots of the Justice and Development Party's EU Stance." *Turkish Studies* 6(3): 421–437.

Dressler, Markus. 2015. "Historical Trajectories and Ambivalences in Turkish Minority Discourse." *New Diversities* 17(1): 9–26.

Duyulmuş, Cem U. 2008. "Europeanization of Minority Rights in Turkey 1999–2007." Presented at the 7th Biennial Conference of the European Community Studies Association-Canada (ECSA-C), September 25–27, Edmonton, Alberta.

Eldem, Tuba. 2013. "The End of Turkey's Europeanization?" *Turkish Policy Quarterly* 12(1): 125–135.

Eligür, Banu. 2009. "Turkey's March 2009 Local Elections." *Turkish Studies* 10(3): 469–496.

———. 2010. *The Mobilization of Political Islam in Turkey*. Cambridge: Cambridge University Press.

Elmas, Esra and Dilek Kurban. 2011. *Communicating Democracy- Democratizing Communication Media in Turkey: Legislation, Policies, Actors*. Istanbul: TESEV Publications.

Engert, Stefan. 2010. *EU Enlargement and Socialization Turkey and Cyprus*. London and New York: Routledge.

Engert, Stefan, Heiko Knobel, and Frank Schimmelfennig. 2003. "Costs, Commitment and Compliance: The Impact of EU Democratic Conditionality on Latvia, Slovakia and Turkey." *Journal of Common Market Studies* 41(3): 495–518.

Esmer, Yilmaz R. and Sabri Sayarı. 2002. *Politics, Parties, and Elections in Turkey*. Boulder, CO: Lynne Riener Publications.

Eurobarometer. 2002. Candidate Countries Eurobarometer- CCEB. http://ec.europa.eu/public_opinion/archives (September 12, 2011).

———. 2003. Candidate Countries Eurobarometer- CCEB. Autumn 2003.2. http://ec.europa.eu/public_opinion/archives (September 12, 2011).

———. 2004. Standard Eurobarometer 62 National Report Turkey. Autumn 2004. http://ec.europa.eu/public_opinion/archives (September 12, 2011).

———. 2005. Standard Eurobarometer 64 National Report Turkey. Autumn 2005. http://ec.europa.eu/public_opinion/archives (September 12, 2011).

———. 2006. Standard Eurobarometer 66 National Report Turkey. Autumn 2006. http://ec.europa.eu/public_opinion/archives (September 12, 2011).

———. 2007. Standard Eurobarometer 68 National Report Turkey. Autumn 2007. http://ec.europa.eu/public_opinion/archives (September 12, 2011).

———. 2008. Standard Eurobarometer 70 National Report Turkey. Autumn 2008. http://ec.europa.eu/public_opinion/archives (September 12, 2011).

Bibliography 139

———. 2009. Standard Eurobarometer 72 National Report Turkey. Autumn 2009. http://ec.europa.eu/public_opinion/archives (September 12, 2011).

———. 2010. Standard Eurobarometer 74 National Report Turkey. Autumn 2010. http://ec.europa.eu/public_opinion/archives (September 12, 2011).

———. 2011. Standard Eurobarometer National Report Turkey. Autumn 2011. http://ec.europa.eu/public_opinion/archives (June 16, 2015).

———. 2012. Standard Eurobarometer National Report Turkey. Autumn 2012. http://ec.europa.eu/public_opinion/archives (June 16, 2015).

———. 2013. Standard Eurobarometer 74 National Report Turkey. Autumn 2013. http://ec.europa.eu/public_opinion/archives (June 16, 2015).

———. 2014. Standard Eurobarometer 74 National Report Turkey. Autumn 2014. http://ec.europa.eu/public_opinion/archives (June 16, 2015).

European Commission. 1999. Turkey 1999 Regular Report, October 13, Brussels.

———. 2000. Turkey 2000 Regular Report, November 8, Brussels.

———. 2001. Turkey 2001 Regular Report, SEC (2001) 1756, Brussels.

———. 2002. Turkey 2002 Regular Report, SEC (2002) 1412, Brussels.

———. 2003. Turkey 2003 Regular Report, SEC (2003) 1426, Brussels.

———. 2004. Turkey 2004 Regular Report, SEC (2004) 1201, Brussels.

———. 2005a. Turkey 2005 Progress Report, SEC (2005) 1426, Brussels.

———. 2005b. Communication from the Commission: 2005 Enlargement Strategy Paper, COM (2005) 561 final, November 9, Brussels.

———. 2005c. Negotiating Framework, October 3, Luxembourg.

———. 2006. Turkey 2006 Progress Report, SEC (2006) 1390, Brussels.

———. 2007. Turkey 2007 Progress Report, SEC (2007) 1436, Brussels.

———. 2008. Turkey 2008 Progress Report, SEC (2008) 2699, Brussels.

———. 2009. Turkey 2009 Progress Report, SEC (2009) 1334, Brussels.

———. 2010. Turkey 2010 Progress Report, SEC (2010) 1327, Brussels.

———. 2011. Turkey 2011 Progress Report, SEC (2011) 1201 final, Brussels.

———. 2012. Turkey 2012 Progress Report, SWD (2012) 336 final, Brussels.

———. 2013. Turkey 2013 Progress Report, SWD (2013) 417 final, Brussels.

———. 2014. Turkey 2014 Progress Report, SWD (2014) 307 final, Brussels.

———. 2015. Turkey 2015 Progress Report, SWD (2015) 216 final, Brussels.

European Commission against Racism and Intolerance. 2005. Third Report on Turkey, Council of Europe, CRI (2005)5, February 15.

European Council. 1993. Copenhagen European Council, Presidency Conclusions, June 21/22.

———. 1999. Helsinki European Council, Presidency Conclusions, December 10/11.

———. 2001. "Council Decision of 8 March 2001 on the Principles, Priorities, Intermediate Objectives and Conditions Contained in the Accession Partnership with the Republic of Turkey." *Official Journal of the European Communities L 85* March 24.

———. 2008. "Council Decision of 18 February 2008 on the Principles, Priorities, Intermediate Objectives and Conditions Contained in the Accession Partnership with Turkey and Repealing Decision 2006/35/EC." *Official Journal of the European Communities L 51* February 26.

European Parliament. 2013. European Parliament Resolution on the Situation in Turkey, B7–0305/2013, June 11.

European Roma Rights Center (ERRC). 2013. Turkey Country Profile 2011–2012. http://www.errc.org/cikk.php?cikk=4160 (August 22, 2015).

Eylemer, Sedef and Ilkay Taş. 2007. "Pro-EU and Eurosceptic Circles in Turkey." *Journal of Communist Studies and Transition Politics* 23(4): 561–577.

Falkner, Gerda, Miriam Hartlapp, and Oliver Treib. 2007. "Worlds of Compliance: Why Leading Approaches to European Union Implementation are Only Sometimes-true Theories." *European Journal of Political Research* 46(3): 395–416.

Falkner, Gerda and Oliver Treib. 2008. "Three Worlds of Compliance or Four? The EU-15 Compared to New Member States." *Journal of Common Market Studies* 46(2): 293–313.

Freedom House. 2005. Countries at the Crossroads. Country Report – Turkey. http://www.freedomhouse.org (December 10, 2010).

———. 2007. Countries at the Crossroads. Country Report – Turkey. http://www.freedomhouse.org (December 10, 2010).

———. 2008. Turkey in Transit Democratization in Turkey. http://www.freedomhouse.org (December 10, 2010).

———. 2009. Freedom in the World – Turkey. http://www.freedomhouse.org (December 10, 2010).

———. 2010. Freedom in the World – Turkey. http://www.freedomhouse.org (May 10, 2013).

———. 2013. Freedom in the World – Turkey. http://www.freedomhouse.org (June 20, 2016).

———. 2014. Freedom in the World – Turkey. http://www.freedomhouse.org (June 20, 2016).

———. 2015a. Freedom in the World – Turkey. http://www.freedomhouse.org (June 20, 2016).

———. 2015b. Freedom of Press – Turkey. http://www.freedomhouse.org (June 20, 2016).

Galbreath, J. David and Joanne McEvoy. 2013. "How Epistemic Communities Drive International Regimes: The Case of Minority Rights in Europe." *Journal of European Integration* 35(2): 169–186.

Gençkaya, Ömer F. and Ergun Özbudun. 2009. *Democratization and the Politics of Constitution-Making in Turkey*. Budapest and New York: Central European University Press.

Gezen, Burak and Vural Bozok. 2015. "Gökçeada Özel Rum Ortaokul İlk Kez, Lisesi ise 40 Yıl Sonra Tekrar Açıldı." *Hürriyet*, September 28.

Gilbert, Geoff. 1996. "The Council of Europe and Minority Rights." *Human Rights Quarterly* 18(1): 160–189.

Gökçe, Mehmet and Elif N. Özbudak. 2010. "Min Dît" Director Miraz Bezar Wants to Restrain Violence with His Film." *Todays Zaman*, April 11.

Göksel, Diba N. 2009. "Turkey and Europe: The Importance of Predictability." In *Turkey's Accession to the European Union: An Unusual Candidacy*, ed. Constantine Arvanitopoulos. Berlin and Heidelberg: Springer-Verlag, 31–44.

Göksel, Diba N. and Rana B. Güneş. 2005. "The Role of NGOs in the European Integration Process: The Turkish Experience." *South European Society and Politics* 10(1): 57–72.

Grigoriadis, Ioannis. N. 2006. "Upsurge amidst Political Uncertainty: Nationalism in Post-2004 Turkey." *SWP Research Paper*, October 11.

———. 2008. "On the Europeanization of Minority Rights Protection: Comparing the Cases of Greece and Turkey." *Mediterranean Politics* 13(1): 23–41.

———. 2009. *Trials of Europeanization Turkish Political Culture and the European Union*. New York: Palgrave Macmillan.

Gül, Ayşen Akkor. 2011. "Monopolisation of Media Ownership as a Challenge to the Turkish Television Broadcasting System and the European Union." *Ankara Avrupa Çalışmaları Dergisi* [Ankara European] 10(2): 27–46.

Gülmez, Seckin Barış. 2013. "Rising Euroscepticism in Turkish Politics: The Cases of the AKP and the CHP." *Acta Politica* 48: 326–344.

Gümüşcü, Şebnem and Deniz Sert. 2009. "The Power of the Devout Bourgeoisie: The Case of Justice and Development Party in Turkey." *Middle Eastern Studies* 45(6): 953–968.

Gürsoy, Yaprak. 2011. "The Impact of EU-Driven Reforms on the Political Autonomy of the Turkish Military." *South European Society and Politics* 16(2): 293–308.

Haber3. 2008. CHP'li Öymen'den 301 Çıkışı [The Reaction about the Article 301 from the CHP Member of Parliament Öymen], April 9.

———. 2012. Sezeryan Yasası Kabul Edildi! [The Cesarean Law is Adopted], June 4.

Haber Türk. 2009. Asker-Sivil Ilişkilerinde Tarihi Yasa [Historical Legislation in Civil-Military Relations], June 27.

———. 2014. Seçim 2012. http://www.haberturk.com/secim/secim2014/yerel-secim/ (September 23, 2015).

Hale, William. 2003. "Human Rights, the European Union and the Turkish Accession Process." In *Turkey and the European Union Domestic Politics, Economic Integration and International Dynamics*, eds. Ali Carkoglu and Barry Rubin. London and Portland, OR: Frank Cass, 107–126.

Hammarberg, Thomas. 2009. Review Report on Human Rights of Minorities, Council of Europe, CommDH (2009)30.

Heper, Metin. 2005. "The European Union, the Turkish Military and Democracy." *South European Society and Politics* 10(1): 33–44.

———. 2011. "Civil-Military Relations in Turkey: Toward a Liberal Model?" *Turkish Studies* 12(2): 241–252.

Heper, Metin and Senem Yıldırım. 2011. "Revisiting Civil Society in Turkey." *Southeast European and Black Sea Studies* 11(1): 1–18.

Hughes, James and Gwendolyn Sasse. 2003. "Monitoring the Monitors: EU Enlargement Conditionality and Minority Protection in the CEECs." *Journal on Ethnopolitics and Minority Issues in Europe* 1: 1–36.

Human Rights Watch. 2004. A Crossroads for Human Rights? December 15. http://www.hrw.org (June 14, 2010).

———. 2007. Turkey: Human Rights Concerns in the Lead up to July Parliamentary Elections. July 19. http://www.hrw.org (June 14, 2010).

Hürriyet. 2002. AKP'de Ikinci Adam Fırat [The Second Man in the AKP is Fırat], December 12.

———. 2008. TÜSIAD: Türkiye'de Insan Hakları Ihlallerindeki Artış Endişe Verici [TÜSIAD: The Increase in Violations of Human Rights in Turkey is Worrying], December 16.

———. 2009. Kürt Açılımını Başlattık [We Launched Kurdish Opening], July 23.

———. 2010. İşte Hükümetin Kürt Açılımı Paketi [Here is the Government's Package for the Kurdish Opening], January 15.

———. 2011. 2011 Yılı Genel Seçim Sonuçları. http://www.hurriyet.com.tr/secim2011/ (June 16, 2014).

İçduygu, Ahmet. 2011. "Interacting Actors: The EU and Civil Society in Turkey." *South European Society and Politics* 16(3): 381–394.

Ifantis, Kostas. 2007. "Turkey in Transition – Opportunities amidst Peril?" *Journal of Balkan and Near Eastern Studies* 9(3): 223–231.

Bibliography

Internal Displacement Monitoring Centre. 2013. "Turkey: Internal Displacement in Brief." Summary, December. http://www.internal-displacement.org/europe-the-caucasus-and-central-asia/turkey/summary (June 16, 2015).

International Crisis Group. 2007. "Turkey and Europe: The Way Ahead." *Europe Report* 184, August 17.

Johns, Michael. 2003. "Do as I Say, Not as I Do: The European Union, Eastern Europe and Minority Rights." *East European Politics and Societies* 17(4): 682–699.

Johnson, Carter. 2006. "The Use and Abuse of Minority Rights: Assessing Pastt and Future EU Policies towards Accession Countries of Central, Eastern and South-Eastern Europe." *International Journal on Minority and Group Rights* 13: 27–51.

Kadıoğlu, Ayşe. 2011. "The Twin Motives of Turkish Nationalism." In *Symbiotic Antagonisms Competing Nationalisms in Turkey*, eds. Ayşe Kadıoğlu and E. Fuat Keyman. Salt Lake City, UT: The University of Utah Press, 33–55.

Karaosmanoğlu, Kerem. 2010. "Reimagining Minorities in Turkey: Before and After the AKP." *Insight Turkey* 12(2): 193–212.

Kaya, Ayhan. 2013. *Europeanization and Tolerance in Turkey: The Myth of Toleration.* Basingstoke: Palgrave Macmillan.

Kaya, Esra. 2012. "MEB'den Azınlıklara Okul Hakkı [Right of School to the Minorities by the Ministry of Education (Milli Eğitim Bakanlığı – MEB]." *Hürriyet*, March 21.

Kaya, Nurcan. 2009. "Forgotten or Assimilated? Minorities in the Education System of Turkey." *Minority Rights Group International.* http://www.minorityrights.org (July 28, 2010).

Kaya, Raşit and Barış Çakmur. 2010. "Politics and the Mass Media in Turkey." *Turkish Studies* 11(4): 521–537.

Kelley, Judith G. 2004. *Ethnic Politics in Europe: The Power of Norms and Incentives.* Princeton, NJ: Princeton University Press.

Keyman, Fuat E. and Sebnem Gümüşcü. 2014. *Democracy Identity and Foreign Policy in Turkey Hegemony through Transformation.* Basingstoke: Palgrave Macmillan.

Keyman, Fuat E. and Ziya Öniş. 2007. *Turkish Politics in a Changing World: Global Dynamics and Domestic Transformations.* Istanbul: Istanbul Bilgi University Press.

Kılıç, A. Aslan. 2013. "Presidential System Debate Disrupts Constitution-Making." *Today's Zaman*, June 9.

Kirişçi, Kemal. 2007. "The Limits of Conditionality and Europeanization: Turkey's Dilemmas in Adopting the EU *Acquis* on Asylum." Presented at the 10th EUSA Biennial International Conference, May 17–19, Montreal.

Kızılıkaya, Emre. 2014. "EXPLAINED: Turkish Presidential Election Results in a Nutshell." *Hürriyet Daily News*, August 18.

Konuralp, Okan. 2009. "Dağdan 34 Kişi Indi En Az 100 Kişi Daha Bekleniyor [34 Came from the Mountain and At Least 100 More are Expected to Come]." *Hürriyet*, October 20.

Kozan, Ümit. 2013. "İşte Akil İnsanlar Heyeti [Here is the Committee of Wise People]." *Hürriyet*, April 4.Kubicek, Paul. 2005. "The European Union and Democratization 'From Below' in Turkey." Presented at the 9th Bi-Annual EUSA Conference, March 31– April 2, Austin TX.

———. 2011. "Political Conditionality and European Union's Cultivation of Democracy in Turkey." *Democratization* 18(4): 910–931.

Kulahci, Erol. 2005. "EU Political Conditionality and Parties in Government: Human Rights and the Quest for Turkish Transformation." *Journal of Southern Europe and the Balkans* 7(3): 387–402.

Kumbaracıbaşı, Arda C. 2009. *Turkish Politics and the Rise of the AKP.* Abingdon, Oxon: Routledge.

Kurban, Dilek. 2008. "Avrupa Birliği'nin Anayasal Düzeninde Azınlık Hakları: Açılımlar, Fırsatlar ve Olasılıklar." In *Türkiye'de Çogunluk ve Azınlık Politikaları: AB Sürecinde Yurttaşlık Tartışmaları*, eds. Ayhan Kaya and Turgut Tarhanlı. Istanbul: TESEV, 269–286.

Kurdish Human Rights Project. 2004. Turkey's Implementation of Pro-EU Reforms Fact-Finding Mission Report, November 2004. http://www.khrp.org (July 18, 2010).

Kuru, Ahmet. 2012. "The Rise and Fall of Military Tutelage in Turkey: Fears of Islamism, Kurdism, and Communism." *Insight Turkey* 14(2): 37–57.

Kymlicka, Will. 2007. *Multicultural Odysseys: Navigating the New International Politics of Diversity*. Oxford: Oxford University Press.

Larrabee, Stephen F. and Gonul Tol. 2011. "Turkey's Kurdish Challenge." *Survival* 53(4): 143–152.

Lazarou, Elena. 2007. "Theoretical Approaches to the Europeanisation of Turkish National Identity." Presented at the 48th ISN Annual Convention, February 28–March 3, Chicago.

Leiber, Simone. 2007. "Transposition of EU Social Policy in Poland: Are There Different 'Worlds of Compliance' in East and West?" *Journal of European Social Policy* 17(4): 349–360.

Letsch, Constanze. 2014. "Erdoğan Emerges Victorous in Turkish Presidential Elections amid Low Turnout." *The Guardian*, August 10.

Liaras, Evangelos. 2009. "Turkey's Party System and the Paucity of Minority Policy Reform." *EUI Working Papers RSCAS* 56.

Magen, Amichai and Leonardo Morlino, eds. 2008. *International Actors, Democratisation and the Rule of Law Anchoring Democracy?* London and New York: Routledge.

March, James G. and Johan P. Olsen. 1989. *Rediscovering Institutions*. New York, London: Collier Macmillan.

Martinez, Lorena. 2013. "Gezi Park Protests show Erdoğan's Control over Mainstream Media in Turkey." *Media Diversity Institute*, June 14.

Mecham, R. Quinn. 2004. "From the Ashes of Virtue, a Promise of Light: The Transformation of Political Islam in Turkey." *Third World Quarterly* 25(2): 339–358.

MHP. 2011. "2023'e Doğru Yükselen Ülke Türkiye Sözleşmesi Ses Ver Türkiye." *2011 MHP Seçim Beyannamesi*. www.mhp.org.tr (May 12, 2013).

MHP ARGE. 2009. Avrupa Birliği [The European Union], February 9. www.mhp.org.tr (August 18, 2011).

———. 2010. Avrupa Birliği [The European Union], April. www.mhp.org.tr (August 18, 2011).

Milliyet. 2007. Yüzbinler Çağlayan'da Buluştu [Hundreds of Thousands Gathered in Çağlayan], April 29.

———. 2013. 3. Köprünün Adı Tartışma Yarattı [The Name of the Bridge led to a Dispute], May 29.

———. 2014. Internete Yasaklar Getiren Yasa [Internet Law 2014: The Law That Brings Bans on the Internet], February 6.

Minority Rights Group International Report. 2007. A Quest for Equality: Minorities in Turkey. http://www.minorityrights.org (June 22, 2009).

Müftüler-Baç, Meltem. 2005. "Turkey's Political Reforms and the Impact of the European Union." *South European Society of Politics* 10(1): 17–31.

———. 2008. "Turkey's Accession to the European Union: The Impact of EU's Internal Dynamics." *International Studies Perspectives* 9(2): 201–219.

Müftüler-Baç, Meltem and Lauren McLaren. 2003. "Enlargement Preferences and Policy-Making in the European Union: Impacts on Turkey." *Journal of European Integration* 25(1): 17–30.

Bibliography

MÜSİAD. 2005. The Evaluation of Turkish Economy 2004 and the first half of 48. www.musiad.org.tr (June 15, 2015).

———. 2007. Turkish Economy 51. www. musiad.org.tr (June 15, 2015).

Mynet. 2013. Diyanet İşleri Başkanı Kürtçe Seslendi [The President of Religious Affairs addressed in Kurdish], April 15.

Najslova, Lucia. 2008. "Turkey-EU 2008: Time for a New Swing in the Boring Plot?" *International Issues & Slovak Foreign Policy Affairs* 1: 47–62.

Nancheva, Nevena. 2016. "Imagining Policies: European Integration and the European Minority Rights Regime." *Journal of Contemporary European Studies* 24(1): 132–148.

Narbone, Luigi and Nathalie Tocci. 2007. "Running around in Circles? The Cyclical Relationship between Turkey and the European Union." *Journal of Balkan and Near Eastern Studies* 9(3): 233–245.

Nas, Çiğdem. 1998. "The Approach of the EP to the Issue of Ethnic Minorities and Minority Rights in Turkey within the Context of the European Minority Rights Sub-Regime." *Jean Monnet Working Paper* 18, Department of Political Studies, University of Catania.

———. 2007. Org. Büyükanıt'ın Konuşmasının Tam Metni [The Full Text of Chief of General Staff Büyükanıt's Speech], April 13. http://arsiv.ntvmsnbc.com.(October 12, 2010).

Official Gazette. 2002. No. 24841, August 9.

———. 2003a. No. 24990, January 11.

———. 2003b. No. 25173, July 19.

———. 2010. No. 27580, May 13.

———. 2012. No. 28239, March 20.

Oğuzlu, H. Tarık. 2012. "Turkey and the European Union: Europeanization without Membership." *Turkish Studies* 13(2): 229–243.

Onatlı, Mesut. 2010. "Türkiye'de Kürt Sineması: Mîn Dit Öncesi Mîn Dit Sonrası [Kurdish Cinema in Turkey: Before and after Mîn Dit]." *Radikal*, May 24.

Öner, Selcen. 2012. "Europeanisation of Civil Society in Turkey during the Accession Process to the European Union." In *Turkey and the EU Processes of Europeanisation*, eds. Çiğdem Nas and Yonca Özer. Farnham: Ashgate, 99–118.

Öniş, Ziya. 2003. "Domestic Politics, International Norms and Challenges to the State: Turkey-EU Relations in the Post-Helsinki Era." In *Turkey and the European Union Domestic Politics, Economic Integration and International Dynamics*, eds. Ali Çarkoğlu and Barry Rubin. London and Portland, OR: Frank Cass, 9–34.

———. 2007. "Conservative Globalists versus Defensive Nationalists: Political Parties and Paradoxes of Europeanization in Turkey." *Journal of Balkan and Near Eastern Studies* 9(3): 247–261.

———. 2008. "Turkey-EU Relations: Beyond the Current Stalemate." *Insight Turkey* 10(4): 35–50.

———. 2009. "The New Wave of Foreign Policy Activism in Turkey Drifting away from Europeanization?" *Danish Institute for International Studies* 5, Copenhagen.

———. 2010. "Contesting for the "Center": Domestic Politics, Identity Conflicts and the Controversy over EU Membership in Turkey." *Istanbul Bilgi University European Institute Working Papers* 2, Istanbul.

———. 2013. "Sharing Power: Turkey's Democratization Challenge in the Age of the AKP Hegemony." *Insight Turkey* 15(2): 103–122.

Öniş, Ziya and Umut Türem. 2001. "Business, Globalisation and Democracy: A Comparative Analysis of Turkish Business Associations." *Turkish Studies* 2(2): 94–120.

Oran, Baskın. 2004. *Türkiye'de Azınlıklar Kavramlar, Teori, Lozan, İç Mevzuat, İçtihat, Uygulama*. İstanbul: İletişim Yayınları.

———. 2006. "Minorities in Turkey and in the EU." In *Deutsch-türkisches Forum für Staatsrechtslehre III*, eds. Otto Depenheuer, Ilhan Dogan, and Osman Can. Münster: LIT Verlag, 49–54.

———. 2007. "The Minority Concept and Rights in Turkey: The Lausanne Peace Treaty and Current Issues." In *Human Rights in Turkey*, ed. Zehra F. Kabasakal Arat. Philadelphia, PA: University of Pennsylvania, 35–56.

———. 2009. "Western Impact and Turkey." Seminar Series in Harvard Kennedy School of Government, Cambridge, MA. http://baskinoran.com (June 15, 2010).

———. 2014. "Azınlıklar Nasıl Azınlık Oldu." In *Azınlıklar, Ötekiler ve Medya*, eds. Yasemin İnceoğlu and Savaş Çoban. İstanbul: Ayrıntı, 17–49.

Ozbilgin, Ozge. 2013. "Turkey Bans Alcohol Advertising and Curbs Sales." *Reuters*, May 24.

Özbudun, Ergun. 2014. "AKP at the Crossroads: Erdoğan's Majoritarian Drift." *South European Society and Politics* 19(2): 155–167.

Özdemir, Burcu. 2014. "The Role of the EU in Turkey's Legislative Reforms for Eliminating Violence against Women: A Bottom-Up Approach." *Journal of Balkan and Near Eastern Studies* 16(1): 119–136.

Özkırımlı, Umut. 2011. "The Changing Nature of Nationalism in Turkey Actors, Discourses, and the Struggle for Hegemony." In *Symbiotic Antagonisms: Competing Nationalisms in Turkey*, eds. Ayşe Kadıoğlu and E. Fuat Keyman. Salt Lake City, UT: The University of Utah Press, 82–100.

Özsel, Dogancan, Armağan Öztürk, and Hilal Onur İnce. 2013. "A Decade of Erdoğan's JDP: Ruptures and Continuities." *Critique* 41(4): 551–570.

Pasquier, Romain and Claudio M. Radaelli. 2007. "Conceptual Issues." In *Europeanization New Research Agendas*, eds. Paolo Graziano and Maarten P. Vink. Basingstoke: Palgrave Macmillan, 35–45.

Patton, Marcie. J. 2007. "AKP Reform Fatigue in Turkey: What Has Happened to the EU Reform Process?" *Mediterranean Politics* 12(3): 339–358.

Pınar, Candas. 2013. "Religion-State Relations in Turkey since the AKP: A Changing Landscape? Evidence from Parliamentary Debates on the Alevi Matter." *Journal of Muslim Minority Affairs* 33(4): 507–530.

Polat, Rabia K. 2009. "The 2007 Parliamentary Elections in Turkey: Between Securitisation and Desecuritisation." *Parliamentary Affairs* 62(1): 129–148.

Posch, Walter. 2007. "Crisis in Turkey: Just Another Bump on the Road to Europe?" *Institute for Security Studies Occasional Paper* 67, Paris.

Preece, Jennifer J. 1998. "National Minority Rights Enforcement in Europe: A Difficult Balancing Act." *The International Journal of Peace Studies* 3(2): 35–54.

Radaelli, Claudio M. 2003. "The Europeanization of Public Policy." In *The Politics of Europeanization*, eds. Kevin Featherstone and Claudio M. Radaelli. Oxford, New York: Oxford University Press, 27–56.

Radikal. 2004. Özkök: AB Yolu Hata Kaldırmaz [Özkök: The EU Path Does Not Tolerate Any Mistakes], October 30.

———. 2007. Müktesebat Bizi Parçalar [The EU *Acquis* Disintegrates Us], April 13.

———. 2008. 301 Görüşmeleri Hararetli Başladı [Talks on 301 Started Vehemently], April 17.

———. 2012. Erdoğan: Kürtaj yasasını çıkartacağız [Erdoğğan: We Will Enact the Abortion Law], May 29.

———. 2013a. Gelin Türkiye'yi Şangay İşbirliği Teşkilatına alın [Let's take Turkey into the Shangai Cooperation Organization, November 22.

Bibliography

———. 2013b. Erdoğan'dan AP'ye Rest: Senin haddine mi? [The Response of Erdoğan to the EP: How dare you?], June 14.
Ram, Melanie H. 2003. "Democratization through European Integration: The Case of Minority Rights in the Czech Republic and Romania." *Studies in Comparative International Development* 38(2): 28–56.
Rechel, Bernd. 2008. "What Has Limited the EU's Impact on Minority Rights in Accession Countries?" *East European Politics and Societies* 22(1): 171–191.
———. ed. 2009a. *Minority Rights in Central and Eastern Europe.* Milton Park: Routledge.
———. 2009b. "Introduction." In *Minority Rights in Central and Eastern Europe*, ed. Bernd Rechel. Milton Park: Routledge, 4–16.
———. 2009c. "The Way Forward." In *Minority Rights in Central and Eastern Europe*, ed. Bernd Rechel. Milton Park: Routledge, 227–232.
Risse, Thomas, James Caporaso, and Maria Green Cowles, eds. 2001. *Transforming Europe: Europeanization and Domestic Change.* Ithaca, NY and London: Cornell University Press.
Rose, Richard. 1991. "What Is Lesson-Drawing?" *Journal of Public Policy* 11(1): 3–33.
———. 1993. *Lesson-Drawing in Public Policy: A Guide to Learning across Time and Space.* Chatham, NJ: Chatham House Publishers.
Rumelili, Bahar. 2011. "Turkey: Identity, Foreign Policy, and Socialization in a Post-Enlargement Europe." *Journal of European Integration* 33(2): 235–249.
Rumford, Chris. 2001. "Human Rights and Democratization in Turkey in the Context of EU Candidature." *Journal of European Area Studies* 9(1): 93–105.
Saatçioğlu, Beken. 2010. "Unpacking the Compliance Puzzle: The Case of Turkey's AKP under EU Conditionality." *KFG Working Paper Series* 14, Freie Universität Berlin.
———. 2011. "Revisiting the Role of Credible EU Membership Conditionality for EU Compliance: The Turkish Case." *Uluslararası İlişkiler (International Relations)* 8(31): 23–44.
———. 2014. "AKP's 'Europeanization' in Civilianization, Rule of Law and Fundemantel Freedoms: The Primacy of Domestic Politics." *Journal of Balkan and Near Eastern Studies* 16(1): 86–101.
Sabah. 2009. Ilk çıkış Özal'dan: Anneannem Kürt! İşte Özal'dan Gül'e Devletin Zirvesinin Kürt Açılımı [The First Opening from Özal: My Grandmother is Kurdish! From Özal to Gül the Kurdish Opening of the State], May 15.
Sabah. 2012. Köşkte İlk Muharrem İftarı [Muharrem Fast-breaking Meal First Time in the Manor House], November 27.
Sasse, Gwendolyn. 2005. "EU Conditionality and Minority Rights: Translating the Copenhagen Criteria into Policy." *EUI Working Paper RSCAS* 16.
———. 2008. "The Politics of EU Conditionality: The Norm of Minority Protection during and beyond EU Accession." *Journal of European Public Policy* 15(6): 842–860.
Satana, Nil S. 2012. "The Kurdish Issue in June 2011 Elections: Continuity or Change in Turkey's Democratization?" *Turkish Studies* 13(2): 169–189.
Sayarı, Sabri. 2007. "Towards a New Turkish Party System?" *Turkish Studies* 8(2): 197–210.
Saylan, İbrahim. 2012. "The Europeanization Process and Kurdish Nationalism in Turkey: The Case of the Democratic Society Party." *Nationalities Papers* 40(2): 185–202.
Schimmelfenning, Frank. 2008. "EU Political Accession Conditionality after the 2004 Enlargement: Consistency and Effectiveness." *Journal of European Public Policy* 15(6): 918–937.
———. 2009. "Entrapped Again: The Way to EU Membership Negotiations with Turkey." *International Politics* 46(4): 413–431.

Schimmelfenning, Frank and Ulrich Sedelmeier, eds. 2005. *The Europeanisation of Central and Eastern Europe*. Ithaca, NY and London: Cornell University Press.
———. 2007. "Candidate Countries and Conditionality." In *Europeanization: New Research Agendas*, eds. Paolo Graziano and Maarten P. Vink. Basingstoke: Palgrave Macmillan, 88–101.
Schwellnus, Guido. 2001. "Much Ado about Nothing? Minority Protection and the EU Charter of Fundamental Rights." *Constitutionalism Web-Papers* No.5.
———. 2005. "The Adoption of Non-Discrimination and Minority Protection Rules in Romania, Hungary and Poland." In *The Europeanisation of Central and Eastern Europe*, eds. Frank Schimmelfennig and Ulrich Sedelmeier. Ithaca, NY and London: Cornell University Press, 51–70.
Schwellnus, Guido, Lilla Balázs, and Liudmila Mikalayeva. 2009. "It Ain't Over When It's Over: The Adoption and Sustainability of Minority Protection Rules in New EU Member States." *European Integration Online Papers* 2(13): 1–28.
Secretariat General of the Turkish Republic for EU Affairs. 2007. Political Reforms in Turkey, Ankara.
Sedelmeier, Ulrich. 2011. "Europeanisation in New and Candidate States." *Living Reviews in European Governance* 6(1): 1–52.
Şimşek, Sefa. 2004. "The Transformation of Civil Society in Turkey: From Quantity to Quality." *Turkish Studies* 5(3): 46–74.
Somer, Murat. 2010. "Media Values and Democratization: What Unites and What Divides Religious-Conservative and Pro-Secular Elites?" *Turkish Studies* 11(4): 555–577.
———. 2011. "Democratization, Clashing Narratives, and 'Twin Tolerations' between Islamic-Conservative and Pro-Secular Actors." In *Nationalisms and Politics in Turkey Political Islam, Kemalism and the Kurdish issue*, eds. Marlies Casier and Joost Jongerden. London and New York: Routledge, 28–47.
Soner, Ali B. 2010. "The Justice and Development Party's Policies towards Non-Muslim Minorities in Turkey." *Journal of Balkan and Near Eastern Studies* 12(1): 23–40.
Sozen, Süleyman and Ian Shaw. 2003. "Turkey and the European Union: Modernizing a Traditional State?" *Social Policy & Administration* 37(2): 108–120.
Sözeri, Ceren. 2015. "Türkiye'de Medya-İktidar İlişkileri Sorunlar ve Öneriler." *İstanbul Enstitüsü Medya ve İletişim Merkezi*, May.
Srivastava, Mehul and Funja Güler. 2015. Turkey Extends Clampdown on Media. *Financial Times*, October 27.
Sugden, Jonathan. 2004. "Leverage in Theory and Practice: Human Rights and Turkey's EU candidacy." In *Turkey and European Integration Accession Prospects and Issues*, eds. Mehmet Uğur and Nergis Canefe. London and New York: Routledge, 241–264.
Sümer, Burcu 2011. "The Turkish Media Landscape." In *Türkei: Medienordnung auf dem Weg nach Europa?* eds. Christoph Schmidt and Rolf Schwartmann. Bonn: International Media Studies 3, Deutsche Welle Mediendialog, 55–67.
Tanıyıcı, Şaban. 2010. "Europeanization of Political Elite Discourses in Turkey: A Content Analysis of Parliamentary Debates 1994–2002." *Turkish Studies* 11(2): 181–195.
Taşkın, Yüksel. 2008. "AKP's Move to "Conquer" the Center-Right: Its Prospects and Possible Impacts on the Democratization Process." *Turkish Studies* 9(1): 53–72.
Thornberry, Patrick. 2001. "An Unfinished Story of Minority Rights." In *Diversity in Action: Local Public Management of Multi-Ethnic Communities in Central and Eastern Europe*, eds. Anna-Maria Biro and Petra Kovacs. Budapest: LGI, 47–73.

Tocci, Nathalie. 2004. "Anchoring Turkey to the EU: The Domestic and Foreign Policy Challenges Ahead." In *Towards Accession Negotiations: Turkey's Domestic and Foreign Policy Challenges Ahead*, eds. Nathalie Tocci and Ahmet Evin. EUI RSCAS, 193–206.

———. 2005. "Europeanization in Turkey: Trigger or Anchor for Reforms?" *South European Society and Politics* 10(1): 73–83.

———. 2007. "Report Unpacking European Discourses: Conditionality, Impact and Prejudice in EU-Turkey Relations." In *Conditionality, Impact and Prejudice in EU-Turkey Relations*, ed. Nathalie Tocci. IAI-TEPAV English Series, Roma, 7–32.

———. 2008. "The EU and Conflict Resolution in Turkey and Georgia: Hindering EU Potential through the Political Management of Contractual Relations." *Journal of Common Market Studies* 46(9): 875–897.

———. 2010. "Unblocking Turkey's EU Accession." *Insight Turkey* 12(3): 27–31.

Today's Zaman. 2008. Court Links Ergenekon to Malatya Murder Case, November 22.

Toggenburg, Gabriel. 2000. "A Rough Orientation through a Delicate Relationship: The European Union's Endeavours for (Its) Minorities." *European Integration Online Papers* 4(16), 1–30.

Toktaş, Şule. 2006. "EU Enlargement Conditions and Minority Protection: A Reflection on Turkey's Non-Muslim Minorities." *East European Quarterly* 40(4): 489–518.

Toktaş, Şule and Ümit Kurt. 2010. "The Turkish Military's Autonomy, JDP Rule and the EU Reform Process in the 2000s: An Assessment of the Turkish Version of Democratic Control of Armed Forces (DECAF)." *Turkish Studies* 11(3): 387–403.

———. 2010. Transatlantic Trends Key Findings. http://trends.gmfus.org (May 22, 2011).

Turkish Armed Forces Press Release. 2007. Turkish General Staff, April 27, Ankara.

TurkishNY. 2009. France Seeks Alternative to Turkey's EU Membership, September 3.

Turkishpress. 2006. November 30. http://www.turkishpress.com/news.asp?id=153633 (January 10, 2011).

TÜSIAD. 1997. Türkiye'de Demokratikleşme Perspektifleri [Perspectives on Democratization in Turkey], Istanbul.

———. 2001. Democratization Perspectives in Turkey and EU Copenhagen Criteria, Views and Priorities, July 2001, T/2001–07/305.

———. 2004. "TÜSIAD: 'European Commission's Report is a Historical Step in the Right Direction in EU-Turkey Relations'." *TÜSIAD Press Releases*, October 6.

———. 2007. Türk Demokrasisi'nde 130 Yıl [130 Years in Turkish Democracy], Istanbul.

———. 2008. Turkey Should Move Forward with the EU Membership Process Avoiding Political Polarization at the National Level. *TÜSIAD Press Releases*, March 24.

Uğur, Mehmet. 2003. "Testing Times in EU–Turkey Relations: From Helsinki to Copenhagen and Beyond." *Journal of Southern Europe and the Balkans* 5(2): 165–184.

Uğur, Mehmet and Dilek Yankaya. 2008. "Policy Entrepreneurship, Policy Opportunism, and EU Conditionality: The AKP and TÜSIAD Experience in Turkey." *Governance* 21(4): 581–601.

Ulusoy, Kıvanç. 2007. "Turkey's Reform Effort Reconsidered, 1987–2004." *Democratization* 14(3): 472–490.

———. 2009. "Europeanization and Political Change: A New Research Agenda for Cyprus Studies." *Turkish Studies* 10(3): 393–408.

UN Committee on the Elimination of Racial Discrimination. 2007. Reports Submitted by States Parties under the Article 9 of the Convention Third Periodic Reports of States Parties due in 2007 Turkey, November 12, CERD/C/TUR/3.

———. 2014. Reports Submitted by States Parties under the Article 9 of the Convention Combined Fourth to Sixth Periodic Reports of States Parties due in 2013 Turkey, February 10, CERD/C/TUR/4–6.
UN Human Rights Council. 2010. National Report submitted in Accordance with the Paragraph 15 (a) of the Annex to Human Rights Council Resolution 5/1 Turkey, February 22, 2010, A/HRC/WG.6/8/TUR/1.
USCIRF. 2015. "Turkey." United States Commission on International Religious Freedom Annual Report. http://www.uscirf.gov/reports-briefs/annual-report/2015-annual-report (May 25, 2016).
Uysal, Ayşen. 2011. "Continuity and Rupture: The 'New CHP' or 'What Has Changed in the CHP?'" *Insight Turkey* 13(4): 129–146.
Vachudova, Milada A. 2005. *Europe Undivided: Democracy, Leverage and Integration after Communism*. Oxford: Oxford University Press.
Visier, Claire. 2006. "Euroscepticism in Turkey: European Ambiguity Fuels Nationalism." *European Institute of the Mediterranean*, Barcelona. http://www.iemed.org/anuari/2006/aarticles/aVisier.pdf (June 15, 2011).
———. 2009. "Turkey and the European Union: The Sociology of Engaged Actors." *European Journal of Turkish Studies* 9: 1–11.
Wright, Jane. 1996. "The OSCE and the Protection of Minority Rights." *Human Rights Quarterly* 18(1): 190–205.
Yanık, Lerna K. 2008. "'Those Crazy Turks' that got caught in the 'Metal Storm': Nationalism in Turkey's Best Seller Lists." *EUI Working Papers RSCAS* 4.
Yankaya, Dilek. 2009. "The Europeanization of MUSIAD: Political Opportunism, Economic Europeanization, Islamic Euroscepticism." *European Journal of Turkish Studies* 9: 1–19.
Yavuz, Devrim. 2010. "Testing Large Business's Commitment to Democracy: Business Organizations and the Secular-Muslim Conflict in Turkey." *Government and Opposition* 45(1): 73–92.
Yeğen, Mesut. 2006. "Müstakbel Türk"ten "Sözde Yurttaş"a: Devlet ve Kürtler." In *Tesev Uluslararası Konferans Tebliğleri: Türkiye'de Azınlık Hakları sorunu: Vatandaşlık ve Demokrasi Eksenli Bir Yaklaşım*. Istanbul: TESEV, 105–111.
Yıldız, Ilhan. 2007. "Minority Rights in Turkey." *Brigham Young University Law Review* 3, 791–812.
Yılmaz, Hakan. 2011. "Euroscepticism in Turkey: Parties, Elites, and Public Opinion." *South European Society and Politics* 16(1): 185–208.
Yılmaz, Gözde. 2011. "Is There a Puzzle? Compliance with Minority Rights in Turkey." *KFG Working Paper Series* 23, Freie Universität Berlin.
———. 2012. "Exploring the Implementation of Minority Protection Rules in the 'Worlds of Compliance': The Case of Turkey." *Perspectives on European Politics and Society* 13(4): 408–424.
———. 2014a. "EU Conditionality Is Not the Only Game in Town! Domestic Drivers of Turkey's Europeanization." *Turkish Studies* 15(2): 303–321.
———. 2014b. "It Is Pull-and-Push that Matters for External Europeanization! Explaining Minority Policy Change in Turkey." *Mediterranean Politics* 19(2): 238–258.
———. 2016. "Europeanisation or De-Europeanisation? Media Freedom in Turkey (1999–2015)." *South European Society and Politics* 21(1): 147–161.
Yılmaz, Gözde and Diğdem Soyaltın. 2014. "Zooming into the "Domestic" in Europeanization: Promotion of Minority Rights and Fight against Corruption in Turkey." *Journal of Balkan and Near Eastern Studies* 16(1): 11–29.

Index

Accession Partnership 63, 65
Agos (minority newspaper) 44, 49, 121
AKP *see* Justice and Development Party (*Adalet ve Kalkınma Partisi*-AKP)
Aksoy Group 120
Alevi Opening 45, 53
ANAP *see* Motherland Party (*Anavatan Partisi*-ANAP)
Anatolia News Agency 49
Ankara Agreement 33, 88–9
Aras, Bülent 109
Aşkale labour camp 32
Association for Human Rights and Solidarity with the Oppressed (*İnsan Hakları ve Mazlumlar İçin Dayanışma Derneği*-Mazlum-Der) 116
Association for Supporting Jehovah's Witnesses 45
Aydın-Düzgit, Senem 5, 67, 80, 113–14

Bahcheli, Tozun 99
Balyoz (Sledgehammer) case, 2010 95
Bardakçı, Mehmet 84
Başbuğ, Ilker 95
Bayır, Derya 29
Baykal, Deniz 102, 122
BDP *see* Peace and Democracy Party (*Barış ve Demokrasi Partisi*-BDP)
Bektashi Association 40
Bianet (online news portal) 121
Börzel, Tanja A. 3–4, 126
Bugün (newspaper) 121
Bülent Arınç 120
Büyükanıt, Yaşar 82–3

Çalık Group 120
Capotorti, Francesco 24, 27
Çarkoğlu, Ali 6, 67, 74
Central and Eastern European Countries (CEECs) accession process 2, 23

Charlie Hebdo 54
CHP *see* Republican People's Party (*Cumhuriyet Halk Partisi*-CHP)
Çiller, Tansu 20
"Citizen! Speak Turkish" campaign 32
CoE *see* Council of Europe (CoE)
Committee for the Protection of National Minorities 24
Copenhagen criteria 74–6; Accession Partnership with Turkey and 65; candidate country status and 71
Copenhagen European Council 18
Coşkun, Bekir 121
Council of Europe (CoE) 23–4; Framework Convention for the Protection of National Minorities 26, 34, 55
Criminal Procedure Code 48–9, 51
Çukurova Group 120
Customs Union Agreement 33

Dağı, Ihsan, D. 5, 110
DEHAP *see* Democratic People's Party (*Demokratik Halk Partisi*-DEHAP)
Demirel, Süleyman 20
Demirören Group 121
Demirtaş, Selahaddin 106
Democratic Left Party (*Demokratik Sol Parti*-DSP) 37, 65
Democratic People's Party (*Demokratik Halk Partisi*-DEHAP) 73–4
Democratic Society Party (*Demokratik Toplum Partisi*-DTP) 44; Eastern region votes, 2007 elections 87, 93; Eastern region votes, 2014 elections 106
Dink, Hrant 44, 93
Doğan Group 120–1
Doğuş Group 120
domestic adoption costs, veto players role in 111–14

domestic polarization 94–7
DSP *see* Democratic Left Party (*Demokratik Sol Parti*-DSP)
DTP *see* Democratic Society Party (*Demokratik Toplum Partisi*-DTP)

Ecevit, Bülent 67
Economic Development Foundation (*İktisadi Kalkınma Vakfı*-IKV) 71
Erdoğan, Recep Tayyip 40, 44, 47–8, 68–9, 85, 93–4, 102–3, 105–6, 109–10, 120–1
Ergenekon case, 2008 95, 102
Estonia, Russian language speakers in 1
Eurobarometer Surveys 74
European Charter for Regional or Minority Languages 24
European Economic Community (EEC) 33; Turkey's application to 64
Europeanization 9–21; EU conditionality and, credibility of 17–19; external, research findings 125–7; external Europeanization interaction-oriented mechanism 13–14; external incentives model 9–10; future research for external 129–30; lesson-drawing model 11; mechanisms of 10; media role in 119–22; in minority rights process 1–2; overview of 9–10; policy change expected outcomes 13; policy dissatisfaction and 19–21; pull-and-push model 14–17; social learning model 11–13
European Movement 71
European Union (EU): absorption capacity 78; conditionality, credibility of 2, 17–19; demands of, and response of implementation by Turkey, 2002–2004 41; demands of, and response of implementation by Turkey, 2005–2007 46; demands of, and response of implementation by Turkey, 2008–2014 56–9; demands of, and response of legal adoption by Turkey, 2002–2004 39; demands of, and response of legal adoption by Turkey, 2005–2007 42; demands of, and response of legal adoption by Turkey, 2008–2014 50; minority rights in 1–2, 23–6, 109–10; minority rules, legitimacy of 109; reform process of 2–3; transformative power of (*see* European Union, transformative power of); Turkey conditionality, 2008–2014 91–4; Turkey relations 33–6; Turkish support for membership in 72; unresolved minority issues 60–1
European Union, transformative power of 23–36; big-bang enlargement and minority protection 26–7; concept of minority in Turkey and 28–9; EU-Turkey relations and 33–6; minorities in Turkey and 27–8; minority rights and 23–6; overview of 23; Turkish Republic, minority rights in 29–33
external Europeanization model 3
external incentives model 3, 9–10; *see also* Europeanization; causal mechanism by 10

Facebook 121
Fırat, Dengir Mir 74
Foundations Law 36, 38, 42–3, 45, 47, 52, 85
Framework Convention for the Protection of National Minorities (FCNM) 24, 34, 55
Freedom House 43

Galbreath, J. David 25
GAP *see* Southeastern Anatolia Project (*Güneydoğu Anadolu Projesi*-GAP)
Garden of Religions 40
Gezi Park Protests *see* Taksim *Gezi* Park Protests
goodness of fit 10
Grigoriadis, Ioannis. N. 81–2, 87
Gül, Abdullah 119
Gülen Movement 121
Gümüşcü, Sebnem 100, 118

hate crimes/acts of intolerance against non-Muslim minorities 44
HDP *see* Kurdish People's Democratic Party (*Halkların Demokrasi Partisi*-HDP)
headscarf ban 94–5
Helsinki Summit 64–5
Higher Education Board (*Yüksek Öğretim Kurumu*-YÖK) 49, 51
Housing Administration of Turkey (*Toplu Konut İdaresi Başkanlığı*-TOKİ) 54
Human Rights Watch 39
Hürriyet 121

İhlas Group 120
İhsanoğlu, Ekmeleddin 106
inclusive citizenship 30
Independent Industrialists' and Businessmen's Association (*Müstakil Sanayici ve İşadamları Derneği*-MÜSIAD) 116; Turkey accession process and 118–19
International Covenant on Civil and Political Rights 38
International Covenant on Economic, Social and Cultural Rights 38
İpek Group 121

Justice and Development Party (*Adalet ve Kalkınma Partisi*-AKP) 5–7, 71; Copenhagen criteria and 74–6; domestic polarization and pull within 94–7; Eastern region votes, 2007 elections 87; Eastern region votes, 2014 elections 106; failure diagnosis and rule of 68–70; influence for pull 123–4; legitimacy of 84–6; popular support for 73–4; reform process and, monopolizing of 100–4; self-definition of 123; Taksim *Gezi* Park Protests and 104–6; 2010 Constitutional amendments and 99–100; 2007 elections 86–8

Kadıoğlu, Ayşe 31
Kalaycıoğlu, Ersin 6, 74
Kanal Türk television 121
Kemalist nationalism 30, 81–4, 87–8, 94, 108, 111–14
Keyman, Fuat E. 5, 100, 113–14, 118
Kılıçdaroğlu, Kemal 102
Koza İpek Holding 121
Kurdish initiative 47–51
Kurdish Opening 47–51
Kurdish People's Democratic Party (*Halkların Demokrasi Partisi*-HDP) 106
Kurdish rights 47–51
Kurdish Writers' Association 40
Kurdistan Workers Party (*Partiye Karkeren Kurdistan*-PKK) 1, 31, 47–8, 63, 66

Labour, Democracy and Freedom Bloc (*Emek, Demokrasi ve Özgürlük Bloğu*-EDÖB) 101
Larrabee, Stephen F. 98
Lausanne Treaty 28, 29–30, 108–9
Law on Compensation of Losses Resulting from Terrorist Acts 45, 54
Law on Construction 38
Law on De-mining the Turkish-Syrian Border 48
Law on Elections and Political Parties 51
Law on Foundations 38, 42–3, 45, 47, 52
Law on Private Education Institutions 42
Law on Settlement 43
Lellouche, Pierre 91
lesson-drawing model 3, 11; causal mechanism by 11
Liaras, Evangelos 6
Lisbon Treaty, minorities and 26
Luxembourg Summit 64

Mazlum-Der *see* Association for Human Rights and Solidarity with the Oppressed (*İnsan Hakları ve Mazlumlar İçin Dayanışma Derneği*-Mazlum-Der)
McEvoy, Joanne 25
Mecham, R. Quinn 73
media, Europeanization role of 119–22
Merkez Group 120
Metal Storm *(Metal Fırtına)* 82
MHP *see* Nationalist Action Party (*Milliyetçi Hareket Partisi*-MHP)
Millet (newspaper) 121
millet system 28–9
Min Dît ("The Children of Diyarbakır") (movie) 49
Ministry of Labour and Social Security 54
minorities: Capotorti definition of 24, 27; grouping, in Turkey 27–8; international definition of 28; Lisbon Treaty and 26
minority-related change in Turkey, 1999–2014 115–16
Minority Report 113–14
minority rights: big-bang enlargement and 26–7; CoE role in development of 24; EU role in development of 25–6; Europeanization process in 1–2; OSCE role in development of 24–5; in Turkey (*see* Turkey, minority rights in)
Minority Rights Group International 32–3
minority rights reform in Turkey, 1999–2014 37–62; EU demands and legal adoption, 2005–2007 42–5, 46; international agreements and, ratification of 38; legal adoption of minority rules, 2002–2004 38–41; mapping policy change in 61–2; overview of 37–8; registration of names and 43–4;

religious associations, registration of 45; revival of legal adoption and implementation, 2008–2010 45, 47–55, 56–60; selective policy change, 2008–2014 55, 60–1
Motherland Party (*Anavatan Partisi*-ANAP) 37, 65–6
MÜSIAD *see* Independent Industrialists' and Businessmen's Association (*Müstakil Sanayici ve İşadamları Derneği*-MÜSIAD)
Muslim minorities 28–9

Narbone, Luigi 78
national identity 108
Nationalist Action Party (*Milliyetçi Hareket Partisi*-MHP) 37, 65–6, 102–3; influence for pull 122; re-entrance of, to Parliament 92–3
'New CHP' 102
Noel, Sid 99
non-Muslim minorities: foundations, legal status of 44, 52; hate crimes/acts of intolerance against 44; Kurdish rights 47–51; newspapers run by 48; non-Sunni Muslims rights 53; places of worship 44; property rights of 38, 44, 52; Roma rights 54
non-Sunni Muslims rights 53

Öcalan, Abdullah 37, 63, 66, 102, 113
Onatlı, Mesut 49
Öniş, Ziya 65, 81, 83, 87, 100
Operation Sevrés 82
Oran, Baskın 29–30
Organization for Security and Co-operation in Europe (OSCE) 23–5
OSCE *see* Organization for Security and Co-operation in Europe (OSCE)
Ottowa Convention 38
Öymen, Onur 93
Özal, Turgut 47
Özbudun, Ergun 105
Özkırımlı, Umut 30–1
Özkök, Hilmi 72, 82

Patton, Marcie. J. 81, 87
Peace and Democracy Party (*Barış ve Demokrasi Partisi*-BDP) 101–2
Perspectives on Democratization in Turkey (TÜSIAD) 117
PKK *see* Kurdistan Workers Party (*Partiye Karkeren Kurdistan*-PKK)

pro-government circles 120
pull-and-push model; *see also* Europeanization: AKP party and 5–7; credibility of EU conditionality and 17–19; described 14; domestic factors and implementation of 16; empowerment combinations between 15–16; expected outcomes for policy change 13; external Europeanization and 3–5; policy change and 15; Turkish minority rights and 5–7
pull via societal mobilization in Turkey: business interest groups and 116–19; civil society and 115–16; media and 119–22; MÜSIAD role in 118–19; overview of 114–15; political party influence for 122–4; TÜSIAD role in 117–18
pull without push, 2005–2007 77–90; AKP legitimacy and 84–6; Ankara Criteria and 88–9; EU conditionality, credibility of 77–81; minority protection through 89–90; overview of 77; reactionary nationalism, rise of 81–4; 2007 AKP elections and 86–8
pull without push, 2008–2014 91–107; AKP 2009 elections and 97–9; credible conditionality for Turkey and 91–4; domestic polarization and 94–7; overview of 91; reform process and, AKP monopolizing of 100–4; selective policy change and 107; Taksim Gezi Park Protests and 104–6; 2010 Constitutional amendments and 99–100
push without pull, 1999–2004 63–76; AKP government support and 73–4; coalition government and, 1999–2002 63–4; Copenhagen criteria and 74–6; domestic-level developments and 65–6; EU conditionality and, 2002–2004 70–2; failure diagnosis and 68–70; Helsinki Summit and 64–5; minority protection change through 76; overview of 63; political/economic crises in Turkey and 66–8

reactionary nationalism, rise of 81–4
Republican People's Party (*Cumhuriyet Halk Partisi*-CHP) 71, 102–3; EU accession and 92–3; influence for pull 122
"Return to Village and Rehabilitation Project" (RVRP) 39–40, 53

Risse, Thomas 4
Roma Language and Culture Research Institute 54
Roma People Forum of Turkey 54
Rose, Richard 19–20
RTÜK (*Radyo ve Televizyon Üst Kurulu*- Radio and Television Supreme Council) 49
rule adoption 9
RVRP *see* "Return to Village and Rehabilitation Project" (RVRP)

Sabancı, Ömer 80
Şahin, Leyla 88
Samanyolu Group 120
Sancak, Ethem 120
Savings Deposit Insurance Funds (*Tasarruf Mevduatı Sigorta Fornu*-TMSF) 120
Schimmelfenning, Frank 3, 9, 12, 20
Secret Army for the Liberation of Armenia (ASALA) 31
Sedelmeier, Ulrich 3, 9, 12, 20
Sevrés syndrome 31–2, 66, 82, 108
Sezer, Ahmet Necdet 67, 114
Shanghai Cooperation Organization 94
Slovakia, Roma speakers in 1
social learning model 11–13, 108–11; causal mechanism by 12; components of 108
societal mobilization, pull via 114–15
Solidarity Association of the Families of the Prisoners and the Sentenced (*Tutuklu ve Hükümlü Aileleri Dayanışma Derneği*-TAYAD) 116
Southeastern Anatolia Project (*Güneydoğu Anadolu Projesi*-GAP) 47, 53
Star *(Uzan)* Group 120
"Support for the Development of an IDP Program in Turkey Project" 53

Taksim *Gezi* Park Protests 94, 104–6
TAYAD *see* Solidarity Association of the Families of the Prisoners and the Sentenced (*Tutuklu ve Hükümlü Aileleri Dayanışma Derneği*-TAYAD)
territorial citizenship 30
Tocci, Nathalie 78
Toktaş, Şule 109
Tol, Gonul 98
Transatlantic Trends 78
Treaty of Lausanne 28–30
Türk, ethno-territorial definition of 113

Turkey: Additional Protocol to the Ankara Agreement and 78–9, 91–2; business interest groups in 116–19; citizenship in 30–1; civil society in 115–16; ethnic/linguistic minorities in 28; golden age of Europeanization for 70–2; minority concept in 28–9; minority-related legal adoption/implementation, 2002–2014 62; minority-related policy change, 2002–2014 62; minority-related policy change in, 1999–2004 41; minority-related policy change in, 2005–2007 46; minority-related policy change in, 2008–2014 60; Muslim minorities in 28–9; official nationalism of 30; political/economic crises in, 1999–2002 66–8; public support for EU membership, 2005–2007 80; public support for EU membership, 2008–2014 92; religious groups in 28; "Return to Village and Rehabilitation Project" 39–40; Wealth Tax 32
Turkey, minority rights in: causal mechanisms to explain 12–13; changing, 1999–2014 (*see* minority rights reform in Turkey, 1999–2014); EU reform process and 2–3; Lausanne Treaty and 29–30; minority groups and 27–8; Ottoman Empire and 28–9; overview of 1–8; PKK and 1–2; policy change outcomes of 13; positive development in 1; pull-and-push model and 3–7; secular reforms and 32; Sevrés syndrome and 31–2; unresolved issues 60–1
Turkish Economic and Social Studies Foundation (*Türkiye Ekonomik ve Sosyal Etüdler Vakfı*-TESEV) 71
Turkish Industrialists' and Businessmen's Association (*Türk Sanayicileri ve İşadamları Derneği*-TÜSIAD) 71–2, 80, 116; Turkey accession process and 93, 117–18
Turkish Labour Agency (*Türkiye İş Kurumu*-İŞKUR) 54
Turkishness, replacement of 93
Türkiyeli, ethno-territorial definition of 113
TÜSIAD *see* Turkish Industrialists' and Businessmen's Association (*Türk Sanayicileri ve İşadamları Derneği*-TÜSIAD)
2010 Referendum 99–100
Twitter 121

Uğur, Mehmet 64
Ulusoy, Kıvanç 112
UN Convention on the Elimination of All
 Forms of Racial Discrimination 38
Union of Alevi 40
'Unity and Fraternity Project' 47

Working Group on Minority Rights and
 Cultural Rights 113

Yılmaz, Mesut 20

Zirve Holding 120